Lady Luck and Me

Ben Dobson

This book is licensed for your personal enjoyment only. This book may not be re-sold or given away to other people. If you would like to share this book with another person, please purchase an additional copy for each recipient. Thank you for respecting the hard work of this author.

Some names and identifying details have been changed to protect the privacy of individuals.

Copyright 2014 Ben Dobson

ISBN: 978-1499529791

Copy Editor: Jane Hingston

Cover Design: Louis Fryer

Firstly and most importantly, huge thanks and love to my long suffering mother. Without her patience, understanding and support I do not know what would have become of me. To my sister and pillar, Emma, even if I could choose family I would have chosen you; thank you. Charmian; I thank you for your optimism. Thanks to Paula for her peaceful writing sanctuary. Massive thanks to Edward Douglas, whose love and generosity knows no bounds. The world would be significantly better if more people had just half your heart. To David Llewellyn, thank you for always being there, I genuinely think I'm lucky to have you in my life. Sincere thanks to Ben Major, who has been a light through some very dark times and for his countless hours sat at the computer; without his perseverance and skill, this edition would not have been possible. Sarah Davies, thanks for coming up trumps when I needed it most. Thanks to Beth Howland-Smith, for your belief in me, my writing and your invaluable input. Mr Nigel P, thanks for the timely chats. And of course Louis Fryer, my good friend, thank you. Without each of you, I would never have got as far as I have: I'm forever in your debt.

Finally, thanks to you, the reader. I hope you enjoy it.

Contents

Before the Beginning . . .	1
A Bean is born	15
Ripped from the bosom	27
Big school	39
South African stress	69
Americano	77
Deepest, darkest Devon	85
'Worldly' travels	93
Sunsets, Socrates and sea urchins	109
Univershitty	127
A Question of Sport . . . Careers	133
Welcome to the working world	143
Amsterdamaged	159
Australia	165
The weird, the wonderful; the Australian East Coast	177
One job, many professions	189
The elusive spirit	199
Sorry seas	209
I'm coming for you, Mr Palin	215
Alive and temporarily kicking	223
Contemplating the life of Pai	227
Rest, relaxation, angry wildlife and organ extractions	247
You wanna fight? Fight me	257
The Man from Uncle	269
Oh no you're not . . .	271
World's end	277
Who needs love when….?	293
Where the streets are paved with gold	307
Home sweet home?	313
Watery stools	321
Black dog days	341

Lady Luck and Me

Before the Beginning . . .

'If you cannot get rid of the family skeleton, you may as well make it dance.'
George Bernard Shaw

Have you ever noticed how many biographies and autobiographies there are about people who have 'made it'? Horatio Nelson, Winston Churchill, Nelson Mandela, Kerry Katona . . . all people who have fully achieved their 'potential' and have works published about their extraordinary lives, and rightly so. But what about the people who haven't reached those dizzying heights, those people whose lives seem to be a comedy of errors, predictably jumping from one balls-up to the next? Well, I'm one of them. Again, let me introduce myself. My name's Ben and I'm a knob.

Before you stop reading there, let me assure you that this isn't a depressing account full of remorse about how many times Lady Luck has slapped me across the face. Far from it, my friends. I haven't won world wars, ended apartheid, discovered a new species or done a photo shoot with *OK Magazine*. In fact, I've done nothing of the sort. The closest to that level of fame that I've achieved is having a quote printed on the bottom of the local council's quarterly refuse leaflet. That was eight years ago. I still have it, framed, above my bed. This is the tale of an average man.

Like the vast majority of people, I had parents and grandparents, two and four of them respectively, and it's with my grandparents that the story begins. I haven't traced my family back any further than that. My father

Lady Luck and Me

says our ancestors were French aristocracy and can be dated back to the Norman conquest of the 11th century. That, I find, highly improbable. Judging by the appearance of all the Dobson males in the family, it's far more likely that the Dobson lineage is from a 19th century north Welsh mining community or a Polish farming village. On more than one occasion, my father has been referred to as Shrek and, as my mother constantly reminds me how much I look like him, I feel blessed. Watch out Mr Pitt, your days are numbered at the top of the beautiful pile. For now, I'm happy to go along with Dad's outrageous claim rather than uncover what's bound to be a disappointing truth.

Sadly, my grandparents are no longer with us but, if I'm anything like any of them in my later years and still allowed out in public, I'll be a happy man. All four are worthy of individual mention.

My grandfather on my father's side, Max Dobson, was a metropolitan policeman, patrolling the often violent East End of London, before, during and after the war. As natural order of the world dictates, he was quite old when I was quite young so my memories of him are a little hazy at best. I do remember vividly what he looked like though: Shrek. Granted, an older Shrek, with sprouts of long, coarse hair protruding from his nose, ear lobes and other seemingly impossible places from which hair grows when you reach a certain age. It's strange at the age of five, knowing exactly what you're going to look like in your 80s. It was a constant source of fascination, Grandpa's facial hair and, often, I used to draw a crude picture of his face and try to imagine where the next burst of hair would come from, a little like pin-the-tail-on-the-donkey. Needless to say, I never got close and was always out-done by Mother Nature's imagination. Apart from the alien hair

Before the Beginning . . .

that wouldn't stop growing, Grandpa's bizarre and unique quirks continued in the form of a dog. Or rather, what I'm now starting to come to terms with, an imaginary dog that he would shout at to stop jumping up at the table or order him to fetch his slippers and, at meal times, to stop begging. Over the years, I managed to painfully sprain my neck countless times trying to catch a glimpse of his elusive, disobedient dog. He was so convincing that, every time we used to visit him, I felt compelled to bring something for the dog, hoping I could lure him out of hiding. I never did get to see the dog and, when Grandpa died, his dog died with him. To this day, I'm still not absolutely convinced whether it was indeed an imaginary dog or whether he had a dog that perfectly blended in with the carpet. I'm too old now to ask my mother; too many years have passed and such questions now would certainly be met with endless hours of family ridicule. I guess I'll never know who the crazy one was in that relationship.

His wife, my nanny, was Alice Dobson: a strong, stoic woman who called a spade a spade, not in a racial sense but the straight-talking sense. Again, my memories are a little sparse with regards to Nanny. Not that she was a forgettable woman but I spent such little time with her as I was always pursuing Grandpa's elusive dog. My mother speaks of her with fond memories so I've adopted those memories and filled in the blanks to create a Mary Poppins-like Nanny.

My mother's parents were a different kettle of fish all together. My grandfather, Ronnie, was a numbers man, rising from relative obscurity within the family business to be M.D of Ryman's Stationers and a Burton's board member. He had a meticulous eye for figures and the stock markets, carefully watching every penny, making sure that

Lady Luck and Me

investments were indeed investments and not just dead places to deposit large sums of cash. Like most men who take life seriously, his seriousness about money-making was equalled only by his enjoyment of alcohol consumption. He worked so hard that, in his mind, he justified replacing the contents of his Evian bottle with gin so, when my grandmother reminded him that he hadn't drunk enough water that day, he would gleefully wander to the fridge and charge his glass full of 'water', right in front of her eyes, thereby quenching her duty and his thirst. For that one simple deception, I admired him and one day I hope to be equally as devious. What she didn't know didn't hurt her. Everyone won. Now that's a perfect crime.

My grandmother, Dorothy, was the other side of the coin. She had a significantly more liberal approach to money and to life. It was at the ripe old age at 70 that she first stepped into a bank and 75 when she first put petrol in her car. Actually, that's a lie. She generously tipped the cashier at her local BP garage to put the petrol in for her as she had no clue where it went. In fact, if it wasn't for the AA man, 30 minutes earlier, at the side of the A3, she would have been blissfully unaware for the need of petrol at all. That was quite a day for my grandmother.

That practical side of life had always been taken care of by my grandfather, and, in turn, she looked after the domestic affairs: cooking, cleaning and duck feeding by the river. As was customary back in those days, my grandfather paid my grandmother housekeeping money in the form of pound coins. For years and years, my grandmother squirreled this housekeeping money away in bags of 50 and sewed them into her coats, cardigans, fluffy toys — anywhere and everywhere that my grandfather wouldn't look. By the end of his days she had accumulated vast collections of these

Before the Beginning . . .

bags. I remember hugging her on one of my visits and being genuinely confused that she had developed a cold, middle, lumpy breast that felt nothing like the two I had come to know. I asked nothing of it; I still didn't understand how I hadn't seen my grandfather's dog so the third boob was even further beyond my understanding. In time, I realised what the third boob represented and grew to love the feeling of it against me. She'd open her front door and it pains me to say it but I would stare at her chest hoping there would be an unnatural third boob staring back at me. Those 50-pound bags first introduced me to gambling machines, pay-phone 0898 numbers and novelty condoms. Thanks, Grandma. If my grandfather had known that his careful penny counting had resulted in her hoarding and, ultimately, funding my awkward physical self-discovery, he would have turned in his grave. Sorry, Grandpa.

Despite her lack of grasp on reality, my grandmother was an innocent soul, full of youth and gay abandonment — the complete opposite of my grandfather. When he was reading the business section of *The Telegraph* by the fire with a glass of whisky in hand, happy as Larry, she would be out in the garden using a toilet brush as her divining rod in the annual family Easter egg hunt. Dressed up to the nines, dripping with beautiful jewellery, she would bumble around the garden with a wicker basket in one hand and a soiled loo brush in the other. The brush used to tremble when it came across an egg; it was quite a sight. She could be ten yards from an unseen egg and the brush would start twitching. We, the grandchildren, would stand and watch in amazement as our very ordinary loo brush would guide

Lady Luck and Me

her to egg after egg, embarrassing us and our empty baskets at the end of the hunt, year after year.

Many times during the year, I would head out into the Wiltshire countryside after watching an inspiring episode of 'The Antiques Roadshow' with the loo brush in hand, convinced that I would find a buried Viking hoard worth millions. If it could find my grandmother all those eggs then surely it could find me a gold crown. I'm still out most weekends with the same brush but, alas, I haven't had anywhere near the success my grandmother had . . . yet.

In spite of their differences, my grandparents loved each other dearly. They spent many hours being the glamorous couple, attending career-progressing dinner parties, formal functions and expensive soirees. I remember hearing of a certain episode when they were on their way back from one of these parties (this comes to mind only because, unbeknownst to me, I was to re-live it 40 years later). After a particularly alcoholically fuelled evening out with friends and business colleagues, it was time for my grandparents to head home along the infamous Hogs Back dual carriageway. Nowadays, it's synonymous with dogging and all those other brilliant adult past-times that I've heard nothing of and know nothing about. But, back then, it was a 10-mile stretch of open road, stunning countryside on both sides, and the occasional pheasant to be wary of. Back in these 'golden days' there were no drink-driving laws and, - no social conscience, - it was perfect. During one balmy summer's night, they had been frequenting the Squires Holt Public House and Restaurant on the Hogs Back and were returning home to Guildford as they had done a thousand times before. Out of nowhere, a blue flashing light appeared. My grandfather, being the gent he was, duly obliged and pulled over into the lay-by, on the

Before the Beginning . . .

opposite side of the road. When the officer appeared at the window, it was clear he was going to have problems. The driver's seat, occupied by my grandfather was fully reclined with him gently snoring as my grandmother slouched over the central division, across grandpa's lap with her hands on the steering wheel, eyes half closed, quietly singing to herself.

After Ronnie was woken from his slumber, he was asked to exit the vehicle only to step into a three-foot ditch and disappear from everyone's view. Once rescued, he was resolute in his argument that the car knew its way home and they had done the same thing for the past 20 years to no ill effect. The officer's argument that they weren't actually near the Hogs Back and that they must have taken a wrong turn to be driving down a one-way street four miles from the Hogs Back didn't seem to deter Ronnie from the fact that the car definitely knew its way home. However, the officer didn't agree and bundled both of them into the back of his squad car, waking them once he had driven them safely home. As I say, they were golden years.

When I heard this story, first from my mother and then my grandfather, I was appalled at the lack of responsibility shown and the outright stupidity of the situation. It seems that, with age, my socially responsible views mellowed. Ten years after hearing that story, I was to take inspiration from it and play out an equally inept scenario at the wheel:

I was attending a school reunion day which included an old boys versus current pupils rugby match, dinner and drinks. We lost the rugby match, heavily. In fact, we were humiliated and did as all young men do on any such occasion, drink even more heavily. I was absolutely blind

Lady Luck and Me

drunk when I decided to take my friend, Rob Wickes, back to my place. He lived in Lyme Regis, Dorset. We were attending the school reunion in Taunton, Somerset and I lived in the heart of Devon. It made sense at the time that I give him a lift part way home, and he could pick up the trail the following day. Looking back at it, with no car or train station within 10 miles of where I lived, it was difficult to see how my offer benefitted him in the slightest. However, he took me up on my offer and hoped that he could repay the favour someday. Within five minutes, I immediately regretted the decision that I had made. Like my grandfather before me, I was driving safe in the knowledge that the car knew where it was going. I had driven the country route avoiding the M5 many times before. I was lucky enough to have 'The Chariot' throughout my sixth-form years so the car had known the route very well. I found that as soon as you name a car, you give it personality and therefore you can attach responsibility. In my drunken wisdom, I thought that because I looked after its tyres, windscreen wipers and oil reserves, it owed me and would drive me safely home, incident free.

After the first two miles, it was clear that this was not going to be as 'The Chariot' lurched from hedge to hedge. It was at that point that I thought of the genius of my grandparents plan and employed Rob to work the steering wheel whilst I closed one eye to concentrate on the pedals and the ever-narrowing lanes. By some miracle, it seemed to be working. We weren't going to break any land speed records but we might just make it to our destination unscathed.

The next suggestion of Rob's led me to believe that he genuinely wanted to hurt himself. It was as though he was not happy flirting with death but actually wanted to

Before the Beginning . . .

poke death in the eye with a stick. 'Dare you to drive with just the hazards on,' he mumbled with his head buried deep in the driver's side foot well. I laughed, as you would at an already absurd situation that's just been pushed to a suicidal level. He wasn't laughing. 'Are you serious?' I questioned in disbelief. 'Go on.' As if my hands were possessed by a higher force, I saw my fingers reach for the hazard lights and then turn off the headlights. I giggled, he giggled and then very quickly neither of us giggled. To this day, we don't know whether it was his brake control, my steering or the fact that we couldn't see a sodding thing that crashed us headlong into the only bridge within eight miles.

We were fine. 'The Chariot', however, was not. It was no longer an option to use the headlights as they, along with the bumper, grill, number plate and various liquids were strewn across the dark country lane. The irony was that the only lights that were still working were the lights that had got us into this mess in the first place. We eventually limped home via the M5 hard shoulder, taking three hours rather than the usual 40 minutes. God only knows why there weren't any police out that night. So, for once, thank you Lady Luck, I salute you.

Having been raised in a strict Victorian household, it was always a surprise that Grandma seemed to be so open-minded towards sex. She was the one who always informed us of Channel 5's late-night, risqué programmes and had quite an extensive VHS library to prove it. They lived in Guildford and regularly made the short journey over to see us in Aldershot. After one particular Friday-night visit, we were all surprised to see Grandma and Grandpa's car pass our drive a further three times with what can only be described as shrieks of joy coming from Grandma who

Lady Luck and Me

was half in the car and half hanging out of the passenger window.

Mum, being naturally concerned, phoned them later that evening to make sure all was right. Grandma picked up the phone and excitedly informed Mum of their highly eventful journey home. It seems that as soon as they had turned out of our driveway, they had been met by a unit of paratroopers running up the road towards them. With Aldershot being the home of the British army at the time, there was nothing unusual about that. What was a little different that night was that the paratroopers were as naked as the day they were born, much to my grandmother's delight. She had demanded that my grandfather drive around the block not once, not twice but thrice in order for her to take as many pictures from as many different angles as possible. She drove over every Friday evening for the next two months hoping for a repeat viewing but, sadly, to no avail. If any of those paratroopers ever read this, I thank you. You gave an aged lady a smile that lasted many weeks.

Incidentally, there's also a very good chance that a couple of months later, the same unit witnessed my mother stepping out of a pair of used pants that had got caught in the trouser leg the night before. As if that wasn't embarrassing enough for her, our dog, which she was walking, shot past, picked up her pants in his teeth and sprinted towards the on-coming exercising company with Mum in hot pursuit bellowing at the dog to let go. Thankfully I wasn't there. If I had been, I fear I would have lost a lung laughing.

My father was a bit of a rogue, albeit a lovable one. He knocked around southwest London for much of his youth, flitting in and out of art college with no particular purpose. A talented cartoon artist but with little motivation,

Before the Beginning . . .

he resorted to finding work as hired muscle. As a tall man with a short temper and karate training, he drew attention from various unsavoury characters that made their living collecting gambling and other such debts. There are tales of him hanging around in stairwells armed with two razor blades with a matchstick sandwiched between them. The theory being that, when the unlucky victim was sliced, it would be a nightmare to stitch back together without leaving a nasty reminder.

Although a questionable choice of career, he did have some redeeming elements to his character. He could dance. My God, he could dance. Dressed up like John Travolta in 'Saturday Night Fever', he would frequent the dance halls of London during the sixties and clear dance floors with his wondrous snake hips. Women were powerless to resist his moves. Equal to the shapes he threw on the dance floor was his gift of the gab. He could woo a rhino at two thousand yards with his dulcet tones and impregnate them at five hundred with just one revolution of those magnificent hips. And all the time looking like Shrek. It was his smooth talking that led him into the office of my mother. She was working at Centre Point in London as a PA when he waltzed his way into her life. As well as her PA role, she was also modelling for window companies, spreading herself across state-of-the-art double glazing and pointing at corners of conservatories. He had come in to blag a job way out of his league which, somehow, he got. But also, with that velvet tongue, managed to secure a date with my mother.

She had attended a ladies' finishing college where they taught her to walk with books on her head, curtsey, laugh far too enthusiastically and adhere to all the social etiquette that is expected of aristocracy. If family folklore

Lady Luck and Me

is to be believed, she was being thoroughly groomed to be Prince Charles's suitor. No word of a lie. It was my grandparents will that she should marry Bonnie Prince Charlie. My father and the Prince of Wales couldn't have been from two more different walks of life, chalk and cheese doesn't come close. She was, of course, putty in my dad's hands as soon as they stepped onto the dance floor, as was anyone else who came into contact with him. Their dates became regular and more serious and, - eventually they were engaged.

When the news was broken to my grandparents, it was welcomed like a cup of cold sick; my grandparents' dreams of a royal wedding and a life of peculiar waving were dashed. Even when he turned up in expensive cars with arms full of my grandmother's favourite flowers, they were having none of it. My parents genuinely thought of eloping to Canada and would have if it hadn't been for Mum falling pregnant with the first of her children, my sister Charmian. Her arrival scuppered any emigration plans and they settled in a little house on the outskirts of Guildford, Mum continuing to work at Centre Point and Dad doing the majority of his mysterious and murky dealings within the confines of dingy, tobacco-stained pubs.

Apart from the vast quantities of alcohol consumed before, during and after negotiations, there were plenty of other vices to keep my father's mischievous mind occupied. With a pint glass in his left hand and a dart in his right, he became well known in many of the surrounding pubs, not only for his silver tongue but also for his talent in front of the dart board. Tactical or not, it was a truly genius move on my father's part. It just so happened that my grandfather was also a keen darts player and, before long, my father and Ronnie were spending countless hours together, either

Before the Beginning . . .

standing at the bar or at the oche, much to the annoyance of my housebound mother. As a result, my father won the hearts-and-minds game with my grandparents, so much so that my grandparents were more than happy to contribute to Mum and Dad's first family starter home. Dad had neutralised the initial hostility and had actually turned it to his advantage. He was Nelson-like in his strategic execution.

Three years drifted by before Mum acquired a second bump. Nine months later, Emma, the middle sibling, popped out. She was a rotund, squealing little thing, reminiscent of a newborn piglet but, to grandparents and parents alike, a very welcome addition to the family. That's where I'm going to leave Emma for the moment; she'll rear her adorable piglet head later on. So now, the immediate family numbered four: one very alpha male and three females, two beneath the age of five. As a result, the pub outings increased enormously and the dart rivalry between my father and Ronnie intensified. Apart from that, it was life as usual. Dad philandered with pub-goers, a string of random women and suspect business contacts whilst Mum worked her well-trained airs, still doing the daily 11-hour corporate nonsense, with the occasional photo shoot.

Eighteen months later, another bump appeared. Whether it was planned or whether it was a celebratory shag that produced that kidney bean, I'll never know. In fact, I tell a lie. I know that's exactly what it was. It just so happens that my father's birthday falls in November whilst my mother's falls in early December. Now, I'm no Stephen Hawkins, but even Kerry Katona could work that nine-ish months from then is August . . . I, the kidney bean, was born in early August. Emma was born in early August and Charmian was born in late August. We were definitely

Lady Luck and Me

the products of birthday shags; whose Happy Birthday we were remains a thing of sibling speculation. If I am indeed anything like my father then my money's on it being Dad's birthday. Not that I know how many times he dips his wick annually; that's not the kind of thing I or anyone, for that matter, should ask. It's just best you don't. But if he is anything like me, then it wasn't only his birthday that such shenanigans occurred.

A Bean is born

It's only in hindsight that you realize what indeed your childhood was really like.
Maya Lin

Dad was doing his usual pub-going business when Mum got the urge or, as I like to see it, Ben's break for freedom. Mum and Dad were fighting like wild animals through much of the pregnancy and, as the stress diminished Mums capacity to produce the necessary serotonin for either of us, she was convinced there would be something wrong with me. Once wheeled into the appropriate room at the hospital with me banging on her organic doors, we were then promptly left alone as the Duty Nurse wandered off, as they did back in those days. Childbirth, especially the third, was seen as a formality. Sure enough without a struggle or delay, I emerged victorious; tiny, hairless and hung like a pixie. Ben the Knob had been born! My mother maintains it was a beautiful moment between mother and son. Alone, in a clinical, sterilised, white room was probably the exact opposite to what Mother Nature had intended the glorious beginning of new life to be. Don't get me wrong, there are hundreds of more horrendous ways to be brought into this world but the one constant is the immediate bond between mother and child, so much more so when their introduction is completely private. Intimate. Maybe it was that I was the last to be born, the only male, or simply the first trying moments that we had with each other, but a special bond was formed — I feel, I think, I hope. I spent many hours of those first few weeks wrapped in swaddling in the arms of mother as she cut shapes in

Lady Luck and Me

the living room to the soothing sounds of Electric Light Orchestra.

As far as I know, the first few months of my life were pretty unremarkable. That was until I started being potty trained. My potty training was very confusing. I had my mother telling me that a little blue plastic bowl was to be my target. Charmian, aged seven, thought differently. She thought it was fun to lead me to believe that the potty was everywhere, including the Swiss cheese plant. The genius of her plan only became clear later; the flower pots, of course, were hidden by the plants' canopies and the soil was the perfect disguise for a number two. I literally soiled many plants around the house, much to my sister's delight and my mother's bewilderment. Still tiny, hairless and hanging like a pixie but now pooing anywhere, indiscriminately.

It wasn't until about the age of four that the first blond ringlets appeared and, with that, my fascination with other people's hair. It was not uncommon thereafter to see me twiddling with complete strangers' hair, on the bus, in the post office queue. Wherever there was hair to be twiddled, I was there, twiddling. Like a moth to a flame. It must have been a tragic sight. I was like a malnourished cherub, without the harp or the wings and with an even smaller penis.

At this stage, we, the family, had moved to a little village called Wood Street on the outskirts of Guildford. Dad was wheeling and dealing in bigger circles in London so we, the family, saw him less often and Mum was left holding down a job, raising three children and wondering what the fuck was going on with her husband and father of her children. When I was knee high to a grasshopper, the inevitable happened. Dad was having an affair and intended

A Bean is born

to move in with his new squeeze. I'm not sure Mum was that surprised. The numerous knife-throwing episodes in the kitchen and exchanges of words that only two devils could muster were clear indications that something had to give.

And so there it was. Mum, who had been destined for such aristocracy, was left with three young children to support, a mortgage to pay and the 'I-told-you-so' self-righteous bullshit from her parents. She did it though. She absorbed the abuse from her parents, held down her job and was nothing short of a perfect mother, caring for our every need. Remarkable, really. I'm in such awe of single mothers who manage to look after themselves, their household and their children and rarely in that order. Remarkable, again, as I can barely look after myself, let alone a brood.

The first six years of my life were occupied with school, eating cheesy mashed potato and wearing shoes three times too big for me, courtesy of our next-door neighbours son, three years my senior. Although Mum had the baggage of three children she was an attractive woman and never short of suitors. That was until one of her friends introduced her to a young Lieutenant Colonel. He was rising quickly through the ranks of the British Army and was seen as one of their brightest officers. Like Mum, he was a single parent, having lost his wife to cancer a few years prior. The inaugural drinks date went smoothly between them and, as a result, we, the family, were invited to dinner. For the first time and after many failed couplings, Mum saw a potential future with dickhead. For the sake of legality, which is a damn shame, that's how I shall refer to him hereafter. He was bright, silver-haired, financially sound and successfully raising his daughter. The match was undeniable. In a bid to win his affections, we were dressed

Lady Luck and Me

to the nines and under strict instructions to eat and drink whatever was in front of us, without question. Now, I ask you, who the hell lays a table for four children under the age of fifteen, me being six at the time, and charges all the glasses around the table with white wine? Who would do that? Dickhead would, that's who.

I was too young and, ten minutes into the lavish meal, too drunk to see the warning signs. Like the good son I was, I polished off the white wine in a matter of seconds. I can still taste it now. It was a cross between Blue Nun and cat's piss and tasted just as bad on the way up as it did on the way down. I can't remember much of the meal but vividly remember the feel of the bannister as I crawled my way along it, hourly, to reach the bathroom throughout the night, all the time over-hearing the exchange of apologies between Mum and dickhead, both desperate not to look like the fool. That was my first introduction to wine and dickhead and I was to have a passionate dislike for both for many years.

The courting between Mum and dickhead continued until marriage was proposed. It made simple sense; for an aspiring army officer there was nothing greater for career progression than walking into the officers' mess with a well-spoken, attractive wife on his arm and, for her, a brighter future for her children.

It seemed like the marriage worked for dickhead as, not long after we moved in with him and his daughter, he was promoted to Colonel and, with that, a posting to Dusseldorf, West Germany, as it was back then. Our new Dusseldorf house was a huge, great, white, characterless cube with a Joseph Fritzel-style basement, two living floors and a shooting range as an attic. The rest of the street was

A Bean is born

populated with other military officers' families, ranging from Military Police to the Intelligence Corps. All one, big, happy, British forces family. We were initially sent to heavily guarded Forces schools where wandering soldiers with M16s and helicopter landings were a regular occurrence during the school day. It was a strange, insular existence, being bussed to and from school and spending the rest of the time socialising and living on the one street.

There were others of my age on the street. One of my peers was a chap called Peter Figg who had the most stunning sister, Claudia. I wonder where you are now, my sweet princess. Even aged eight, we can all appreciate true beauty and it was her, personified. Long, flowing, brown hair, and a body that defied her fourteen years. I befriended her geek-like brother just so I could spend more time in her company, giggling awkwardly whenever she chose to speak to me. She was the apple of many young men's eyes. I'm sure I was making headway for her to be my future wife when it was cruelly nipped in the bud. The Figgs had two large dogs that regularly delivered healthy loads twice a day in their garden and, as entertainment was in short supply, I came up with the Dog Shit Game which was exactly what you'd expect it to be. After liberally applying a twig with as much canine excrement as you could find, you would chase your opponent around the garden, flinging the shit at the best opportunity. It was my game and I excelled at it, so much so that it was detrimental to my life-long plans with Claudia. Having discovered a recent dump, I hastily covered my stick with gravity defying amounts, cornered Peter and unleashed the hell that clung to my stick. With sniper-like accuracy, I struck my target full on the open mouth causing instant vomiting, tears and a house ban from his very angry mother. I don't think I ever got the opportunity to formally

Lady Luck and Me

apologise for what I can only imagine must have been the most distressing experience of his childhood. Peter, if you ever get to read this, I am truly sorry. That afternoon, I lost a friend but, more importantly, the mother of my children.

Having been banished from the Figg's house, I spent my free time in the garden aimlessly kicking a football around whilst being stung by hornets which frequented the apple tree in the middle of the lawn. This quickened my feet and gave me a life-long resentment of all flying creatures which was to be cemented years later. Meanwhile, down in the basement, dickhead was constructing an intricate five-foot, balsa wood glider. Once made, he took it to the hill at the end of the German part of the estate and flung it into the air, time after time, watching it meander down in the gentle currents until it landed beautifully a kilometre away from its launching site. It was my honour to go and retrieve it for him to throw again. And I did, day after day, you bastard, like some obedient yet retarded shooting dog. That was until the one Sunday afternoon that I found the basement door unlocked. Seizing this rare window of opportunity, I headed down the stairs and into the usually secured glider hangar. My trembling hands grasped the delicate wooden frame and, whilst shitting myself, I bolted back upstairs with it and into the garden, feeling overjoyed that I had just stolen the devil's trident. Not only did the 25 square metre back garden have an enormous apple tree smack bang in the middle of it, it also had the most foreboding 50-foot pine trees surrounding it. With a run up and a great leap, I hurled the glider into the air, not thinking of either its flight path, descent or landing. Majestically, it climbed high above the tree-line and house until it seemed to hover momentarily before nose-diving and then hurtling back towards earth, increasing with murderous speed. Like

A Bean is born

a boomerang, it was heading straight back towards me. In fear of decapitation, I leapt out the way just in time for the glider to whistle past me, past the apple tree and smash through the sitting room window, showering a surprised dickhead in shards of glass and balsa wood splinters. It was awesome. What had taken him months to build took me 15 seconds to destroy. I didn't wait around to see if I could reason with dickhead and hot-footed it out of the garden as fast as my twig legs could carry me.

The other lad of the same age on my street was Rupert King-Evans who lived opposite. The main thing I remember about Rupert King-Evans was his invitation to Camp Beaumont. I know, it sounds like a Brighton gay cruise; it was actually an activities holiday for youngsters in the UK. I think it still exists today. I accepted the invitation with relish and embarked on a 10 day holiday which included archery, quad-biking and potholing. Unfortunately, being only 10 years old, I didn't qualify for any of those activities; in fact, the only activities that I qualified for were wildflower collecting, bird watching and country walks (the country walks were getting to the flowers and birds and then back again). It was the most elaborate, ballsy, baby-sitting business that has ever been conceived by man. It was shit. Ten days of shit.

There was one highlight, or lowlight maybe, that happened on the last night of the 'activity holiday'. It was customary for Camp Beaumont's last night to be fancy dress and they held nothing back in making it the biggest night of the holiday. Everyone but me, it seemed, was aware of this and had packed accordingly. Some were sporting crazy Star Trek uniforms, whilst others wore weird vegetable suits. I had nothing but the clothes I'd been wearing for the previous nine days. It just so happened that an older boy

Lady Luck and Me

took a shine to me, not in a sexual way I assure you, but probably because he could see the pain written all over my young face, witnessing a small boy's worst nightmare. He wore an impressive Storm-Trooper suit and was obviously old hat at these last night shin-digs, commanding respect from the other long termers. He offered help and I very gladly accepted, seeing him as a solution to my potential public humiliation.

I asked no questions and, obediently, wore the clothes he had found for me. Fully dressed, I was the perfect image of Judy Garland in the original 'Wizard of Oz'. Looking back, it was uncanny and really quite impressive. As soon as the make-up had been applied with a trowel, I was led down the corridor and thrust not only into the main hall but onto the stage where everyone had gathered for the crowning of the 'Best Dressed'. After a brief argument with the organisers as to which gender category I fell into, my mentor led me up onto the stage and left me standing to rapturous applause from the 200 oddly dressed bastards in the room. The stage cleared rapidly. There wasn't a vote, short-list or any other finalist there with me on that stage. To complete the humiliation, my hand was thrust in the air like I'd won a heavyweight title fight, stirring the prepubescent crowd into a fever. My eye was caught by my mentor, enthusiastically waving his arms at the crowds and making me feel increasingly like a shrinking cross-dressing penis. I received a five pound gift voucher for Woolworths which was promptly stolen whilst changing back into my 'holiday' clothes. I didn't want to go on another activities holiday after that.

Not long after my return, the decision was made that we, the children, should be sent abroad for private schooling. My sisters were interred in the prestigious

A Bean is born

St Georges School for Ladies, Ascot and I was sent to Holmewood House in Kent, another highly revered private school for young gentlemen. The relocation was tough for all of us. Like my sisters, Mum had been a daily constant since birth so it was quite an ordeal adjusting to seeing them once every couple of months, if I was lucky. Mum has since had to answer some painful questions regarding that separation and although she regretted the decision she made, she did so selflessly and with her children's best interests at heart. Dickhead, the sick fuck, took pleasure in taking sad, soul-destroying photographs of Mum sharing the same pain thousands of kilometres away in Germany.

Now that my sisters and I were somebody else's responsibility, dickhead could focus fully on his career and the arse-licking that is required in order to rise up through the ranks, of which he had become a grand master. He regularly held dinner parties for other officers at our house, using his own Army chefs to do the catering. It was during one of these pretentious willy-waving evenings that I first encountered the real dickhead. I must have been about 10 at the time and on holiday from school and, as the meal was in full swing, questions of education and careers were raised. Next to me, an Infantry Colonel in black tie asked my sister, Emma, what she wanted to do when she grew up. Before Emma had time to answer, I loudly announced that Emma wanted to be a hooker when she grew up. Dickhead, at the head of the table, choked so hard on his pork chop that the Officer sitting next to him panicked and started giving him the Heimlich Manoeuvre. Once dickhead had recovered, he apologised to his guests and then solemnly told them and me, that I had no idea what that word meant. He sent me upstairs to my room, sternly

Lady Luck and Me

instructing my bewildered mother to re-join our esteemed guests at the table.

A couple of hours crawled by as I nervously awaited my fate. As soon as the door closed behind the last guest, I heard him climbing the stairs. He slammed my bedroom door behind him and came at me, eyes widening, pupils dilating with his right hand raised above his head, 'I want respect, not love.' And with that, his hand thundered down on my puny body. That wasn't the last time he tried to beat that lesson into me, the twat. In the years that followed, I went to extraordinary lengths to be prepared for that one day I might accidently see him again. I know where he lives; always have done but, so far, my compassionate side is keeping the vengeance at bay. Let's hope that that continues.

Aside from his cowardly beatings, he was also emotionally and socially retarded. One Sunday morning during holidays, my mum, my three sisters and I were all sitting around the kitchen table when dickhead walked in with shopping. He had an enormous grin on his face. He tipped the bag up, laughed, and walked out of the room. On the table for all to see were two hardcore gay porn magazines, some kitchen roll and a packet of Rowntrees Winegums. I ask you, who the fuck does that? Nobody ever got to the bottom of that one. I could write a novella on dickhead's countless social faux pas and very peculiar 'heterosexual' antics but I won't as I'm already beginning to feel queasy having spent already too long writing about him. Just before I throw up, I'll conclude dickhead by saying he was a confused, lonely, immature, sexually ambiguous fuck up. Those are the best compliments I can give him. In spite of what I thought of him, the British Government and Her Royal Majesty didn't seem to agree with me and, in their

A Bean is born

wisdom, rewarded him with a CBE. I've never been able to work that out; how a man who's incapable of looking after his own family and, with so many psychological problems, is seen fit and able to command thousands of heavily armed men all over the world. Who makes these decisions? No doubt other equally fucked up individuals.

Lady Luck and Me

Ripped from the bosom

'Loneliness and the feeling of being unwanted is the most terrible poverty.'
Mother Teresa

Holmewood House was anything but a house. Discipline and punctuality were its foundations and everyone adhered to its philosophy. There were two cultures within the school: the full-time boarders and the day pupils. There seemed to be a shared sense of helplessness and therefore camaraderie between the boarders and a sense of pity and arrogance by the day pupils, smirking as their lifts arrived at the end of the day. As boarders, we were marked out of five daily, on our cleanliness, uniform folding and personal space organisation. At the end of the week, the scores were tallied and the victor was allowed an extra 15 minutes TV time on Saturday night. At the age of 10, that was a big deal as it meant bedtime became 7.45 rather than the usual 7.30. In our boarding house, the dormitories were separated by four glass partitions, each sleeping a separate year group of around 10 pupils on five bunk beds. Over the space of an hour, there would be three stages of light until complete darkness descended. You could set your watch by it.

Back then, the common understanding between boarders was that we were there because our parents didn't like or want us at home. The fact that my mother and new family now lived overseas only reinforced this schoolboy thinking. Boarding should really mean abandonment. The countless hours that I invested in trying to convince the housemaster's wife to let me make just one phone-call

Lady Luck and Me

never paid off. Instead, she tried to break my yearning by giving me a needle and thread and bits of offcuts, telling me to try and make something for Mummy to show how much I missed and loved her. A lot of tears went into some really shit cushions and several sad bits of crudely stitched mismatching fabric from attempts at purses. However, by the end of my needle-working days at Holmewood, I was accustomed to most stitching techniques and a dab hand with knitting needles. On the odd occasion I would be drafted into the laundry room to help clear a pant-naming backlog.

Being unable to reach home by phone, the letter-writing sessions after chapel on a Sunday morning was my last hope to let Mum know just how much I missed her and my sisters and just how much I would love to hear her voice on the phone. I also wrote about what was happening in class, which teachers I didn't like, how much I hated it and again how much I missed her. As I wrote, I hoped the tears rolling down my cheeks would land on the words so they would smudge and offer another means of expressing just how much I was missing her. At the end of the session, when we handed our letters in for posting, each letter was scrutinised for spelling and punctuation and then placed in one of two piles on the teacher's desk. Only after the teacher had read and sorted each letter were we allowed to leave, in silence. No-one knew what the two piles were for and we still had blind faith and no reason not to believe that the teacher would rush out immediately to post them, as a matter of urgency.

It took a while for me to catch on that anything derogatory written about the school or anything about me not enjoying it would lead to a visit to the Housemasters study after lunch on Sunday afternoon where the pupil

Ripped from the bosom

would be quizzed about why and what they had written in their letters home. Often the letters and postcards that I received from mum made no mention of any post arriving for her with simple questions often going unanswered. It was almost as if the letters were never posted.

Thankfully, I wasn't at Holmewood House for long; a couple of years at best. Apart from my prowess with a needle and thread, the only other lesson that has served me well from that experience was not the discipline or wardrobe maintenance, but that teachers can be cold and heartless.

My next school was in Berkshire. An old renovated stately home tucked away deep in the Home Counties countryside. A majestic building surrounded by woodland, open fields and so much more importantly, girls. For an imaginative, pre-pubescent Shrek, it was a wonderland and I immediately felt more comfortable there. There were no more than two hundred pupils sharing oodles of space, both in the classrooms and in the dormitories. The animosity between the boarders and the day pupils was non-existent with there being a genuine family atmosphere throughout the school. When it came to boarding, I was seen as hardcore as I was pretty much the one and only boarder that stayed the weekends as well as some half terms, not through choice, but by the lack of anyone willing to host me.

My memory tells me I had friends, but maybe I was a massive arsehole and never knew it? I suppose that would explain the rarity of the invitations. Anyway, as they were picked up in their 80 grand cars, I was looking forward to a late night bath with the duty housemaster that used to oversee our cleanliness. I vividly remember him sitting in the bathroom in the evenings and the shower room

Lady Luck and Me

after games, legs crossed on a raised platform watching us rub ourselves down, checking each and every armpit on the way out. Looking back on it, it was the seediest experience of my life . . . to date. At the time, of course, I didn't know any different. The other questionable guardian was my housemaster/French teacher and cricket coach who used to stroke the back of my legs when I handed work in, whispering to me I was his number one.

Strangely enough, this was also the time I discovered my party trick. Whilst others inverted their eyelids, I calmly drove thick safety pins into my arms until they hit bone and then invited others to do the same until my arms looked like pin cushions. I found it soothing and almost addictive, each day finding different areas where I could push through until the dull ache of the bone was reached. In the time that I was there, no-one out-tricked me. Years later, it was diagnosed as self-harming, but in that ignorant time I saw it simply as fun because I enjoyed doing it.

During my time there, I developed a fascination for the Middle Ages, more specifically the Norman Conquest, all thanks to the most engaging, non-paedophile, Canadian, history teacher, Mr Embury who resided in a tiny broom cupboard/study room hastily arranged by the matrons at the end of the boarder's corridor. Heaven only knows why he took such a position but, to this day, I thank Lady Luck for him. Not only did he teach with animation, he taught with passion and real enthusiasm giving all of us a genuine reason to want to be in his class. It was during these lessons that my imagination was properly fired, creating a world in which I was the lead character.

For some reason, as soon as I put pen to paper I'd drift off into a fictional, medieval time where I was a jester

Ripped from the bosom

wandering from town to town, brushing the tops of the barley as I travelled. If I close my eyes now, I can still see my character dressed in a typically quartered red and yellow jester's suit, bells included; arms spread wide, skimming the tops of the barley ears, sporting what can only be described as Freddie Mercury's face, with the great, big moustache being the focal point. I used to roam through beautiful glades, forest trails and by waterfalls, never engaging in conversation or ever actually even seeing another person. The places that I imagined were places I had never been or seen in any book; they were very much imaginary places and yet there was always a familiar knowledge of the place and time without ever having any points of reference to confirm it. From my waking moment, I used to look forward to the earliest opportunity when I could escape into that other world. Occasionally, when I was alone, I used to sit and cry at being born in the wrong time period, convinced I would have been far happier living as my character in his time.

As the writing continued, word spread amongst the teachers and, due to me being the most permanent member of the school, I was given special privileges of being able to write care-free during English and history lessons. It was feverish at times, writing in a trance-like state as I travelled through what I now know to be the beautiful, sunny, Wiltshire countryside. It was escapism at its very best and still serves as a sanctuary of peace and freedom when I close my eyes in trying times. Fifteen school writing pads later, I produced my first historical fiction novel, *The Everlasting Druids*, an epic tale set in England, post-Norman Conquest, during the early reign of William the Conqueror but centring round his half-brother Bishop Odo. Odo was the spearhead of a ferocious, fighting Catholic force that was at war against the nature-loving, pagan natives that

Lady Luck and Me

disguised themselves as creatures of the forest to seduce and kill the naive Catholic occupiers. It was a simple tale of good versus evil with relatively few but accurate, historical facts thrown in for good measure.

I gave mum my scribblings during my summer holidays which she dutifully typed up and proudly presented as a beautifully bound manuscript. Considering I had been allowed to forfeit many hours of expensive education in order to write it, she gave it to me with unmistakable pride, so much so I think that was the catalyst that has made writing the fondest of all my hobbies. A couple of years had passed since I had first put pen to paper and, in that time, my writing style had changed dramatically. By the time I had finished writing the book, I thought the beginning was so awful it would all have to be rewritten. Mother Nature, however, had other ideas and intervened by giving me raging hormones and a new-found interest in my penis. Suffice to say, *The Ever-lasting Druids* was put to the back of a cupboard to be forgotten about.

So I spent most weekends at the school and, more often than not, on my own. It was a huge ex-Edwardian stately home, with countless wings and corridors stretching on for what seemed like miles. The hardest weekends were during the winter months when the temperature plummeted and the winds whipped through the aged windows. With only me rattling around the place, the powers that be decided to turn the heating off as it wasn't financially feasible to have it on for one person. I was pretty much left to my own devices and went to bed when it suited, usually after watching some horrendously frightening movie or, if I was lucky, some late night soft porn on Channel 4. It forced me to enjoy my own company and also to learn how to make friends quickly. With so few people around,

Ripped from the bosom

I learnt that the more adaptable I made myself, the longer I kept company. Falling into a social chameleon role like that, at such a young age, was necessary not only for the companionship but to prove to myself I could be liked. I still thought that I wasn't wanted at home because they simply didn't like me.

In my quest, I often sacrificed far too much of my soul, rolling over far too easily if there was any whiff of any disagreement or confrontation. In order to keep people happy, I gave them complete control, carrying out exactly what I was told, when I was told, which, gradually over time, I think rendered me unable to think for myself or have any belief in myself. I don't think dickhead helped with that.

These days though, I still enjoy my own company but my need to befriend everyone has abated the older I've become. Now, thankfully, my belief that I'm not an absolute bastard and wasn't sent away because no-one liked me has taught me I can choose the people I surround myself with, rather than accepting and being thankful to anyone willing to speak to me.

Away from the main school building but in the grounds, the headmaster had his family home. Matt, his son, was a year or two younger than me and fell into the category of 'Right Little Shit'. Arrogant and with a sinister streak, he was not well thought of by many, including his own parents. Tammy, the daughter, was two years older than me and schooled elsewhere. She had developed into a sporty, physically mature young woman years before she should have and, because of this, became every hormonal boy's fantasy. The same could also be said for the headmaster's wife. Although she was middle-aged and not particularly

Lady Luck and Me

attractive, she had a flirty, dirty quality about her and she knew it. We all knew it and she knew that we knew it. As well as teaching drama she also taught swimming. Our swimming classes were split into boys and girls classes, in an attempt I suppose to stop the boys leering at the girls in their swimming costumes. What this meant though was that she had the undivided attention of 10 horny boys watching her and her alone in her swimming costume getting in and out of the pool numerous times a class. On more than a dozen occasions we asked her to show us her back stroke technique just so we could stare at her ample breasts bobbing up and down. Regularly, peers of mine would have to make up woeful excuses to leave in order to escape the growing embarrassment in their Speedos. She knew it and, I'm absolutely sure, loved it.

The headmaster was a caring, light-hearted fellow who seemed to spend most of his time on the school's nine-hole golf course than he did in his office. He always wore a smile and I genuinely believe he had his pupils' well-being as his highest priority. Out of school hours, the family pottered around the school and its grounds making full use of the facilities and, with me doing the same, it wouldn't be uncommon to come across one or all of them. Over time, we saw more and more of each other resulting in me being adopted as a second, surrogate son. I would be invited to dinner at the weekends and often offered a bed for the night under their roof, one, to keep Matthew occupied in the evening and two, so the rest of the family could get a break from him. As the headmaster was a history Doctor, I didn't mind hanging around with Matthew so long as I got to quiz his dad on the specific points of history that interested me. The other pay-off I got for spending time with the family was the attention I received from Tammy.

Ripped from the bosom

As I was the only boy with whom she had regular contact, she must have seen me as someone upon which to hone her flirtatious skills. I was like a rabbit in headlights in dealing with her affections, not knowing how, or even whether, I should reciprocate them.

Time passed and I was spending more and more time at the weekends with them and loved being part of a family again, albeit a temporary one. Tammy's affections were also growing in boldness until, one weekend; they finally came to a head. It was like any other weekend, I had free reign of an empty, desolate school and had decided to try my hand at being the schools number one rollerskater, so was spending as many hours as I could racing around the indoor sports hall. Tammy, not a skater but a hockey player, thought it would be funny to use me as moving target practice, thankfully not with real hockey balls but hollow, light ones. We were both thinking it was hilarious when one struck me in the groin unbalancing me and sending me full pelt into the wall. I crumpled in a heap, not through the pain but with the understanding that such an accident would definitely result in endless sympathy. Sure enough, Tammy was distraught and rushed over to help me to my feet and then escorted me into the adjoining room where I could sit comfortably.

After inspecting my fictitious injuries on my elbows, Tammy, being thorough in all that she did, insisted she had a look at my bruised knees. Despite my assurances that my knees felt absolutely fine, I was no physical match to fight off her ambition or aggression in getting my trousers off. Before I really knew what was going on, she was having sex with me on the gym mats. I lay there as she did all the work not knowing what I was supposed to do or how I was supposed to do it. It wasn't

Lady Luck and Me

good, it wasn't bad; it was just different and had come somewhat out of the blue. It certainly wasn't how I had imagined my first proper sexual encounter to be. When the realisation of what was happening kicked in and just when I thought to myself I should be enjoying this rather than feeling violated, we heard the unmistakeable creak of the gym doors. Familiar whistling was heard as footsteps got closer and closer. Tammy shot off me, pulled up her tracksuit bottoms and darted behind a long cupboard that housed the hockey sticks. No sooner was she in place, her father, the headmaster, rounded the corner to see me lying on the gym mats, trousers around my ankles, roller skates on, trying to catch my breath. It can't have looked good. Obviously startled, he looked at me, raised his eyebrows and simply said, 'Oh, sorry to interrupt, Ben.'

Resuming his whistling, he carried on walking through the door and out of the gym. Tammy reappeared from behind the cupboard, smiled and said, 'Wow, that was close' and left the gym the way her father had come in.

I lay there, recapping the last five minutes. I really wanted to run after him and explain that I wasn't masturbating, that his daughter had just taken my virginity and had leapt off just in time to leave me in that compromising position. I didn't and sheepishly pulled my trousers up, removed my roller skates and hid in the dormitory for the rest of the day. I hardly saw Tammy at all after that and whenever I saw the headmaster he smiled and winked as if to say, don't you worry, your secret's safe with me. Well, Doctor, if you ever read this, now you know the truth and it wasn't at all what you think it was.

Aside from the extra-curricular time spent with Tammy, I also enjoyed the school's more official extra-

Ripped from the bosom

curricular activities. I was never happier than when I was on the sports fields and excelled at the hand/eye sports such as cricket and hockey, captaining the school in both. According to my coaches at the time, I had the potential to go all the way in cricket, although sadly they were very wrong; lack of passion and a shortness of talent saw to that.

When not in the classroom or on the playing fields, my time was taken up practising my singing, which is now laughable. In the days before my voice broke, I had a reasonable treble's voice and headed our school choir, leading my flock into chapel on Sunday evenings carrying a huge brass cross. I'm sure I was appointed Head Chorister only because I was always at school at the weekends and would therefore never miss a service. As well as carrying the cross, I proudly displayed my three Church of England music awards around my neck and over the white cassocks we were all given. The sight would have been a paedophile's dream come true. As a reward for being Head Chorister, I got special privileges from the Choir Master Mr Miles, namely that I was allowed to go to his flat, which was in the school grounds, most evenings to watch any one of his hundred horror videos whilst he made me toffee apples and cake. At the time it felt like a great privilege but looking back at it now, it was a wholly inappropriate gesture that smacks of grooming and certainly wouldn't be allowed in this day and age.

Christmas was always the most important time for the choir and in my final year at St. Andrews it was decided that I would do 'The Snowman' solo before the service got underway and the first verse solo of 'See Amid the Winter Snow'. I rehearsed feverishly in the preceding months, and when the event finally came around, I was ready. I absolutely nailed 'The Snowman' solo, feeling like God

Lady Luck and Me

himself when I had finished and actually looked forward to my second solo of the evening. Alas, the second was not quite so successful. After missing the first line I looked up to see my mother and grandparents visibly in pain at my silence. The organ started again with the same result. Not only had I now forgotten the words, I now felt the 500 people in the church waiting for my next fuck up. The third time the hymn was started, my friend next to me, Nick Holloway, gave me a sharp jab in the ribs with his elbow which caused me to produce a sound not to dissimilar to that of air escaping from a bagpipe. My timing was out and I was hopelessly out of tune but I had started so had to carry on. Eventually, after what seemed like an hour, my verse was over and so was my singing career. To my mum's and grandparents' credit, they congratulated me on a fine 'Snowman' performance but mysteriously never said a word about my second effort. Even today when I have to sing, those awful memories come flooding back. There'll be no 'X-Factor' for me, I fear.

Big school

> *'Anyone who has been to an English public school will always feel comparatively at home in prison.'*
> Evelyn Waugh

The move from Berkshire to Somerset was a tough one. My biggest fear of leaving was that my showering and bathing time would not be quite as thorough as, unfortunately, certain individuals would not be there to make sure my awkward places had not been missed. However, if the public school rumours were to be believed, there would no shortage of willing replacements.

My prep school had been a sleepy, untouched haven buried deep in the Berkshire countryside, hidden away from the perils of modern-day life. It had an insular, large-family feel to it with my peers being more like brothers and sisters and the teachers like guardians rather than cane-wielding megalomaniacs that most people associate with the old private schools. For the most part, it was a happy, comfortable environment to be in, especially in my last year as I managed to rise to the enviable position of Head Boy and, coupled with my sporting success, I was well-regarded by both pupils and masters.

It was sad to leave, but this next school offered a reunion with my sister Emma, who had been suspended from her school, St Georges, for an underage drinking binge on Lambrusco. It was Mum's and dickhead's decision that she should be taken out of St Georges to prevent further rebellious misdemeanours, much to Emma's annoyance,

Lady Luck and Me

and inserted into the Sixth Form to complete her last two years of schooling before university. That was their excuse, but I have an inkling that the real reason was money and convenience. St Georges was a highly respected all-girls school that cost considerably more than where I was and as Charmian and my sister had now finished at St Georges, it made more sense logistically and financially that we should be schooled together at the cheaper sibling rate. If alcohol and a bad crowd were the problem at St Georges, I couldn't possibly see how a co-ed school surrounded by off-licences and pubs would be less of a distraction to her studies. Whatever the real reason for her move was, it was good news for me. I'm not so sure if Emma thought the same though. During our first year together, Emma came to see me and, being the dutiful and watchful brother that I was, I was sure I could smell alcohol on her breath. Fearful she was going to relapse and turn into a fully-fledged alcoholic that you might see on the Jeremy Kyle show, I immediately phoned home once she had left. Mum then phoned Emma's housemistress and the housemistress interviewed Emma, much to Emma's annoyance. She hadn't been drinking and I had just caused an utter shit storm for her. Emma, I'm really sorry about that.

I hadn't been to school with either of my sisters since the age of six, when we all attended a Convent school in Hampshire which, as the name suggests, was run by mothers and sisters of the cloth. They masqueraded as servants of God when all was fine and dandy or when a parent was present, but were the Devil's assistants when they doled out their punishments. Stray paper aeroplanes in the playground were met with sharp, ruler slaps to the back of bare legs, resulting in redness, tears and a stern reminder that God was watching and was not pleased. It

Big school

was also the place where I came up with the genius decision to change my surname. Now that Mum and dickhead had married, I was entitled to change my sir-name, which I did, giving me the desirable initials B.A. Nowadays it doesn't mean much, but back in the mid-eighties, the A-team dominated Saturday evening TV and BA was Baracus the biggest, bad-ass, black man on it. I, on the other hand, was the smallest, skinniest, weakest white boy in the year. The contrast between my initial namesake and me couldn't have been greater. It did, though, for a while a least, give me huge kudos points in the playground. As the news of the new initials got around, the more respect I was shown. The marble pit, once an area reserved for the cool kids, was where my new homies and I hung out. It's amazing at that age that a name change, no matter how ridiculous it is, can dramatically change your fortunes. If only it was that easy in adulthood. In time, it backfired somewhat. It wasn't long before fellow pupils caught on that I wasn't actually the massive black man mountain on TV but still the weak, spaghetti-limbed runt that I was before the name change, except now they could take the piss as well. Not only that, I was stuck with the dickhead's surname throughout my early years of education and it served as a constant and raw reminder that he was part of my life. Starting at a new school gave me the long-awaited opportunity to finally shed the dickhead's surname and reinstate my true family name. All in all, as much as I loved the school, I was glad to be moving on. It felt very much like the end of one chapter and the beginning of a bigger one.

It was a huge foreboding building dating back to the late nineteenth century, complete with the original dodgy plumbing and cold dark stoneware. Even on a glorious summer night it would have been the perfect set

Lady Luck and Me

for a hammer horror movie and wouldn't have taken much of a stretch to imagine Christopher Lee patrolling the tall dimly lit, artic cold corridors in his high-collared cape.

The front of the building was dominated by a clock tower that overlooked the front playing pitch, which in the winter months was the first XV rugby pitch and in the summer months the first XI cricket pitch. As a result, the cricket outfield could be a little unpredictable with a seemingly innocuous cricket ball suddenly leaping from the ground and smashing an unsuspecting fielder in the face. For the home side it was expected and thus watched with caution, for the away side St John's ambulance was on standby.

Away from the main building, the grounds were smattered with other buildings which had been added at later dates. Most of the additional academic blocks which were dotted around were gaudy 1960s and 70s eyesores which had been given absolutely no aesthetic thought whatsoever and were to serve solely as practical learning centres. If fact, I would go so far in saying that if Stevie Wonder had been the architect I would still have been surprised, they were that grim that anyone with a heartbeat should have been ashamed of what they had created. The boarding houses weren't much better, slightly more modern but in dire need of TLC. Regardless of the vast sums of money which the school demanded from its boarding patrons, it was clear that the boarders' comfort was not a high priority. There was a chapel which we all had to attend on alternate days before school started and which also hosted marriages, baptisms and confirmations. It also had a choir which I got press-ganged into joining soon after I arrived due to my choral credentials from prep school, but sadly by then my voice had properly broken and the sound that I produced

Big school

was more akin to a dying buffalo than the assumed angelic cherub. I was ejected pretty quickly and that I was thankful for, early teenage peers can be very unforgiving in their judgements to boys singing in choirs.

I was housed in School House, the only boarding house to be located within the actual main building itself and the oldest house in the school. My first year's dormitory was in the clock tower and shared one of its walls with the headmaster's office. Six of us slept there on three bunk beds, with a grandstand view of the front playing fields. Great location with the only downside being that whenever the clock chimed (hourly), our beds would vibrate and we would suffer tinnitus for the best part of an hour until the bell signalled the passing of another hour. One of my new room-mates, Goldy, was a giant of a man at the age of 14. A regular player for Bristol youth rugby club who required three shaves a day to stay fresh faced, even the upper sixth formers admired his manly attributes. Even though he was able to strangle an elephant with his bare hands, he wasn't blessed intellectually and at times it would be a struggle to have the most basic conversation with him. Having said that, get him onto either the capitals of the world or Bristol Rovers football club and Jeremy Paxman or Stephen Fry wouldn't get anywhere close to him. He was like a hairy rain man on steroids.

Being on the lowest rung of the school ladder meant we were given chores every morning and, in true public school tradition, mine was looking after and tidying 'Belly's' room. He was an upper sixth former who lived in squalor and had a striking resemblance to Lenny in John Steinbeck's 'Of Mice and Men'. The honour bestowed upon me was to pick up his soiled pants from the night before, make him tea and generally be his bitch as he slumbered in

Lady Luck and Me

bed passing wind and barking orders. This master and slave relationship didn't stop once I had completed my morning duties but continued throughout the day. If I was in the vicinity and Belly wanted something I would be summoned to do his bidding or face one of his club fists reigning down on me. Irrespective of my schedule or timetable, Belly had to come first, landing me in considerable trouble for tardiness with most of the teachers, most of the time. Everyone in my year in School House was assigned a sixth former to 'help ease their everyday pressures' and Belly was unanimously voted the most demanding to look after.

During breaks or at lunchtimes, the sixth formers huddled together in their groups like some sort of court of law, passing judgement on everyone in the years below, thinking and acting like they were the gods of the playground. Regularly Belly would call me over, unleash a fist into my arm and then send me off on a menial mission just so he could exercise what little power he had. They had some sort of competition going on to see who could be funniest by making their 'helper' do the most pointless tasks. The vast majority of his year had a conscience and would actually ask, not threaten, their 'helper' to do relatively useful things like pass messages on or fetch something from their room which they had forgotten. But not Belly, oh no, Belly had no conscience, so after the usual punch on the arm he would shout at me to go to the garage half a mile away and bring him back a one penny sweet with a receipt as evidence that I had been there. And all this was against the clock. He would then re-join the others in mocking fellow students who passed by. But my fortunes

Big school

with Mr Bell were to change and in the most unexpected way.

It was midway through the summer term, Belly and his crew were nearing the end of their A-levels and their time at school, so the atmosphere was relaxed and generally pretty carefree. My arm had lost most of its black-and-blue bruising and, for the first time in many months, was mainly skin-colour again. Prep had just finished and, like every day, we were all making our way to the School House common-room for the final roll call of the day. En route, Belly spotted me and called me in to another sixth-formers room. Belly had his back to me fiddling with something I couldn't see. He swung around sharply and thrust something towards my stomach. Naturally, and without thinking, my hands flew up to protect myself and, at that moment, I felt something cold and metallic on my thumb's knuckle. Looking down I was shocked to see blood oozing from an open wound, dripping onto the floor. I looked at Belly and the instrument he had in his hand. He stood there staring at the cut, mouth open, whilst the butterfly knife he had been playing around with went limp in his hand and then fell to the floor.

Meanwhile, Mr Brown the assistant housemaster – who had just returned shaking from the police station after Edwin had anonymously phoned 'Crimestoppers', informing them Mr Brown matched the photo they had shown on television - had begun the roll call in the room next door. For something that should have been very painful and distressing, it was actually one of the most pleasurable experiences I had had all year. The sheer panic and horror on Belly's face was a delight to see and still to this day fills me with warmth every time I picture it. Through the air we could hear my name being called by Mr Brown, Belly

45

Lady Luck and Me

responded, yelling out I was with him which seemed to suffice as Mr Brown continued reading out names. Before the list had been completed, Belly had bundled me out of the room down the corridor and outside to his car. He drove like a man possessed to the local hospital all the while apologising profusely and swearing at himself for his own stupidity. I loved every minute of it and creamed the situation by rolling my head from side to side, gentle groaning in false agony. This twat who thought he was the bollocks had now been reduced to a pitiful child, shitting himself at the potential repercussions this incident might have. Sitting in A & E with a towel wrapped around my hand, Belly began pleading with me not to incriminate him. Knowing that I had him by the short and curlies, I sat there watching him squirm like an obese grub, giving nothing away. By the time I was called through to see the doctor, Belly was in tears and knew the sword of Damocles hung over him, and I alone had the power to let it fall or take it away.

The doctor removed the towel and inspected the thumb. Belly sat next to me nervously shuffling from cheek to cheek. Inevitably, the question of how I came to have this injury arose. I looked at Belly who looked at me, then at the doctor who looked at me and Belly and then back to Belly. The silence was deafening yet glorious. It was the sound of ultimate power. Finally, I looked at the doctor and told him I had carelessly slipped with the bread knife. Belly let out a huge sigh of relief and then desperately did his pathetic best to try and disguise it as the beginning of a cough. The fool had clearly just incriminated himself, even I felt embarrassed for him. The doctor, smelling a sizeable rat, looked at Belly and then at me and told us this wasn't a bread knife wound and repeated his original

Big school

question again. Before Belly could fuck it up even more, I quickly answered that it had been caused by my clumsiness with the bread knife. He looked at both of us and raised an eyebrow. Credit to him though, his questions ceased and he began stitching the wound, telling me, but looking at Belly, that I was lucky it wasn't deeper and in the future to be considerably more careful with bread knives.

From that day forth, Belly became my bitch. Nobody could quite understand what had taken place for there to have been such a complete role reversal. For the remaining few weeks of that summer term, I had Belly picking up my ruined underwear each morning and making me tea. I only sent him to the garage once and that was to get a refund for the penny sweet he had told me to get the month before. He didn't much like that but was bright enough to know that I still had the power to make or break him. Whenever I look at the small scar these days, I can't help but smile. Although the power was short-lived it was oh-so-sweet and would gladly take a knife all over again just for the pleasure of those final summer weeks.

Apart from most of the first year being taken up accommodating Belly's every whim, it was a year that passed quite quickly. Most of the time, I was being governed by hormones with weird growth spurts coming and going and acne which was always coming but unfortunately never going. I become so self-conscious of my ever-increasing range of mini volcanoes, it started to seriously have an effect on my mental wellbeing. The combination of Belly's demands and my facial eruptions drove me to spend many afternoon's sitting in my dormitory overlooking the front field, listening to Dire Straits' 'Brothers-in-Arms' on repeat for hours as tears rolled down my face. Knowing nothing about depression at the time, I thought I was sad

Lady Luck and Me

or hormonal. I had tried all the over-the-counter remedies to no avail and, in desperation, had started buying bizarre Chinese concoctions in an attempt to stem the ailment. I actually have no idea whether the cream that I was smearing all over my face twice a day was for acne but it had a drawing of a face on the front and lots of Chinese writing on the side and, as I had tried everything else, I thought I would give it a go. My face didn't improve in the slightest that year but my cock doubled in size which I can only attribute to the Chinese and their magical cream.

The last hope was the school doctor and maybe a prescription. My step-sister had been prescribed Roaccutane which essentially burns the top layers of the skin on the face off, leaving a red, swollen, delicate and hopefully spotless face behind. It wasn't ideal but necessary at the time. At the first consultation, after the usual questions of diet and exercise, I was rather surprised when he asked me to take down my trousers and cough whilst he held my balls in his freezing hands. I didn't think too much of it as it was an initial assessment for my general health. I was asked to return the following week and then the week after that and the week after that. The questions dried up and the appointment now just consisted of me taking down my trousers and coughing for five minutes. Apparently it was all in aid of me getting the best possible treatment. A month later and no prescription in sight, I decided not to go back to the school doctor and actually never set foot in the sanatorium for the rest of the time I was there.

It was in the second year that I met the first love of my life, Clare. She was slightly rebellious (she wore Doc Martin shoes), athletic (she ran the 100 metres), from a religious family (Catholic), was attractive (she had developed sizeable breasts) and bright (she sat at the front

Big school

of the class). She was also going out with one of the cool guys in my year, Ross. He was rebellious, often coming back after the weekends talking of his clubbing nights and how many Marlboro red cigarettes he had smoked. They had been dating for a while and it was common knowledge that they had been around all the bases, a number of times. I had only managed the home run once, with Tammy, and that had been disastrous.

My communication with Clare all started as a bit of a joke. We were in the same English class but rarely spoke. She was part of the cool girl gang who had all gone to school together at the prep school so had grown up together and knew each other well. I was shy, nervous, self-conscious, not from Somerset and still trying to find my feet socially. Sitting at the back of the class with my new friend James, I began writing her little notes. The notes worked and soon Clare and I were in the early stages of courtship. Ross didn't seem to object and reacted with indifference when it became public knowledge we were dating. It was all very new and exciting for me and I was, for the first time, experiencing feelings for a female that weren't penis-driven.

The rest of the second year was pretty featureless. Clare and I grew closer and I was accepted into the cool social groupings mainly due to my sporting prowess rather than my rapier wit. The week before speech day and the end of term, Clare and her non-boarding friends had been given permission to go to Wimbledon to stay in one of her friend's family flats. I, of course, being a boarder and, more importantly, dating Clare, was flatly refused permission to go with them. Clare's mother had raised concerns about her eldest daughter and myself being left alone, overnight, miles from her watchful eye. I was not going to let an opportunity to get out of school to sleep in the same bed

Lady Luck and Me

with my girlfriend pass me by, so I hatched a cunning plan. I made my dormitory peers swear an oath of silence to me, told my housemaster I was going on a two-day Royal Shakespeare Company seminar and packed my bag happy with my flawless deception.

The morning of my departure didn't start well. Somehow, I had managed to misplace my wallet and the phone number of the flat in London. Obviously, it was imperative that I had the number as I hadn't told Clare or any of her company that I would be making the trip to see them. I didn't want the cat to escape the bag and scupper my plans before I had even left the school premises. Searching frantically, I enlisted the help of my fellow dorm member Edwin, a Hong Kongese wily ferret, and it wasn't long until he appeared from under a bed, wallet in hand, smiling from ear to ear. In my excitement and relief, I thanked him, not in the orthodox fashion but the way Inspector Clouseau thanks his sidekick Cato, thinking that if it's all right for him to say then it's got to be fine for me. My 'thank you my little yellow friend' quickly extinguished Edwin's smile and his face started turning a crimson red. I died inside, immediately registering that I had committed an almighty faux pas and that my thanks had actually been the worst possible insult. My explanation of the Pink Panther story fell on deaf ears and Edwin exited the room, visibly fizzing with anger. Not only had I seriously racially abused a good friend but had very probably blown my cover for my London expedition. Wallet in hand, overnight rucksack on back and with a heavy sense of guilt, I made my way to the coach station.

The coach pulled in to Waterloo station and I disembarked. I hadn't spent any time in London on my own before and as I stood in the station pondering my next

Big school

move, it dawned on me how poorly prepared I was. The landline number in my hand gave me no indication as to where in London I should be heading, all I could remember from the conversation that I had had with Clare was that the flat was in a part of London that began with a P. When Clare had told me of its actual location I hadn't committed it to memory, thinking that London was just a little bigger than Taunton and couldn't have too many areas that began with P. Now, as I looked at the snaking underground map, it was clearly evident that I had seriously underestimated the vastness of the capital and I was a total arse not to have taken more details. If I had remembered the second letter following the P, it would have reduced the possible list significantly, but I couldn't. So, after getting no reply from the number I had been given, I began working my way through the underground stations beginning with P. At each of the stations I would try the number again, and each time the phone remained unanswered. What occurred to me quite quickly was the fact that they had come up to watch Wimbledon, so there was a very good chance that's where they would be all day until probably, at the earliest, dusk and as it was only midday. I realised I was going to have a very long afternoon indeed. By 3 o'clock I had completed the District line, Central line and Circle line twice, by accident, and the enormity of the challenge ahead of me had really hit home. By 5 o'clock I had done the Piccadilly and Bakerloo lines and had made countless, unanswered phone calls. It was whilst I was waiting for the Victoria line that the exhaustion, thirst and hunger set in, forcing me to wobble and then collapse on the platform. It was a middle-aged, pin-striped businessman that assisted me to a nearby bench and then kindly fed the vending machine for water and a Mars bar. I briefly told him of my woes before he smiled sympathetically and boarded his

Lady Luck and Me

train, leaving me gathering my thoughts and fighting back the tears.

Night was beginning to fall when I got off at Pimlico and I was now worried, no frightened, as I didn't have enough money for a B and B, knew no-one to stay with and had missed the coach back to Somerset. Simply put, I was in a proper pickle. Once again, the phone rang out and I cursed loudly, much to the bemusement of passing commuters . . . going home . . . to their families . . . and their evening meals . . . and their beds. The bastards. Sitting outside Pimlico station next to the pay phone I had no other option but to sit, wait and dial frequently, hoping Clare and co hadn't decided to go out for the evening meal. I was moved on from two doorsteps by disgruntled residents and sat on the pavement feeling more and more like a down-and-out as the minutes ticked by.

With all hope seemingly lost and the idea of sheltering under a park bench becoming a real possibility, I decided to make one last phone call. Crossing the road to the phone box, the yellow neon street lights picked out four people walking away from me. The more I looked and willed, the more familiar they became. Bypassing the phone box, my weary walk turned into a stumbling trot and then, convinced it was them, into a record sprint. By the time I reached them I was like Sly Stallone at the end of 'Rocky', crying out for Adrianne. Clare turned around just in time for me to fall into her arms and start sobbing like a child who's just lost its teddy. With friends under each arm I was taken/carried the short distance to the flat and collapsed on the sofa, thoroughly embarrassed about my naivety towards the whole episode but also mindful and appreciative that a small miracle had just taken place. What were the chances of my being in the middle of London,

Big school

lost, after dark and my friends appearing at just the right time? Needle in a haystack of haystacks comes to mind. All my efforts hadn't been in vain though: I did get to share a bed with Clare for the first time that night.

Having watched Wimbledon after scrounging a spare ticket, we all took the coach back to Taunton. Aware that all their parents, including Clare's, would be waiting to pick them up, I pulled up my hoodie and made sure I was the last to leave the coach in the hope I would slip away unnoticed. As I stepped off the coach, head down making my way across the car park, my huge hood blinded me to everything but the ground directly in front of me. Just when I thought I had made it, I heard a screech of tyres and long, angry horn. Looking up in order to offer my apologies, my eyes locked with Clare's mothers, and she was not happy. She glared at me, with pursed lips shaking her head. Of all the cars in the car park, Lady Luck let me stumble into the only one I was trying so desperately hard to avoid. Before I gave her a chance to lower her window and abuse me, I was gone, weaving my way through the parked cars and down an alleyway, heart pumping. It had been a disastrous outing all in all but a memorable one nonetheless. I had learnt that London was a place where an address is absolutely necessary, that hoodies ruin discreet getaways and that miracles can happen when all hope seems lost.

My GCSE year flew by and, before I knew it, I was sitting the exams. Revision had been compulsory, but I had managed to think of a thousand other things to occupy my time as I sat at my desk. So, as each subject paper was placed in front of me, I was already thinking of excuses to

Lady Luck and Me

give disappointed teachers and furious parents for my poor performances.

During that summer term I had sat the Morrisby Test, which was a complicated aptitude test designed to ascertain which career I would most likely be suited to and when the results came back I was convinced that the papers had been muddled as mine suggested I would make a good customs and excise or police officer. To this day I can't think of a worse or more poorly suited career and, after having spent hundreds of pounds on absolutely nothing, Mum and dickhead now hoped my grades would shed light on where I should focus my studies. I was glad when I laid my pen to rest for the last time and worked out I had about six weeks to enjoy before the exam results were in and I was in serious trouble. Some friends of mine had mentioned escaping to Antibes in the south of France for a cheap, two-week holiday. A lad's holiday away where we could sun ourselves and legally get drunk seemed the ideal solution for forgetting the shit storm which was coming my way, so I put my name down. I'd never been on a coach for more than about four hours before our two-day journey and, when we finally arrived at our destination, I was already in fear of the journey back. I thought I was a patient man but two straight days of a baby wailing and smelling the contents of its nappies cook under the mid-summer sun as I sat next to the toilet on a non-ventilated coach, would test even Buddha's resolve.

It turned out that our self-catering holiday was so cheap because our accommodation comprised of a large tent that slept four, a plastic table and chairs and a dangerous-looking camp stove. The toilets and showers were shared with the other thousand people on site and on more than one occasion daily showers were skipped after

Big school

watching turds glistening with bubbles float out with the used shower water. We were one tent in a row of 30, and in one row of 40. Each row seemed to accommodate each nationality as all the holiday-makers in our row were British with the row behind us being Dutch and the row over from them, German. It was a rather strange national segregation that created an unwanted tension throughout the campsite, with spats regularly occurring between individuals of different nationalities. By the end of the second week, small militia groups had formed, thinking that safety in numbers was the safest way to travel. We divided our time between the shitty, overpopulated, polluted little beach that was awash with used condoms, tampons and the odd forgotten sandal during the day and in our tent drinking the cheapest Bavarian beer at night. Thankfully the holiday went pretty much incident free as we did the best we could to avoid trouble, grateful to just be away getting drunk without the worry of a unmarked mini bus rounding the corner at any minute.

The final night came and the plan was simple: get as drunk as possible as quickly as possible because one, we could for the last time and two, if we were so hung-over we wouldn't notice the painful journey back. Cheap spirits took the place of the beer and within a couple of hours we had our first warning from security guards on bikes to turn down the music. By nightfall civilised conversation was way beyond our ability so we had resorted to simple drinking games that required very little brain power. On the second visit, the security guards confiscated our portable stereo and, after another stern warning, peddled off leaving us to make up our own woeful tunes.

To spice up the dying night, one of our party thought it would be a good idea to introduce industrial-

Lady Luck and Me

sized firecrackers that had been bought from a dodgy market stall outside the front gates of the campsite. As he stumbled and fumbled around trying to light the fuse, the rest of us hung on supporting each other, watching and giggling. The fuse burnt surprising quickly, far more quickly than the fire-starter had expected, turning his drunk mischievous face into a sight of sheer panic. This caused him to launch the cracker high over his shoulder, over our tent and clatter loudly on the roof of a huge four-by-four in the German row, the fuse still sparking away. We winced and waited. First we heard the fiddling of the zip at the German tent just before shitting ourselves at the most enormous explosion I'd ever heard. Bottles fell off the table in the after-shock as 30 car alarms sang in unison, waking what sounded like every sleeping child in the campsite. One of our group unplugged the light in our tent, leaving us standing in darkness and silence, listening to the German car/tent owner going absolutely ballistic. Thinking our time was up, we waited and swayed from foot to foot, expecting the most savage beating of our lives. But, as more and more irate foreign voices joined in, it became clear that the blame had been laid squarely at somebody else's tent. After cowering like little scared girls for a couple more minutes, we crept out of the tent and peered through the thin, straggly hedge just in time to watch a half-naked, hairy German pick up a plastic chair, hold it over his head and then fling it with all his might at the Dutch tent opposite.

The ripple effect was unimaginable. Twenty minutes after the fire-cracker had taken a chunk out of the car, widespread brawling between the Dutch and the Germans was well underway with a couple of the rogue militia groups stopping by for an indiscriminate punch or

Big school

two. We watched on in horror as it slowly spread to the rows around us, eventually involving Spaniards, Italians and most of the security staff. Our light stayed off, letting us wander through the shadows drinking gin and watching the mayhem unfold all around us. I passed out late into the night, fully clothed, on one of the plastic chairs outside our tent, successfully blind drunk. The next morning I woke to find my only shoes, on the floor next to me, full of my own sick. My shirt, shorts and legs also had traces of undigested two-minute super noodles on them. Numerous tables and chairs were scattered, upturned, around me, along with other random bits of debris you would expect from a full-scale riot. About a third of the German tents were intact and standing, the rest had been flattened, bent metal tent poles sticking out at awkward, irreparable angles. Beyond their row, the Dutch tents had fared even worse. Barbeques had been tipped over tents, burning and scarring the ground and tents that the coals had set on fire. Cars had acquired sizeable dents overnight, with some missing wing mirrors and windscreen wipers. Suitcases, blankets and soft toys littered the ground, giving the impression that some sort of human-rights atrocity had taken place during the night.

None of this concerned me as much as the thumping pain which had originated in my head but had now spread to the rest of my body, rendering me incapable of leaving my soiled seat. At that moment, I vowed never to drink gin again. I sat there being slowly cooked and shrivelled by the hot morning sun, eyeing up the life-saving bottle of water lying on its side on the ground, genuinely unable to make the 10-yard journey. Gin and various other aromas sweated through the pores in my skin, reminding me and my stomach of the liquid diet the night before. What finally got my legs stumbling to life was the sight of

Lady Luck and Me

a French police car slowly slaloming its way down the eerily abandoned Dutch/German road. Lurching from object to object I entered the tent, kicking my fellow holiday-makers lifeless bodies as I went. We only just escaped our tent with our belongings as two French police officers disappeared into the tent next to us, working their way along the row making their enquiries.

We all sat in silence at the coach park, sun beating down, nervously looking over our shoulders expecting a police car to pull up any moment to take us away. When the doors of the coach closed and the engine roared to life, a wave of relief washed over me. That was until the air-con suddenly stopped working, the broken toilet door swung open and the same baby that we had travelled down with, began a two-day, merciless tantrum, regularly filling and overflowing its ill-fitting nappy. I've never wanted a gun as badly as I did for those two days and when the coach came to a halt 48 hours later in Bristol, I was a broken man, in need of a holiday.

France has never been a good holiday destination for me. The second and last time I went was after my A-levels, again with friends. The week itself was a bit of an alcoholic blur but what I do remember is the ferry journey there and back. Both for embarkation and disembarkation, the loading of the ferry had to be stopped just for me as I struggled with my clutch control on the ramp. The 1000 other people had to wait and disapprovingly watch as the P and O official had to drive my car up the ramp whilst I hid in the back seat too ashamed to be seen. I have no intention

Big school

of holidaying in France again, nothing but bad memories. I really am a true Brit.

Having achieved pretty mediocre GCSE results, it was unclear which A-levels I would be best suited for. In the end it was decided that I would do Geography, History, English and Social Biology. Soon after I started I dropped Geography so that I could concentrate on the other three. Why? I have no idea. I had no clear focus what I should do with my life, never mind what I wanted to study at university. History and English were straight forward essay subjects, not that I found them easy, quite the opposite in fact. I thought learning about great conquerors and experimenting with different writing techniques would fuel my imagination and inspire me, instead English was about the subtleties and speculative meanings of Seamus Heaney's poetry, and history was dates, dates and essays with dates about obscure and pointless fifteenth-century parliamentary legislation. To compound the issue, the classes were both taught by the dullest, most cantankerous two men I've come across to date. There was also definite gender favouritism. I remember the pain and boredom of studying Germaine Greer's 'The Female Eunuch' and then having to do a critique of it. It was of little surprise to me that myself and my two other male classmates all got a C whereas Kiko, a Japanese exchange student who couldn't say her name in English let alone write it, managed to produce a piece of work apparently worthy of a very respectable B+. That left us all scratching our heads.

So what could and should have been my two most interesting subjects were blighted by decrepit teachers trying to teach a woefully obsolete syllabus. The only redeeming factor was I that spent both classes with Amelia Bailey and her magnificent breasts. She was the apple of everyone's

Lady Luck and Me

eye, including most staff members both male and female, and she knew it, playing both staff and students like an electric keyboard. I've always wondered what happened to her and her glorious assets.

Social biology was also predominately essay based but was modular, so the essays and exams were taken throughout the two years. It was considerably more interesting than my other two subjects, due to the lessons having more relevance and practicality to current life. I enjoyed it so much it became the nucleus of my study and I was determined that my university course should encompass it. At the time, I quite fancied myself as a psychologist or psychotherapist. My room/study during my lower sixth year happened to be situated on the ground floor, directly opposite the two girls boarding houses, and in those houses resided a group of five upper-sixth stunners. They stuck together like one big ball of honey, dominating all social situations they entered into. For a school comprising mainly of horny boys, these beauties were elevated to goddess status. They had leaped over that imaginary line smack bang into the middle of womanhood. Fully developed and brimming with self-confidence, they were in a league of their own.

For some bizarre, unknown reason, one of the group, Mishka, a petite dark-haired, blue-eyed wonder, had taken a shine to me. I was lanky, awkward and already becoming follicly challenged. Opportunities such as these very rarely came my way which left me with a sizeable dilemma. Clare and I were in good shape and I had vowed to myself that I wouldn't make the same mistake my father had, blaming that mistake for robbing me of a happy childhood. For a couple of months I staved off the temptation, exchanging self-conscious smiles, still expecting that any day her

Big school

affections would turn elsewhere. The days went past and still Mishka was making her intentions known. With the first social biology module creeping ever closer I was putting in my hours and slowly becoming more confident that I was going to nail this one. Preparations completed, I turned in early on the eve of my first stepping stone to being a psychologist. At around midnight I was rudely awoken by an incessant rapping at the window and, since the upper sixth had just finished their A levels, I was not all that surprised. Drawing back the curtain in my pants I expected to see some drunk, vomit-soaked upper sixth verbally abusing me, desperate to get in the house as it was way past curfew. Instead, Mishka was standing there made up to the nines beckoning me outside like some mythical siren. What with it being hours away from what, at the time, was my most important exam of my life, every sinew in my body and every brain cell bar one screamed 'NO, NO, NO', whilst one rogue cell screamed 'YES, YES, YES!' I was dressed in about 15 seconds and quietly climbed out of my window into the night, feeling like the man from the Milk Tray advert. Parked a short distance away was her cream and purple 2CV, engine running, doors open. It was a perfectly crafted getaway. Out of the school gates, through Taunton and then deep into the Somerset countryside twisting and turning through miles of deserted country lanes until eventually arriving at a thatched, chocolate box country cottage in the middle of nowhere. Surrounded by corn fields basked in the moonlight, it was a scene to behold. The interior didn't disappoint either. Elegantly decorated throughout, I had the sense that we weren't the first to come here for a lustful evening. The giant double bed, complete with black silk sheets, dominated the master bedroom and could well have been a feature in *Country*

Lady Luck and Me

Life magazine. After we hastily finished a bottle of red, the night really began . . .

I was woken by bright sunlight and the terrible feeling that something was very wrong. First the guilt kicked in, then the much more horrifying feeling of not knowing what time it was and not knowing where the fuck I was. Those two terrible realisations didn't bode well for me being calm and collected for my first A-level exam. Tearing the duvet off me, I hurtled out of the bedroom in search of Mishka and the all-important time. It was only when I ran through the kitchen door that I regretted not taking the extra three seconds to put on any clothes. I was greeted by Mishkas peers: the three other most attractive women in school. Like a rabbit in the headlights, I stood there, terrified and shrinking, metaphorically and literally. With my hands cupping my crotch I backed out of the kitchen and sprinted back upstairs desperately trying to ignore the giggles that followed me.

Whilst dressing I heard the front door close and the muffled giggling continue until the sound of a car engine filled the air. Tentatively, I crept back downstairs and peered around the corner to thankfully see Mishka on her own nursing a cup of tea. Since being caught by the school beauties with my trousers down, or not on at all as the case was, I had momentarily forgotten about the all-important time. Now, as I looked at Mishka, I couldn't help but notice the four foot circular clock that was hanging on the wall directly above her head, almost as if it had been just placed there by the devil determined to remind me of the mountain of shit that I was in. And I was in shit, piles of it. As hard as I stared at the clock, its hands wouldn't stop or go back, but mercilessly kept ticking away each second with a sickening mechanical thud. If the clock was

Big school

accurate, and I had no reason to believe it wouldn't be in this perfect country cottage, I had 15 minutes to make the start of my exam. With quick, very optimistic calculations, I reckoned I could just make it. As long as Mishka's 2CV could reach 120 mph, it was a completely clear, gun-barrel straight Roman road all the way back and the gods were on my side. My urgency wasn't lost on Mishka as I desperately tried to explain my somewhat sizeable predicament. Her expression turned from amusement to horror as I quite clearly frightened her with my incoherent rant. I was out of the door before she knew what was going on, leaving her to surrender her cup of tea and follow me out to the car.

The Somerset country lanes weren't clear or Roman and her 2CV was barely managing 25 mph and checking my watch every 30 seconds did little to help my stress levels or slow down time. Five minutes into the very hopeful 15 minute drive back, the car began to bunny hop, inducing my heart to almost go into cardiac arrest. Before I had time to take a deep breath and pray, the engine died and we ground to a sudden halt, flanked on both sides by high hedges and fields. There was to be very little chance of immediate assistance. My fate was sealed. In the days before mobile phones, situations like this were only solved by old-fashioned leg work. After a speculative look under the bonnet, not that I had the faintest idea of what I was supposed to be looking for, I left Mishka with the car as I took off looking for help or a way back to school, whichever came first.

Just when all hope had faded, I was almost run over by a rather jolly farmer driving an aged tractor. Having successfully flagged him down and briefly described the size of the shit that I was in, he invited me to sit alongside him as we drove back to the knackered 2CV and Mishka

63

Lady Luck and Me

sunbathing in the adjacent field. Neither of them had any empathy or concern that I was teetering on the edge of seriously fucking up my life and on the verge of a breakdown. The farmer, John, or as his friends called him, Maggot (only in Somerset) set about inspecting the fragile engine and within a minute was chortling loudly as he extracted a maimed but living rabbit from the engine casing. Holding it by the neck and flinging it around like a rag doll, he proceeded to tell us occurrences such as these are all too common on the lanes. Mid-sentence and with both of us watching on, he nonchalantly smashed the rabbits head on the wheel arch leaving a bloody stain and Mishka squealing. He held the now dead, twitching rabbit in front of us offering it to us as some sort of souvenir.

We left Maggot still clutching the rabbit as we bundled back into the car and started the engine. Thanking him through the securely wound up windows we continued on our way, having lost 20 minutes and any notion that farmers were sensitive, misunderstood souls. I was now late for my exam and it had now become a case of damage limitation. If the car could reach 150 mph and time stood still there was still a slim chance I could apologise my way into sitting the paper after all. As I watched the speedometer needle flirt with 30 mph and my watch's second hand continue on its unwavering march, I began to conjure up a multitude of excuses for the many individuals who would be asking what the hell I'd been doing and where the hell had I been doing it. Mishka remained oblivious to my impending doom and quite gaily began to sing along to George Michael on the radio, which subsequently made me screw up my hands into white, knuckled, little balls. Finally, we arrived at the school gates 40 minutes after my exam had started, Mishka kissed me goodbye on my cheek

Big school

and wished me a good day, still unaware that this little tryst had almost certainly cost me a university place and probably a few broken bones and bruises from the people I had let down.

As I sat in my room watching the seconds tick by, guilt began to creep in. Not guilt for missing the exam, I had a story to last me a lifetime why I had missed that, the guilt was for Clare. It was the first time I had really experienced the very depths of guilt and agonised over the thought that I was just like my father, and would live my life womanising and squandering relationships that would have been wholesome and nourishing rather than ending life alone, sad and remorseful. The longer I sat, the worse the thoughts became, snowballing into ridiculous predictions that I would never have another girlfriend again if people knew what I had done. By the end of my guilty session, my story was written all over my face and if anyone had asked me how I was at that particular moment, I would have broken down and confessed all. As it was, no-one asked me a thing and I recovered sufficiently in time not to come to the attention of any of my peers.

The housemaster, Mr Wales, did however hear that I had missed my exam and took me into his study to question me, and when I say question me, I mean that literally, in the singular. He asked, 'So, Ben, Mr Cook tells me you missed your first Social Biology module?' in the strongest welsh accent you can imagine. To which my reply was, 'Yes, Sir.' At that, he raised his bushy eyebrows, turned and left his study, leaving me recapping the conversation

Lady Luck and Me

thinking maybe I had missed something. I hadn't and nothing more was said between us regarding the incident.

I therefore dropped Social Biology and concentrated on my two other subjects. I kept the whole night a secret, even from my closest friends. It had been exciting but very wrong and the whole episode had made me question my morals and left me feeling like the biggest shit alive for months after.

During the holidays, I usually had the weekends off from doing odd jobs here and there and made regular trips to see Clare and spend time in her family's garden, competing with Tony, her father, pitching golf balls. Tony was a lovely man, Lancastrian by birth and a past Wasp's captain, England International and Barbarian rugby-playing legend. He had semi-retired, working from his home office organising wooden spoon charity events and, bizarrely enough, selling neoprene matting for stables and other animal enclosures. He was a devoted family man who welcomed anyone to join him and his bow tie for a glass of wine, cheese and a good old natter. Clare's mother was a staunch Catholic, a little neurotic and more than happy to put anyone in their place for the smallest faux pas. If he was the cheese, she most certainly was the chalk. They lived in a comfortable, detached house in Corfe, just outside Taunton, which, according to local friends of theirs, had the most cloudless sun hours in the entire country.

It was a haven to me, not only during the holiday weekends but also during term time and, as girlfriend's families go, they were lovely. Since they were practising Catholics (mother's insistence), sleeping with Clare in the same bed was absolutely forbidden, but they weren't that archaic or idealistic to know about modern teenagers

Big school

urges and often turned a blind eye to public displays of affection. Clare and I could have many hours in her bedroom during daylight hours but, as soon as the moon rose, our activities were closely monitored by her mother. On saying our goodnights, I would embrace them, wish them a sound night's sleep, turn to Clare and say the same. I would wait until all the lights were out, give it 30 minutes for the parents to fall into their slumber and then tip toe out of my room, down the creaky mid landing into Clare's room. This 10-yard manoeuvre could take me anything up to 25 minutes depending on: 1) how sozzled I was, 2) how sozzled they were, and 3) how horny I was.

For months this routine was practised and I never thought my movements went unnoticed. As I've said, Clare's parents were pretty savvy and the floorboards were ear-splittingly loud in the otherwise silent house; only a dead, deaf person wouldn't have heard me making the journey. Credit to them though, nothing was ever said, ever. Not even after one particular midnight's visit when, returning to my room, clothes in hand and paying detailed attention to my foot placing, I didn't notice the used condom fall from my clothes onto the stairs for the entire family to see before I emerged hung over from my room the following morning. There it was, with a ray of sunlight capturing it perfectly. It was as if an invisible hand had placed it there. Nothing was said at the breakfast table. Perplexed and very definitely bashful, I decided not to raise the point or even remark on it. All I got was a somewhat strange but reassuring wink from Tony.

Unfortunately that wasn't the only sexual misdemeanour that I got into trouble with at the Clare's house. After one particular Valentines night ball, Clare and I returned a little worse for wear, Clare more so than I.

Lady Luck and Me

Once I had deball-gowned her and we'd said our discreet 'good-nights', I tip-toed downstairs, not needing to sleep yet, to watch television. Halfway through the sign language news at two, Juliet, Clare's stunning younger sister, walked in having been a waitress at the ball. The sign language news reader now came second and before I knew it I had a breast either side of my nose.

The detailed memories of that night have long been used up on lonely nights, but I will say we didn't complete the deed. Suffice to say it was pleasurable and yet again morally very bad. This second fuck-up seriously kicked my conscience in the nuts, rightfully telling me I was, as previously thought, an arsehole and that Clare deserved to be treated better, by someone better. My guilt grew, finally overwhelming me, and resulted in me telling my closest friend at the time, in an attempt to share and ease my burden. Unbeknownst to me, he secretly harboured feelings for Clare and sensed an unmissable opportunity to get into her pants. He virtually sprinted from my room, making a bee-line straight for Clare and repeated exactly what I had told him, adding a couple of his own, imaginative untruths. When confronted by Clare, I admitted and repented and amazingly stayed in the relationship for many years after. I lost what I thought was a friend and had gained, thereafter, the nickname 'The Rat' from the family, which was freely used every time I visited.

South African stress

'He who laughs last, laughs longest.'
English proverb

My final school connection was a rugby tour to South Africa when 30 players and four ex-staff, all suited and booted, boarded a plane for the six-week tour. We were to be billeted in twos and threes and hosted by the parents of the schools we were about to play. Our first hosts were a black family in Cape Town who were mightily keen to impress upon us the hospitality of their people, so decided to take us to one of the city's most lively clubs, Club Lenin. Under instruction from tour management, all excursions were to be conducted wearing our tour blazers, so we felt a little like fish out of water when we were dropped off outside the club in the heart of a very questionable neighbourhood. Our host had a long conversation with the biggest, most evil doorman I'd ever seen whilst the three of us stood awkwardly in our suits at the front of a huge queue of exclusively black club-goers. As hundreds of angry eyes poured over us, I thought it was only a matter of time before we were ripped apart by an angry mob. I was seriously resenting management's ridiculous dress code policy when the doorman, sensing the growing unease in the queue, sensibly ushered us in. We were given priority going through the metal detectors and frisk searches and escorted quickly through the confused onlookers and seated in our own booth directly behind the DJ. We were told toilet trips must be when only absolutely necessary and only then with him, and the dance floor or indeed

Lady Luck and Me

anywhere outside our current booth, was strictly off limits. Other than that we were free to enjoy ourselves.

Our host wandered off into the club, leaving us to nervously look over shoulders as the bass speaker, which we were virtually sitting on, made our ears bleed. A beer arrived for each of us, delivered by a mute, solemn-faced waiter just in time for the music to be cut and the curtain pulled back to reveal 1000 very disgruntled black faces staring at us. The DJ came over with the microphone and introduced us individually, thrusting the microphone under our noses as we took it in turns to say our name, where we were from and do we have a message for Club Lenin. We mumbled as little and as quickly as we could, wishing the ground would swallow us as the 1000 black faces stared at us in silence. With the introductions awkwardly completed, the DJ turned the microphone to the crowd, asking Club Lenin whether they had a message for us. Nothing, not a word, not a sound; graveyards at midnight are noisier. He then wished us luck on our tour, whipped the curtain back across and cranked the music back up.

Again, we sat back down; beer spilling in sweaty shaking hands, convinced we weren't ever going to get back out of the club alive. When the curtain twitched for the second time so did my bowels. Thankfully it was our host, but this time, without the beaming smile. He beckoned us out of our booth and, with substantially more security on both sides of us, we were quickly jostled across the dance floor down the stairs and, almost at a run, into the street and the waiting car. As we sped away down the road, we all craned our necks around to see revellers pour out of the club and 'warmly' send us on our way. The next day at

South African stress

training, our issues with our enforced attire was listened to and subsequently revised.

We beat our first hosts comfortably and left to stay with our next hosts at the rival white school, having formed surprisingly close bonds with them in the short time we had been with them. This created a rather tense atmosphere when the entire school turned up to support us against the wealthier, far more racist, white school. They were, of course, segregated and by the time the final whistle sounded, our victory and their celebrations had pushed the host school to boiling point. Fearing a violent flash fight was about to break out, we the players were rushed off the pitch and into the safety of the changing rooms as staff from both schools and our management team did their best to quell the increasingly volatile situation. I don't know what was said, but by the time we re-emerged an hour later, the last of the school buses carrying our hosts was leaving the car park, not to be seen or heard of again, sadly.

With one more game to win to have an unbeaten tour, our last game was against the might of an extremely wealthy, highly regarded private school. I was paired with James, mischievous classmate, the firecracker starter in Antibes, and good friend. Our hosts were an extraordinarily rich farming family who had maids, drivers and even a pilot on hand, willing to do their bidding at the drop of a hat. Dinner was a four-course affair, served with white-gloved hands and solid silver spoons. Animal hunting trophies hung on all four walls beneath which stood half a dozen beautifully dressed servants, keenly watching, making sure we wanted for nothing. With three generations around the table, all dressed up to the nines, it was as if we had fallen directly into a period drama television scene. Even in our suits and blazers, we felt overwhelmingly under-dressed.

Lady Luck and Me

The gentle murmur around the table was brought to a silence by the father, at the head of the table, striking his silver knife repeatedly on one of his four crystal wine glasses. He stood up and, in a broad Afrikaans accent, formally welcomed us to his house. He then gave us a brief family history before being interrupted by his mother in Afrikaans and promptly sat back down. She turned to us, smiled and apologised to us for her son's behaviour and for speaking in Afrikaans. With the intention of changing the mood, she enquired whether either of us spoke any other language. Not wanting to waste such a gilt-edged opportunity to embarrass and humiliate James, I quickly responded that James spoke fluent French and was hoping to study it at Oxford the following year. James couldn't speak a word of French but knew this game well and knew that to challenge me would only embarrass both of us and worse still, could be interpreted as taking the piss out of our hosts. Through a tight-lipped smile, he concurred and told the impressed dinner guests that he thought the interview for Oxford had been promising. The more they quizzed his interest in the language and French culture, the more I was dying of silent hysterics, desperately trying to stay in control of my weakening bladder.

As the meal and all-things-French questioning came to an end, we withdrew to the drawing room for after-dinner cognacs and cigars. I was exhausted after trying to contain myself for so long and, as our cigars were lit for us, congratulated myself on a gag perfectly executed. My glory basking was to be short lived however, as James, determined on revenge, slipped in to the conversation that as well as being a rugby player I was also the county champion at snooker. I then proceeded to spit my very expensive cognac over our hosts father as he went on to explain that snooker

South African stress

was taken very seriously in that household and that their son was the national under-16 champion, practising up to six hours a day in their purpose-built games room next door. I had played pool a few times before but never snooker and never on a full-sized table. The bastard had me. I said nothing but died painfully inside when the father excitedly and loudly announced to the room and the rest of the house that the following evening there would be a best of 11 games match between the South African under-16 champion and the English County champion to the applause of everyone. In an attempt to limit the forthcoming humiliation, I said that something had been lost in translation and I certainly wasn't the English County Champion. My protest fell on deaf ears as word spread through the house. Out the corner of my eye, I saw James double up and creep quietly out of the room. The night was brought to an abrupt end in order that a good night's sleep should be had before the encounter the following day. As James and I climbed the stairs in very different moods, I saw two of the servants whisper, point at me and walk away giggling. Even cocooned in the Egyptian cotton bed linen on an extra-large king size bed, in a beautifully decorated room with views stretching across miles of moonlit fields, I didn't get a minute's sleep.

The next day dawned and, with heavy eyes, we left the house in a flurry of activity to do our day's training. James didn't let me forget for a second what was waiting for me back at the ranch and constantly reminded me of the ever-ticking clock. Training over, one of the household cars drove us back to the ranch and, on entering the gates, my heart missed a beat. It seemed word had spread far and wide as both sides of the long drive were jam-packed with cars. Inside the house, the servants were working overtime

Lady Luck and Me

to keep the hundred or so guest's glasses full. I was politely informed by the host's mother that it would be in keeping with tradition that I wore a tie and formal presentable footwear and if my shoes needed a polish, somebody would be provided immediately.

I entered the games room to polite applause with the spectators above me on the overlooking balcony quietly whispering amongst themselves. The room was packed. At the far end of the vast snooker table sat the 15-year-old son, cross-legged, wearing a tailor-made three-piece suit, complete with bow tie, looking like a young Stephen Hendry. Once again I cringed when the father introduced me as the English County Champion and shrank at the roars of support for the young South African. Losing the coin toss at the very beginning of the match was the start of what turned out to be a two-hour, 6–0, utter and complete humiliation, which included propelling the white ball off the table towards the surprised grandmother with such velocity it decimated the bone china tea cup and saucer she held in her hand, resulting in disapproving whispers from the onlookers and my profound apologies to her and the maid who was sent to clear it up.

James hid in the shadows with tears of joy running down his cheeks as my vigil from my chair continued. In the six games played, I think I potted four balls, two of them being the white, only adding to James's delight. After the trophy presentation and speeches, the guests applauded once more and then quietly dispersed back to their cars brimming with national pride. After a sympathetic handshake from the host's father and a poisonous stare from his mother, I sat in my chair, listening to the glasses being clinked in the next room and watching James roll

South African stress

around on the floor, loving my pain and congratulating himself on a brilliantly executed plan.

The ensuing rugby match and our victory mattered very little to our host family and, when it was time for our goodbyes, all the talk was of snooker and what the potential was for their son in Europe having beaten the English County Champion so emphatically. I wished him all the best for what I was sure to be a dazzling snooker career and thanked the family for the unforgettable stay. With the tour ending unbeaten we spent the last two days in Swaziland, relaxing and watching how the local tribe went about daily life using what they assured us was the old traditional methods and wearing old traditional dress which was actually ill-fitting, usually on the small side, thongs. Our suspicions to their claims were aroused when, on the second night, Friday night as it so happened, we saw the thong wearing tribal members transform into P-Diddy lookalikes, wearing expensive leather jackets and Armani sun-glasses, speeding away into town on highly polished Harley Davidsons. It was an amusing way to finish the tour and we returned back to the UK with the same, original personnel. The rugby had been fun, but the people, the land and the ever-present racial tension will stay with me far longer and one day I hope to return so that I can add to those memorable experiences, maybe even returning to Club Lenin.

Back in Devon, I returned to work, picking up what jobs I could. I tried my hand at bar work at a pub on the quay in Exeter, only to last a week due to a local man who propped up the bar, constantly asking me to bend down to get him salted peanuts so that he could thank me with a wink and tell me in a dirty, husky voice that I would look great wearing white hot pants. Living at home I had no

Lady Luck and Me

outgoings, so slowly started to save enough funds to take a month's holiday to the States with my friend Rob Wickes.

Americano

> *'America is at that awkward stage, it's too late to work within the system, but too early to shoot the bastards.'*
> Claire Wolfe

We landed in the grotesque city of LA and quickly decided not to stay but take the Greyhound bus up to Las Vegas, the party capital of the world. Although we were under the legal drinking age, we relied on the kindness of strangers and our well-honed Queen's English, public school accents to get us into the revelling spirit. We booked in to the Queen of Hearts Hotel just outside the Freemont Arcade which was exactly the kind of depressing, dilapidated place you would see on an episode of 'CSI', complete with a dry swimming pool and an ex-Vietnam veteran wheeling his drunk, legless body around in a pimped up wheelchair. It was he, after we'd had to listen to countless old war stories, who agreed to get us booze from the local bottle shop. We politely listened to more of his sorrowful stories whilst drinking Jim Beam and Coke around the dry pool before excusing ourselves and staggering off into the bright Vegas lights.

After seeing the various casinos put on their free shows, we stumbled past the brilliantly named 'world famous Las Vegas tattoo parlour'. Keen to see what made it world famous, we took a stroll in and, adorning the walls, saw the hundreds of celebrities who had apparently had their body art done there. Skwiffy-eyed and inspired by greats such as Joan Collins and Barry Gibb, we decided we would join the ranks and agreed to be permanently

Lady Luck and Me

inked. Barely focusing with one eye, I shot out a finger and told the resident artist I wanted that one on my back. As I laid down on his table, inanely smiling and beginning to dribble, I left Rob thumbing through the countless volumes of options. I was woken by the artist shouting in my ear that he was done and turned to seek Rob's approval, only to be greeted by an empty room and no sign of Rob, the bastard. I hastily paid the 80 dollars and stumbled out, still pissed but feeling a monumental hangover coming on. I finally made it back to our rank hotel, thanks to a friendly transsexual hooker, only to find Rob, lying fully clothed, trousers undone, porn channel flickering away in the background, passed out on his bed. After turning off the television, I followed suit.

The next morning, I woke with a banging headache having had an awful nightmare. As I looked at my swollen, baggy eyes in the mirror, my right shoulder throbbed away. It quickly dawned on me it hadn't been a nightmare at all and, as I turned and saw the bandage, my heart sank. I had no idea what it was hiding and really didn't want to know. Rob joined me at the mirror and pissed himself. Despite my remonstrations with him about reneging on our pact, nothing could stop him from pointing and laughing. Carefully he undid the bandage to reveal what I would carry on my body for the rest of my days. He stared at it expressionless. Tentatively I turned around and saw in the mirror, a black, fist-sized Batman symbol. I don't even like Batman. I had only ever seen one Batman film and really hadn't taken to it, so why, in the name of Kerry Katona, had I decided to permanently mark myself with his symbol is still a mystery.

We soon found out that our English accents didn't give us an all-access-all-areas pass and that the casino's

Americano

security didn't give two shits where we were from only that we were under age to set foot inside. As they manhandled us out of the premises onto the street they gave us a stern warning not to return. Apart from the casinos, we realised there was actually very little else to do in Vegas and started scratching around looking for other ways to lighten our wallets. The Grand Canyon was only a stone's throw away and plenty of operators offered different tours, including donkey trekking, white-water rafting and the one that required the least input from us and the most from our wallets: scenic flights. We signed up and were transferred to the airfield and our waiting tiny Cessna light aircraft. We were joined by the Texan wide-boy pilot and two Argentinean girls of a similar age to us. As we taxied down the short runway, Chad, our pilot, began incessantly babbling about what he had done the night before, including talking us, play by play, through a football game. The two girls at the back of the small plane spoke only Spanish and, seeing the fear in their eyes, obviously hadn't been on a plane that size before. As we banked hard left to run along the Colorado beneath us, turbulence struck throwing us all into the roof of the plane. The Spanish girls behind us emitted ear-piercing screams whilst burying their finger nails into the head-rests of our seats. Chad carried on chatting away, seemingly unaware of his passenger's fear. Whilst we were strapped to the seat with a small string-like belt across our stomachs, Chad had some sort of Formula-one racing harness on that went over both shoulders, across his chest and around his button-straining stomach. As the plane continued to weave its way over the canyon, the updrafts threw us around the aircraft like rag dolls.

The sick bags proved too small to capture our breakfasts and, when we finally landed, we had seen about

Lady Luck and Me

five minutes worth of one of the seven natural wonders of the world which had been spectacular but sadly had become secondary to our fear of self-preservation. Of the two girls behind us, one had passed out covered in her hysterical friend's sick and required being brought around with smelling salts once we were stationery. The other girl simply sat there, mute and trembling with the remnants of her breakfast running down her chin. Chad gaily bounded out of the cockpit, thanking us for flying with Chad Air and strode away across the tarmac whistling, leaving his ground crew to help us regain our legs and start the mammoth job of cleaning the interior of the plane. That was it for Rob and I, we had had enough of Vegas and booked ourselves on the next bus out of there to San Francisco, stomachs wobbling and shoulder blade throbbing.

In comparison, San Francisco was a joy. We found ourselves a nice, cheap hostel close to the centre of town and discovered that San Franciscans were a lot more liberal with the drinking laws. The tram system and world-famous steep streets made every journey an eye-opener. For the first week we were more than happy just to potter around, feeling the town's free-love history and watching old men play hours of chess in the parks. We took the mandatory boat trip around Alcatraz and under the Golden Gate Bridge and gorged ourselves on the many authentic Italian pizza joints and, for the first time since landing in the States, were genuinely relaxed and beginning to dismiss the idea that all Americans were small-minded simpletons. That was, until one Tuesday afternoon.

Rob's funds had run low and we were enjoying an evening in front of the hostel's television, casually supping on beer whilst watching endless episodes of 'The Simpsons'. As with all extended beer-drinking sessions,

Americano

toilet journeys had become regular and it was during one of these trips that I encountered the darker underbelly of San Francisco. Everyone knows that San Fran is the gay capital of America and, thus far, we had seen little evidence of this. I was weeing in the urinal when the door opened and a skinny, malnourished black guy came in, stood next to me on my right and began to relieve himself. With his flamboyant clothes, lisp and swinging hips, there was no mistaking his sexuality. Halfway through he asked me the time and in my innocence, raised my right hand, letting go of my cock and thereby giving him the opportunity to stare at my exposed manhood. Before I could answer his bogus question, he had pinned me against the toilet wall and was fighting to get my trousers off. Not taking my rebuttal seriously, he aggressively started pulling me into a cubicle, desperately trying to bolt the door behind us. I lashed out, kicking and punching as I tried to free myself from his gay-grip. Thankfully, I landed a knee square in his nuts and, as he doubled over, I escaped his cock-hungry clutches and ran out into the corridor, shouting to Rob as I passed the television room, making for our room to gather my belongings and head out of the hostel onto the street. We spent Rob's last night in America in the safety of the airport and, once Rob had left, I felt vulnerable and that any further stay was pointless. I brought my flight forward and lived in the airport under the watchful eye of the many CCTV cameras for the remaining couple of days, ate Big Macs and only entered public toilets when I was sure I was alone. My American dream had been more of a nightmare if the truth be told. Thankfully though, I would be reminded of it every time I caught a glimpse of my ridiculous tattoo.

The next time I saw Rob was a couple of weeks after returning; down on his patch in the picturesque

Lady Luck and Me

Dorset countryside. By then, our American memories could be laughed at and were regarded as character-shaping adventures. During my stay, Rob's family had rented out their three self-catering cottages to a film crew who were shooting a film at one of the many, large, period country houses that are dotted all over the Dorset landscape. One day, there came a knock at the door and, as I was the closest, I opened it to a well-dressed, middle-aged man who initially began enquiring about the cottage's heating before stopping and then enquiring about my movements over the next couple of months. It transpired that he was the wardrobe manager of the production and bizarrely thought I had the look that would be ideally suited to the period feature film they were working on. As it happened, I had nothing to do before joining Clare in Romania so, after insisting that Rob who was also at a loose end should be involved, I agreed and followed his instructions to turn up at the production's temporary office in Bridport the following day which we duly did.

We were employed as extras and paid 40 pounds a day, cash in hand and, even with me sporting a bright, peroxide-blond hair style, was assured it would be well hidden under my eighteenth-century soldier's hat. On set, we joined other extra soldiers in the wardrobe department and were kitted out in the full regalia, and trained how to use an authentic musket. 'The Scarlet Tunic' was a Thomas Hardy adaptation and starred thespian legend, Simon Callow, Emma Fielding, Linda Bellingham (who really should have stuck to Oxo adverts) and Jean Marc Barr, star of 'The Big Blue' among others. On more than one occasion, I had my make-up applied with Jean who, after I congratulated him on a fine performance in his signature film, told me of his family in Paris and his career since then. He was, without doubt, the most down-to-earth and talented of all the actors there. Like most film sets, I suspect, there was a lot of waiting around and, for 40 quid a day, the production company did well out of us.

Six weeks in and having been left to dress ourselves, I had become complacent. On the biggest, most expensive shoot of the film, production had to halt as the director bellowed through his megaphone at me that I had my leather shin pad things the wrong way round. The wardrobe assistant, who was instructed to help me by the director in the most condescending voice I had ever heard, informed me that my little mistake had cost the production tens of thousands of pounds. The next time I passed Callow, he shook his head at me, mumbled under his breath and minced away with his entourage in hot pursuit. The two months came to an end and all our money had been spent down at the pub at the end of each day, not that it was a regret, on the contrary, we rubbed shoulders with other extras hearing stories of the acting world and being united in the fact that Callow was the most demanding actor that any of them had ever worked with.

I attended the premier in the cinematic capital of the world, Bridport, and saw that I featured very little and, when I did, I could quite clearly see my peroxide-blond hair peeping out from below my cardboard soldier's hat, making the entire film so far from authentic it was blush-worthy. For all the hours that I had marched, shot and ran in front of the camera, most of my silver screen debut seemed to have been left on the cutting room floor. If I was disappointed with it, I can only smile when I think of what Callow's reaction was. I still have the T-shirt and if Spielberg wants me in one of his flicks, I'm available on the

Lady Luck and Me

condition that Callow is at the other side of the planet or six feet under.

Deepest, darkest Devon

> *'Golf and its courses can best be defined as an endless series of tragedies obscured by the occasional miracle.'*
> Anon

As I waited for the call to movie stardom, I returned home to quaint little Trusham and began job hunting once again. It was during this time that I courted one of my more memorable girlfriends, Tanya. A 5' 8" blond with bright blue eyes, slim and completed with a bust Katie Price would be proud of; both of which, I must add, natural. We worked at the Teign Valley Golf Club, waiting on and taking abuse from wealthy, retired patrons. She naturally and quite rightly got all the attention from both lusting men and jealous, scornful women. I can only think that it was because pickings were so meagre that she asked me out for a drink. Every morning I would be greeted with yet more angry pimples reducing my self-confidence to an all-time low. Eye contact had become difficult. More often than not I stared at the ground, doing my best to hide my hideous pustules. I thought that it would be just a matter of time for Tanya to admit to her mistake, make her apologies and quickly move on. Again, to my surprise, our little relationship lasted longer than I had imagined. We enjoyed our intimate moments loudly enough for my grandmother, who on occasion stayed, to remark on the boundless energy of the 'youth of today'.

Two months into our very lustful relationship, I was invited around to dinner at her parents' house, a beautiful fifteenth-century manor house which could well

Lady Luck and Me

have been the centre spread for *Country Living* magazine. Tanya's father was of the old school. He was a former Etonian, Oxford Rugby Blue and successful entrepreneur who was well connected with the upper echelons of society; her mother was a distant relation to the house of Windsor. Wearing my best BHS grey suit, I arrived with the expected flowers and wine in hand. Pleasantries and the first course were served without a hitch. I was on top form, entertaining with my foreign exploits and impressing them with my dickhead stepfather's status in the army. I was certainly doing a good enough job for them to seriously consider me as an appropriate suitor for their daughter and, as the wine flowed, the stories got taller and their respect for me grew. It was palpable; I was in my element.

The second course came and went with the obligatory toast to the chef, health and happiness before I excused myself from the table and headed upstairs to the most decadent bathroom I have ever seen. Nature called not for number one but for a number two. I felt two stone lighter once I had dropped the kids off, and smiling contently, flushed the porcelain throne only to be left with the result of my evacuation staring me straight in the eye. Having flushed once I was acutely aware that the bathroom was located directly above the dining room, and as I could quite clearly hear my hosts laughing, I suspected they had quite clearly heard me flush. If I flushed again, it would give the game away that I had a problem; an ugly, over-sized, nutty problem. So, in a moment of madness, I wrapped my hand in bundles of loo paper and fished out the stubborn turd. Stupidly, I was now holding a turd but had nowhere to put it. As the water was soaking through the paper I knew I was running out of time. Without a

Deepest, darkest Devon

second thought, I unhinged the window and flung the turd and the paper out.

Closing the window and washing my hands, I returned to join the party. On opening the dining room door, I was surprised to see all three standing with their backs to me, looking out of the French windows onto the patio. I joined them and, to my horror, there it was; my tissued turd not three feet from the door, spotlighted under the harsh glare of the security light. I died. We didn't have the final course or the planned cheese and biscuits. In fact, I left pretty much straight away, thanking them for their hospitality which, in hindsight, probably wasn't the best idea with my head hanging very low. I didn't see Tanya or her parents after that. Rumour has it she married a pop star, mothered five children and lives the life of Riley.

Teign Valley Golf club was the source of many of my happiest memories whilst living in Devon. Apart from it providing me with girlfriends, free golf and a cash-in-hand job, it also housed a well-stocked bar. Once my waiting duties had been completed, I was allowed a couple of after-work drinks and, as I was young and relatively new to drinking, it didn't take many to get me on my merry way. Thankfully I got on well with the live-in barman, Laurie, so it wasn't uncommon for me to have many more than I should to drive, and then creep back home nervously along the dark, back lanes.

My car wasn't the only vehicle that I was driving when I shouldn't have been. Laurie and I had got into a particularly bad habit of drinking, hot-wiring the golf buggies and going for joy ride races down the longest holes on the course. Four races in and we were level pegging at two each. For the decider, it was agreed that a longer course

Lady Luck and Me

should be driven, so the first around the back nine would be declared the winner. The heavy cloud cover made the August night black as black can be, with visibility down to about two yards when walking. Behind the Perspex screen of the buggy and travelling at 15 mph with no lights, visibility was down to zero and an intimate knowledge of the golf course was all either of us had to rely on for navigation. Without booze coursing through our veins, it might have just been possible, but, after several pints of strong lager and a couple of pre-race shots of tequila, it was an absurd idea. Even though I was alcohol impaired, I was still alert enough to know that I would have to 'feel' my way around the course and saw that just completing the course would be a worthy achievement. Laurie quite clearly had other ideas. As we accelerated off the tenth tee into the complete darkness, I heard Laurie shoot past me, laughing demonically. Either he could see in the dark and had the race under his belt or, as it turned out, he was blind drunk and had absolutely no care for his own life. I spent the tenth fairway hanging my head out the side of the buggy hoping to get my eyes accustomed to darkness and picking flying insects out of my teeth. By the time I had got to the thirteenth fairway, I hadn't seen or heard Laurie since the start line. I couldn't work out whether this was a good thing or a bad thing. Maybe, I thought to myself, it was going to be a classic tortoise and hare race.

The thirteenth fairway was one of the widest on the course with only two bunkers and a standing stone to steer clear of. It was probably my favourite hole on the course and I knew it like the back of my hand, giving me the confidence to put my foot down and hit top speed. Nearing the bunkers, I slowed enough to hear faint but definite groans coming through the darkness. Stopping,

Deepest, darkest Devon

fearing the worst, I tentatively made my way to one of the bunkers, expecting the worse, and found an overturned buggy with Laurie lying face down in the sand. Once Laurie had been peeled out of the hazard, I righted his buggy and, without a word, he was off, back into the night, seemingly undeterred by his lucky escape. Before I had managed to get behind the wheel of my electric steed, I heard an almighty crash followed by an ominous silence. Again, I followed the groans and my lighter's flame, to find Laurie lying on the fairway, dazed, confused but still adamant he was going to win the epic race. The buggy was on its wheels this time but had an enormous crack on its bumper and was missing the entire Perspex windscreen. The only thing that wasn't damaged was the standing stone that stood in front of the cracked bumper. Helping Laurie to his feet revealed where the missing windscreen had gone; it seemed Laurie had hit the lone standing stone at full tilt, taking and using the windscreen to cushion his fall. The multiple cracks throughout, prevented it from being reattached so it was discarded in the nearby undergrowth and the race resumed against my better judgement.

The remaining holes were taken slowly and, as the alcohol had begun to wear off, the realisation of both Laurie's near-death experiences clearly indicated Lady Luck was watching, and running out of patience. Avoiding all other possible man-made traps, I was on the home straight, the eighteenth fairway. Laurie hadn't been heard or seen since the standing stone prang. Again, I didn't know whether this was a good or bad thing but, considering his recent run, could only be a bad thing. I was not wrong. As the eighteenth hole and the finishing line beckoned, my attention was drawn to the car park next to the Clubhouse which was being bathed in the cold, yellow, security light.

Lady Luck and Me

In the middle of the car park under the full glare of the light were three wheels and the black underside of a golf buggy. Crossing the line, I brought my four-wheeled stallion to a halt and dashed down the bank to the buggy. Laurie was nowhere to be seen, and I could just make out the remnants of a dashboard and a caved in roof. Laurie then appeared in the doorway of the Clubhouse holding two pints above his head shouting 'Champion' with a broad grin on his face. I laughed, shook my head and went to fetch the pint he was holding out for me. It was only when I got close did I see his injuries. Blood ran from his broken nose, and the top of his forehead looked as though an apprentice butcher had been at him. I don't know whether he was in shock, euphoric about his win or adequately inebriated enough to be blissfully unaware of the blood running down his face. All three were likely.

We toasted his fine victory and then I escorted him to the bathroom to deal with his open wounds. Thankfully the cut on his forehead wasn't as bad as first feared, and the alcohol in his system proved enough of an anaesthetic for him to manoeuvre his nose back into position. Nursing done, we retired to the bar for another pint and the tale of how his buggy ended up on its roof in the middle of the car park. It seems he had overshot the finish line and had become airborne off the bank before landing and rolling several times, finally coming to rest in the middle of the car park, wrong way up. We hatched a plan to plead ignorance or, if need be, shamefully blame it on the travelling community that had taken up residence in a nearby wood and, if questioned further, claim that Laurie's injuries had been inflicted by one of the afore mentioned travellers in a random pub fight. Happy with our water-tight alibi, we carried Laurie's ruined buggy back to its space and then

Deepest, darkest Devon

parked mine alongside it. Having said my goodbyes, I drove home at a snail's pace, determined not to follow in Laurie's motoring shoes and dreading what the next day might hold.

Arriving the next morning for work, the golf club was a hive of activity and excitement. Laurie had yet to surface and all kinds of bizarre stories were circulating as to what had happened in the night. Not only had one of the buggies been trashed, but the back nine fairways and greens were so badly scarred by tyre tracks that the annual club tournament would have to be rescheduled in order for the green staff to repair the seriously damaged surfaces. As the police were called, I feigned an upset stomach and headed home riddled with guilt. When I returned a couple of days later, the written-off buggy had been replaced, the greens were still unplayable and Laurie had left, never to be heard of again. The travellers had been interviewed by the police and told to move on and the whole incident was quietly and quickly forgotten about. The pangs of guilt still remain with me to this day.

In need of a break from the golf club, the valley and my guilt I headed to Bristol for a weekend of general recklessness and abandon. The Saturday night had unfolded like many others before it when tragic injury befell one of my friend's girlfriends. Out of the blue, she insisted I gave her a piggy back ride through Bristol city centre. Not listening to my reluctance, she flung herself on my back, throwing me off balance. I began a hopelessly futile attempt to regain my balance by first walking quickly and then running in a final desperate effort to keep us upright. It didn't work. Unable to run any faster, I tripped, catapulting the unsuspecting girl from her nine-foot vantage point, across a road to land head first on the curb on the other

Lady Luck and Me

side. By the time I had dragged myself to my feet, the limp girl was surrounded by a group of horrified onlookers. The anxious crowd was five deep when the ambulance arrived and, from their hostile behaviour towards me, clearly saw me as the cause of the carnage. I was ushered away by my piss-taking, unsympathetic friends as the ambulance roared off down the street, lights flashing and sirens screaming.

Two weeks later and after hundreds of apology texts, I set eyes on her again. The swelling of her broken nose had spread to both her eyes, and the numerous stitches in her forehead looked as though they had been drawn on by a three year old. Once my shock had subsided, I continued on with my apologies. I think she accepted them although it was difficult to understand a word that she was saying due to her new unfamiliar wired jaw and the tube that was protruding from her mouth. I'm not sure whether her new face was to blame, but it was after her lengthy rehab programme that her relationship with my friend abruptly ended.

Thankfully, the day I was to depart to meet up with Clare in the wilds of Eastern Europe was just around the corner. By now I was relishing the prospect of getting away to a different lifestyle, away from the pubs and away from the alcohol-related apologies.

'Worldly' travels

> '. . . there ain't no journey what don't change you some.'
> David Mitchell

Clare, being the loving, warm-hearted, generous soul she was, had decided to spend her year off helping and teaching English in an orphanage in the centre of Bucharest before starting her degree at Birmingham University. The organisation which had made all the arrangements had billeted her with a Romanian family that lived in the heart of Bucharest's poorest district. She slept there at night and carried out her angelic duties during the day, having the weekends off to get utterly shit-faced with other foreign saints. This, of course, put the fear of Lucifer in me, convinced it was only a matter of time before I got a phone call telling me she had met a 7-foot Swedish model named Sven with a cock like an African tribesman. As imaginations go, I have a particularly damaging one when it comes to worst-case scenarios with women. So, within a month of my mother giving me 100 pounds to stop biting my nails, I had to return it to her. I received letters (in the days before emails) about the sights Clare had seen, and who she had seen them with. They always set my mind racing, convincing myself she must have been involved in some weird, Eastern European sex fest; what happens behind the Iron Curtain, stays behind the Iron Curtain.

Despite her reassurances that she loved me and only had platonic friends, I couldn't wait to get out there and put my restless, insecure demons to bed. Our plan was that she carried out her three-month Mother Teresa stint and

Lady Luck and Me

then I would join her shortly after New Year to do three months of travelling around Eastern Europe. As the days ticked by and Christmas came and went, I was champing at the bit to get out there. The same names in her letters became more and more frequent and so my nails became shorter and shorter. Eventually, and with ten bloody digits, it was time to fly and join her. I hadn't thought about what to expect from Eastern Europe or its people; I could only think of being re-united with my beloved. What should have occupied my thoughts was just how fucking cold it was going to be and what I should have packed in preparation. As I parted company with Mum at the airport, she looked me in the eyes and told me she loved me, told me to take care, and as I walked through security waving at her, told me to think about marrying Clare. And then she was gone. With an already fragile mind, this last statement really gave me the willies. It was all I could think about on the four-hour flight, whereas all I should have been thinking is how many sets of thermals I had packed.

It was only when I disembarked from the plane and made the short journey to the awaiting bus and to the terminal that I realised I had made the grave mistake of packing absolutely nothing appropriate for an Eastern European winter. The thin, Ben Sherman, short-sleeved shirt and the linen trousers just weren't going to cut it. Thankfully, I had remembered to pack the one, white fingerless glove that I had found under my bed but had reservations wearing it as I might be mistaken for a Michel Jackson wannabe. In the twenty seconds it had taken from leaving the cosy womb-like plane to the bus doors closing, I had lost feeling in my feet and hands and was sure frostbite had taken hold of my nose. I hadn't noticed any heavily clothed people on the plane, but now, as I looked

'Worldly' travels

around, it seemed as though everyone, apart from me, had morphed into a member of an Artic exploration party. Disregarding my pride and my fellow travellers opinions, I fished around in my hand luggage, withdrew the glove and proudly slipped it on.

Emerging from the airport with both little and large rucksacks in hand, I had no idea where to go or even how to find out where I should go. My instructions from Clare were to meet outside the main entrance of the Gara de Nord, Bucharest's main and busiest railway station, at a pre-determined time. As my only thoughts when I set out from England were of Clare, I hadn't thought about city guides, phrasebooks or again, how frigging cold it was going to be. The alien world around me milled purposefully to and fro as I stood, scanning the foreign signposts, feeling my feet and one naked hand begin to ache with cold. My attempts to communicate with anyone official-looking were met with puzzled looks and, more often than not, a face full of cigarette smoke. Eventually, and only after humiliating myself with a child's train impression, a luggage-handling, cigar-wielding taxi driver pointed down the road before continuing to load up his boot with his fare's belongings. Obediently, I followed the direction of his finger and was rewarded with a train sign pointing me in the same direction. A kilometre later, and unable to move a muscle in my now frozen face, I arrived at the airport train station only to be greeted by the largest English language sign informing people that a free bus transfer service operated between the station and the arrival terminal. Grrrr.

My first attempt at buying a ticket into Gara de Nord was seriously hampered by an uncontrollable chattering of teeth and a particularly impatient, bearded ticket woman. With audibly frustrated people queuing

Lady Luck and Me

behind me, I left the ticket window empty-handed and decided to let my face thaw a little before I tried again at a different window. My second attempt was more successful and, with ticket clutched firmly in gloved hand, I fought my way along the relevant platform and boarded the overcrowded train, exhausted, hungry and still unable to feel most of my withering body. As the train set off, I found myself wedged in the passageway between the window and the cabins unable to move due to my oversized rucksack on my back, the small one on my front, and the sheer volume of people. By inhaling the armpit that was flattening my nose, it seemed Romanians worked hard and showered infrequently, making an already unpleasant journey significantly worse.

Not long into the journey, angry voices could be heard coming along the impassable passageway and watching the speed at which the passengers were inching out of the way, they were putting the fear of God into people. The nearer they got, the more frantic I became. Trying to move was hopeless and, by the time the three hardest, biggest men I'd ever seen got to me, I was out of options and held my hands up submissively. Surely it must have been clear to them that I had nowhere else to go and even with angry remonstrations, nothing was going to change that. The first man went puce in the face just before grabbing me by the collar, shaking me out of my wedged position and then punching me in the face. I fell backwards through a cabin door into an astonished family and onto their groceries. As I lay there like a beetle on its back, my assailant stood over me, laughed, spat on me and

'Worldly' travels

then continued on his journey down the now miraculously clear passageway.

Lip bleeding, it was now time for the family to have a go at me for falling on their weekly shopping. All seven of them were up in arms at my intrusion, with the grandmother stereotypically beating me over the head with her handbag as the father helped me to my feet albeit roughly. Even the six-year-old girl managed to get a kick in before I made it to my feet and, in spite of apologising profusely, I was pushed back out in the passageway with the doors and curtains closed loudly behind me. I kept my head down for the rest of the short journey in fear of unwittingly offending somebody else. If I had learnt anything in the first hour of being in Romania, it was that they weren't the friendliest people that I'd ever come across. Nicolae Ceaușescu's brutal regime had only fairly recently ended and the country was going through a tough transitional phase. The influx of moneyed Westerners wandering about as inquisitive tourists must have seemed as if we were taking pity or, worse still, advantage of their wounded nation.

The first few days with Clare in Bucharest were spent avoiding the cold by hopping from bar to bar and meeting the friends that had given me so much heartache. There were no Swedish models amongst them and they all actually turned out to be friendly, fun, amiable people. The family that Clare lived with resided on the fifteenth floor of a 30-floor grey tower block, surrounded on all sides by other similar high rises, many of them abandoned or derelict. Clare's hosts were a mother and a daughter. The daughter was of similar age to Clare and I. Neither spoke English, but they smiled a lot and generously spooned out whatever had been found that day and thrown in the ever-bubbling pot on the stove. Every meal, every day came from that

Lady Luck and Me

pot. Whenever they came across anything edible it would be thrown in. Offal, fish, fruit all shared the same sauce resulting in each mouthful having to be washed down with their homemade plum brandy. The six meals I had in that flat are, without doubt, the most disgusting six meals I've ever had and, short of eating a rotting camel's arse, I can't imagine anything worse.

Snow lay on the ground as stray, skinny dogs roamed from building to building; it was exactly as the imagination had conjured an Eastern European inner city block to be. The atmosphere was heavy with depression and poverty, leaving me with a very real sense of just how hard life was there. It was a far-cry from the wealthy schools that I attended and a very different way of life to that which I had ever been exposed to before. To say it made a profound impact on me would be a colossal understatement and I still regard those few days in Bucharest as some of my most formative.

Having filled my rucksack with more suitable winter clothing and bade farewell to Clare's hosts, we boarded the train to Transylvania and its world-renowned, stunning countryside. It would be the first time Clare and I would be able to spend some 'quality time together'. The tiny single bed with paper thin walls that we had shared in her host's flat had hardly been conducive to reacquainting ourselves with each other's more intimate places and so private time was eagerly awaited. Clare's hosts had kindly arranged for us to stay with some of their friends deep in the country assuring us, with a wink, that we would have our own double room and privacy.

We were picked up late in the evening from the station and driven deep into the night to a sprawling

'Worldly' travels

farmhouse and, once introductions had been made, shown to our homely room. With our bellies full and our heads a little fuzzy from more homemade plum brandy, we retired for the night, relaxed and excited. Everything went well in the bedroom, until it was discovered that the bastard condom had split. All at once, our world came crashing down. In England, this wouldn't be a major problem what with the morning-after pill, but here, miles from any medical facility, unable to speak the language and without medical insurance, it was our worst nightmare. What made matters worse, of course, was that Clare came from a Catholic family who certainly wouldn't be sympathetic if she phoned home for advice. For a night that had held so much expectation, bitter disappointment didn't come anywhere near. Neither of us got much sleep that night and, as we went over and over her biological timetable and hypothetical scenarios, all of them ended unpleasantly. In the end, we decided to wait and let nature take its course, crossing whichever bridge was presented to us.

The following three weeks were a struggle. As much as we tried to enjoy the breathtaking scenery and the quaint feudal way of life around us, the inescapable cloud of trepidation hung over us. The majority of our conversations quickly descended into ugly arguments as the stress and tension took its toll. Finally, and four days late, we had confirmation that Clare wasn't pregnant, prompting a two-day memory loss bender in a forgettable small town near the Hungarian border. What with that scare, intimate moments between Clare and I became pretty much non-existent during the rest of our time in Eastern Europe.

Most of our travelling was done overland and, wherever possible, by train, mainly for comfort and speed. We had our hit-list and a tight, well-organised schedule, so

Lady Luck and Me

dilly-dallying at obscure towns that weren't on our itinerary was kept to a minimum. We were armed with a European train time table and a selection of 'Lonely Planets' that had been read and re-read and then heavily highlighted. If a town or a point of interest hadn't been highlighted or held any logistical purpose for us then it was avoided or by-passed. To me, nowadays, that's the worst possible way to see foreign lands or experience alien cultures. Spontaneity, advice from fellow travellers, local knowledge and freedom of constraints and time are the key factors to successful travelling. I'm all in favour of seeing the ancient wonders and following in the footsteps of the greats but not because a guide book tells me to but because circumstance and coincidence has led me there. If somebody suggested to me that I did that same route, with the same timetable that I did all those years ago, I would kick them in the shins. If you're going travelling to broaden your mind, then let intervention and opportunity do it for you, otherwise the details and subtleties of cultures are missed.

With Romania and its sights having been ticked off the list, our next port of call, so to speak, was Budapest, Hungary. This involved taking an overnight sleeper train and crossing the Romanian-Hungarian border. The first rule anyone learns when they're going travelling is that your passport and, particularly a British passport, is your most valuable possession and should be cared for like you would care for a newborn baby, never letting it out of your sight. We were both still in recovery mode from the two-day bender and so, when we found out we had a cabin to ourselves, strapped our rucksacks to our beds and put our heads down for some much-needed sleep. It was not to last long though. At around midnight, we were rudely awoken by some rough shaking and a fierce torch inches from our

'Worldly' travels

eyes. As they were determined to wake us, they seemed unlikely to be robbers. As my eyes grew accustomed to their offensive light, I could make out that they were uniformed, carrying guns and quite clearly had not been employed for their friendly customer service. Romanian border guards. Still a little dazed and confused and wearing only a T-shirt and pants, I scrambled around under my pillow in search of my passport. Clare had already given them hers and had had it returned with the necessary stamp in and was semi-consciously rearranging her pillows in preparation to return to the land of nod.

I handed mine over and was immediately blinded as they flitted between my passport photo and me. Romanian words were spoken and then they were off, out of our cabin and along the passageway like two greased greyhounds, still with my passport in hand. Like a half-naked, headless chicken, I gave hot pursuit. With only the occasional street light illuminating my way, I lost count how many times I stubbed my toe, all I cared about was the glimpse of their torch in front of me and my 'baby' which they held in their hand. Finally, at the very end of the train, I caught up with them in the guard's cabin. They both stared at me not saying a word and, despite my best efforts to communicate, stayed silent, just staring at me. The one holding my passport raised it to me and, as I reached out my hand to take it, whipped it away and raised his other hand rubbing his index finger and thumb together. Evidently I was going to have to buy my baby back. As I stood there in my pants and T-shirt, I gestured to them that I obviously wasn't carrying any money. The more I twirled and lifted my top to convince them I didn't have any means to pay them, the more vigorous the finger rubbing became. By the time I turned to head back to our

Lady Luck and Me

cabin to retrieve some cash, I'm sure I could see faint wisps of smoke rising from his grubby little thieving fingers. In the end it cost me about 20 quid to get my passport back and any respect I had for border guards.

Budapest, in comparison, was a joy. The weather hadn't improved but the architecture, food, people and all-round civility was in stark contrast to Romania. If Romania was Kerry Katona then Hungary was Keira Knightley, both unique but worlds apart. As much as I enjoyed being in a civilised society once again, surrounded by stunning buildings and being passed by beautiful women, Budapest lacked an edge. We certainly weren't in a hurry to find its darker underbelly and, once we had visited our must-see sites, we moved on, out of Budapest and into Bratislava, Slovakia, again by rail. That started our whistle-stop tour through Slovakia and the Czech Republic, hopping on and off the train to satisfy our cultural to-do lists.

Prague was beautiful and expensive. There was no doubt that it had been quicker to pick up on its tourist potential than the other ex-communist countries that we had visited, as beer prices weren't too dissimilar to that of London. Boozed up stag groups and scantily clad hen parties rubbed shoulders with bewildered Saga tour groups, one set looking for debauchery whilst the other looked for cultural nourishment. Having seen the late-night prostitutes and inevitable drunken brawls, we had seen enough of Prague and its spires and jumped onto the train to Poland.

We had allowed more time for Poland and had done significantly more research into places which we wanted to visit. Our first stop was to be Krakow. As both Clare and I had studied History at A-level, Krakow was

'Worldly' travels

of particular interest, not just for its renaissance art and museums but also for its role during the Second World War. We wandered around the different parts of the city, inhaling its ever-changing sights and sounds.

Down one side street, we unexpectedly came across the most unusual museum. Actually, it wasn't really a museum, it was more like a travelling circus, but not a people's travelling circus, a creepy-crawlie travelling circus. In a grand baroque-style building, the two heavily pierced German owners of this bizarre exhibition had rented out the entire second floor to showcase their collection of a hundred or so of the world's most poisonous and terrifying tiny creatures, all housed in their individual glass boxes. Stuck on each glass box was a little description of where they had come from, how venomous they were and, in very precise detail, exactly how their poison works on the human body. It was interesting, but ultimately, pretty grisly. Having read the first description of how the fat-tailed scorpion's poison shuts down the body, I took a step back and thereafter eyed the security of the cases more closely. Having seen all but the final one, I was warming my hand up ready to pat myself on the back for surviving the most potentially lethal room in the world when I noticed that the last glass box had a TV monitor next to it. Playing on a continuous loop was Prodigy's 'Breathe' video. The description on the case read that this was the home of the actual millipede in the video and was the David Beckham of the insect world. On closer inspection, the star was not at home and, as the lid had been removed could have been absolutely anywhere. My heart sank and bottom twitched.

Clare hadn't reached it yet and so not to alarm her unnecessarily, I thought I would alert the owners to their star's disappearance. As I got within ear shot, he swung

Lady Luck and Me

round to reveal the millipede standing/sitting/resting along his entire forearm and him stroking it, smiling at me just like a surreal Dr Blofeld in the Bond films. He beckoned me over and, in spite of my objections, insisted in his heavy German accent, that I stroke it. With hesitation and a trembling hand I did as he said, fearful that he could turn this situation into a scene from a 'SAW' movie if I dared to refuse twice. I would say it was more of a token touch than a loving caress and, as expected, the millipede was cold and alien. I did my best to thank him sincerely, paid a donation and quietly left thinking 'That's got to be one of my best claims to fame ever'. Apart from that somewhat wacky sideshow, Krakow had not yet been tarnished too heavily with tacky tourist shops and had thoroughly retained its individuality and charm making it the highlight city of the trip.

Fifty kilometres west of Krakow is the infamous Auschwitz concentration camp. Again we had studied what had happened in these hell holes, but nothing, no matter how much literature anyone can read can prepare you for what you find. I have been told I'm a highly sensitive person so Auschwitz was always going to be particularly testing. The first thing that struck me on seeing those sinister gates was how well preserved it was. Because of this, it was depressingly easy to put yourself in the shoes of the thousands of poor people who had walked underneath it for the first and last time. The information boards which were dotted around were descriptive but unemotional which gave the ambience much more weight. It allowed you to feel it for yourself rather than be guided by someone else's presentiment. The snow which blanketed the ground dampened any noise and concentrated the mind on the eerie silence allowing the imagination to evoke the

'Worldly' travels

agonising screams which must have filled the air all those decades ago. Everything I saw, from the rusty barbed wire to the ground beneath my feet, would have witnessed unimaginable brutality and hatred and that nauseating feeling was present throughout.

Rooms full of human hair, with which pillows were stuffed for the German soldiers, or the rooms full of prosthetic limbs salvaged after the owner had expired in the gas chambers hit me with such severity that I no longer questioned whether there was a God. The entire tour of Auschwitz I was conducted in silence, not because it was insisted upon but because words were of no use. We left Auschwitz I shell shocked and visibly pained.

Auschwitz I was a well-preserved, carefully managed and dutifully cared for site. The second site, Auschwitz II (Birkenau), was walking distance away and not so preserved or well managed. In fact, it was anything but. If I thought I felt giddy at Auschwitz I, Birkenau really did test my mettle and I defy anyone who hasn't been there not to come away questioning everything they thought they knew about the human psyche. We are capable of and carry out the most atrocious deeds imaginable that even the Devil himself would be ashamed of.

Nothing surrounds Birkenau. Flat, featureless fields are bisected by a railway track that leads into the vast red-bricked fortress with its sole purpose to ferry hundreds of thousands of prisoners to their incarceration. Standing in the middle of the tracks, looking at the foreboding gates, it's just possible to make out the tall treeline behind the camp. In both directions, the walls seemed to carry on for miles with watch towers every 100 or so metres. Entering through the gates, the railway stops abruptly with an obvious, roomy gas chamber to the right and rows and rows of huts to the left.

Unlike Auschwitz I, there were no information boards, no guides, no other tourists, just dark deafening silence. No trees grew, no birds sang, nothing moved. It was, in every sense of the word, dead. Venturing into the grey gas chamber with the showers overhead, it was not hard to imagine hundreds of bodies crammed up against each other, nervously listening out for the evil hiss of gas coming through the pipes, knowing that or the sound of choking would be the last horrific noises they would hear. Seconds was long enough to feel the residual pain left in the walls and I only just made it out in time before I was doubled over, dry retching. The huts weren't much better. Around the tiny bunk beds, times tables and stick men had been etched into the walls, making the huts the saddest, smallest classrooms that only a few, if any, of its pupils would graduate from. It was incredibly difficult to spend any time in the huts, and by the third, I had had my belly full and didn't enter any more. We spent about an hour wandering around Birkenau, completely and utterly alone.

Unable to stomach any more, we left through the gates we came through, acutely aware of how lucky we were to be able to do so. That place comes closest to reflecting the blackness that stirs in my stomach. That day, I lost a significant chunk of faith, hope and love that I had for humankind.

The concentration/extermination camps deeply and profoundly affected both Clare and me. Before that afternoon, I would never have thought a couple of hours could change my life views so dramatically. As a result, the remainder of our time in Poland was spent under a reflective, mournful cloud. The colour in things had faded, music wasn't as moving, laughter became harder and any innocence which we had carried from our childhood had all but disappeared.

Lady Luck and Me

Sunsets, Socrates and sea urchins

'Happy is the man, I thought, who, before dying, has the good fortune to sail the Aegean Sea.'
Nikos Kazantzakis

Escaping the dark depressing depths of the Eastern European winter, Clare and I made the sensible decision to head to the Greek islands for some well-deserved sun, sand and serendipity. Our plan was to fly into Athens, join the 'Lonely Planet' can-can around the ancient sites and then make a bee-line to Piraeus, the gateway to the Aegean Sea and its many majestic islands. The Acropolis and surrounding buildings of so-called early wisdom were disappointing. It was clear that, over the years, millions of tourists and hoards of spotty 'don't give a fuck, daddy's paying' school groups had passed through. The empty crisp packets and abusive graffiti that adorned the sad, fallen ruins, where greats such as Socrates and Plato once preached, was a stark reminder of how ideologies are born, temporarily live and then painfully die. There, on top of the Acropolis, with Athens spread out below under a dense cloud of smog, all three stages of this particular ideology, capitalism, were sadly evident.

Deflated, hot and bothered we climbed back down to the city beneath and stumbled across Athens best-kept secret in a nondescript side street. It hadn't been mentioned in 'Lonely Planet', or any other tourist literature we had read, but my goodness me it should have been. The Athenians can keep their underwhelming classical architecture, their ancient philosophic scrolls and proud intellectual history

Lady Luck and Me

but for the love of moustaches, share the secrets of your humble souvlaki. To this day, I have searched for its equal and have always been found left wanting. Six inches of wrapped pitta crammed full of ingredients from God's own garden. Chicken, onion, tomato, lettuce, chilli, some strange tangy sauce and a big dollop of magic ensured that our time in Athens had been a partial success. The following day we sat on the top deck of the ferry under the midday Mediterranean sun and watched the shoreline grow smaller and our skin turn pinker. At that age, a healthy reddish glow was a small sacrifice to make in order to be away from the missing links in man's evolution. Hours drifted by and, eventually, we arrived at our first island, Naxos.

Naxos wasn't really anything to write home about. There were a few more wilting ruins, more hairy Greeks and a shed load of tacky neon bars crammed with 18 to 30-year-olds from all nationalities getting arseholed and trying to shove their tongues down as many throats as possible. The few that weren't in the bars were comforting friends on the pavement or holding back hair as their technicolour yawns ran away along the gutter. The chemists, which flanked most bars, did a roaring trade selling condoms, morning-after pills and antibiotics. The cheap gift shops did equally as well selling tat such as inflatable sheep and Greek gods with enormous cocks. Clare and I gave these bars a wide berth as our quest was to search out the real, authentic Greece and find the local tavernas where they served retsina and ouzo exclusively.

It didn't take long until we stumbled across a really grotty worn-out place where the clientele was 100 percent leather-faced, hairy men . . . and we were welcomed as if we had just stolen and eaten their babies. Music stopped and the barman stood there expressionless as we did our best to

Sunsets, Socrates and sea urchins

order half a carafe of the local wine. Three attempts later and still in silence, two dirty tumblers were slammed on the bar and filled with the rankest smelling concoction my nose has ever been offended by. With 60-odd eyes gauging our reaction, we did our best to ignore the rancid smell and taste, compliment the stony-faced barman on his fine drop and hospitality and left to join other party goers holding back hair on the pavement.

Having been disappointed with our two days and what Naxos, one of the bigger islands, had to offer, Clare and I opted to go for one of the smaller islands, still hoping to immerse ourselves in the real traditional Greek island culture. Our next port of call was to be a tiny island called Schinoussa. Population: not very many. Tour groups: none. Tourist shops: none. Highlights: small sandy beaches and a traditional Greek orthodox village on top of a hill. Equipped with books, sun cream, a rudimentary tent, basic food supplies and a pair of Speedos, we were all set to enjoy some uninterrupted peace and quiet and quality time together.

The ferry pulled in to a tiny, isolated pier and, unlike the other ports we had been to, there were no hawkers, no reps, no taxis. In fact, there was absolutely nothing, not even a building in sight. A long, golden beach spread out either side of us and the mottled turquoise water beneath the pier seemed to call out our names as we made our way along it. Being the first off and in genuine awe of where we had just landed, we hadn't noticed that we were the only two people who had disembarked. It was only when the ferry sounded its horn and we turned round to see it leaving the pier did we think it was strange that no other bastard had got off. In the back of my mind it was slightly unsettling but the adventure and romance of having what

Lady Luck and Me

seemed like the island to ourselves quickly quashed any negative thinking.

As the ferry got smaller and smaller, the feeling of isolation became greater and greater. We dumped our rucksacks under the only shrub on the beach that offered any sort of protection from the merciless sun and hastily climbed into our swimwear. Flitting between the coolness of the ocean and the heat of the beach we thought we had it made. We planned to spend the night there on the beach under the stars listening to the gentle lapping of the waves and the next day venture further into the island and to the village that, hopefully, time had forgotten. Tent erected, bread and fruit consumed, after sun applied, we settled in for the night, congratulating ourselves on a fine location.

The congratulations were short-lived as sandflies and mosquitos seriously hampered any chance of a night's sleep. The following morning, tired, cranky and peppered with various insect welts, we were ruing what seemed like a perfect destination and set about tearing chunks out of each other about whose poor decision it was to spend the night on the beach. Vowing not to spend another night there, we packed up our gear, strapped on our rucksacks and returned to the pier in the hope of picking up the trail to the village. Leaving the pier and cursed beach behind us, we followed the dusty track over the dunes and into the barren wastelands beyond.

A couple of hours into the journey, the track became a path and suddenly forked. There was still no sign of any life and neither fork offered any clue as to which way the village might be — both looked as though they hadn't seen a traveller for decades. The main concern now was what the sun was doing to our fragile, fatigued bodies.

Sunsets, Socrates and sea urchins

Regular lashings of Factor 15 were quickly carried away by rivers of sweat, exposing our naked skin to the harshness of the Mediterranean sun. Our water supplies were healthy as was our thirst.

We didn't have a map of the island as we thought it not necessary. Lonely Planet's entry on Schinoussa had been so short that we thought we would be able to walk around its entirety within a couple of hours, and we therefore hadn't worried or even considered food or water rationing. Four hours in, rationing was introduced. Finally, we found the fork again. It was mid-afternoon and Clare was in a terrible state. We didn't know how far away the village was or even what was there.

The romance of the island and the dreams of finding an untouched ancient village had all but evaporated. We had arrived at the island mid-afternoon the day before and if we continued back along the path to the beach there was a chance we could be in time to catch the ferry off the island. Decision made, we took our weakening legs as fast as they could carry us back over the dunes, to the pier, and waited. Exhausted, in pain and in silence we continued to wait, scouring the horizon for any sign of the ferry, but alas no ferry came.

As the stars came out and the realisation that we would have to stay another night dawned, we reluctantly picked up our rucksacks and made our way back onto the beach, Clare gently sobbing. The remainder of the bread and fruit was distributed and wolfed down, not through enjoyment but sheer necessity. The next day we either had to find the village or get off the island as food and water were now dangerously low. Another cloud also hung over us, the difficulty of the day had taken its toll on our

Lady Luck and Me

relationship, with any form of affection or intimacy being sharply rejected.

We emerged from the sweltering tent into the early morning sunlight with bodies that a fourteenth-century plague victim would have been happy with. Eyes swollen, cheeks inflamed and limbs subconsciously scratched to ribbons in a vain attempt to relieve the incessant itch that radiated from every bite, and that was me. Clare looked more like the Elephant Man, and I mean 'man' as it was difficult to determine which bumps God had given her and which bumps Schinoussa's winged beasts had given her. Both our moods were black and, with no food and limited water there was little to lift our spirits. Clare refused to move and looked forlornly out to sea. After my suggestion that the sea might be a good anaesthetic was met with more silence, I made up my mind there was only one thing for it, so I gathered up the empty water bottles, decanted half our remaining water into one of them, stuffed my pocket full of cash and gallantly headed back to the track, hell-bent on finding the village or indeed anyone who could extend our lives a little longer.

I arrived back at the fork of the path already glistening in sweat, cursed the path we had taken the day before and purposefully strode along what was surely to be the dusty track to our salvation. Over the first small rise, I heard the unmistakeable ding of a bell somewhere in the distance, it wasn't the majestic church that my imagination had convinced me of, but a herd of about twenty emaciated cows with the most feral looking one sporting a rusty bell around its neck. My heart sank as expletives spilt from my dry, chapped mouth. All was not lost though, for out of the corner of my eye, I spied a water trough and a dripping tap. As much as I tried, the rusted tap refused to open any

Sunsets, Socrates and sea urchins

further so I spent the next hour sitting in a field, painfully watching the water bottles fill, drop by drop. Burnt and conscious of time, I decided to venture no further down the path and head back to the beach, hoping once again to catch the elusive ferry back to civilisation. Although heavily laden with several bottles of water and having a mouth like Ghandi's flip flop, I dared not drink any of it until I had dropped the water purifying tablets in, which as Sods Law would have it, were in the rucksack on the beach. Leaving my mangy four legged friends behind, I took one final hopeful look around for other any sign of life and then re-joined the path back to the beach.

Clare hadn't moved in the hours that I'd been gone and, from a distance, looked as though a taxidermist had been at work on her. News that I had found water but no village was received with mix emotions. At least we weren't going to die of thirst, I reassured her, trying in vain to produce a giggle. Purity tablets deployed, we drank until our thirst was adequately quenched whilst doing our utmost to ignore the water's pungent acidic aroma.

For the second time in two days we gathered our things together and made the short journey to the pier, all the while scanning the empty horizon. And, again, for the second time in two days, no ferry or any other water-borne vehicle appeared to rescue us. The situation was now desperate and by the time we left the pier again, Clare acted more and more like a heavily sedated character from *One Flew over the Cuckoo's Nest*. Clare spent the night sitting up awake, swivelling her head from side to side keenly listening out for incoming wings and then slapping herself wildly in an attempt to stem further deformity. When morning broke, it seemed as though her night's vigil had paid off. Her body hadn't suffered any more abuse and the welts had

Lady Luck and Me

visibly subsided but the lack of sleep had reduced her to speaking in tongues not dissimilar to that of a possessed biblical character. After force feeding her water and doing my very best to comfort her with sympathetic words, I once again gathered up water and vowed to her that I would be back once I had located the village.

Head down and through gritted teeth, I trudged back along the beach, back onto the path and back past the now disinterested cows. Not twenty yards further on from where I had filled the water bottles, I saw it. Heaven only knows how I hadn't seen it the day before but just as Lonely Planet had said it would be, there it was, sitting proudly on the hill, white walls shining; the most quintessentially Greek village that any imagination could conjure up. It was a sight to behold. It was beautiful, not just aesthetically, it was more than that, it was our saving; it was life. I hurtled back to the beach and the awaiting Clare and broke the good news.

Finally and well overdue, we left the beach and its sinister inhabitants behind and slowly made our way through the countryside, stopping briefly at the cows for Clare to have the longest conversation and laugh she had had in days. Tearing her reluctantly away from her new bony friends, we made the final ascent to our salvation. On entering the village, our first priority was food. It had been a good thirty-six hours since we had last eaten and, combined with the stress and fluid loss, we had definitely lost weight, and Clare, her marbles. The village was small but relatively busy with the main cobbled street running up through the middle of it. On both sides of the street, in the shade of the overhanging roofs the elders of the village sat on rickety wooden stools playing backgammon and talking amongst themselves. It was difficult to put an age to them

Sunsets, Socrates and sea urchins

but, by their withered features I'm guessing the average age must have been a hundred and a healthy-looking hundred at that! From what I could see, they had certainly benefitted from their distance from the modern world and their diet of feta cheese and fresh vegetables seemed to have prolonged their lives considerably. There there wasn't a sour face among them and, even in their completely black attire, looked more than comfortable in the midday heat than we did. At first we were eyed with caution, almost as if we were lepers bringing death to their picturesque existence, but soon their eyes softened as it must have become clear that both of us were in serious discomfort.

An old lady, complete with black scarf, caught our eye and beckoned us over and began babbling away in Greek. From the outset, it was clear that there was going to be a communication problem and regardless of how much I slowed down my language and she raised the volume on hers, the barrier remained. After some humiliating ape impressions, she finally understood and directed me up the street before continuing her conversation with the two other women she was sitting with, not giving us another glance. Rucksacks back on, we continued up the street, politely yet awkwardly nodding to the villagers as they passed us by. Half way up the street, the most glorious vision possible; a stall festooned with bunches of grapes, hands of bananas, velvety ripe peaches, bulbous tomatoes, freshly baked bread, bottles of wine and sadly, straw donkeys wearing little, brightly coloured sombrero hats. Before I had a chance to mutter a hello to the stall holder, Clare, like a starved rabid animal, started grabbing everything she could get her insect bitten hands on. If I had had a whip or some kind of grown-up baby harness, I most certainly would have used it. By the time I managed to get

Lady Luck and Me

to her, she had consumed two tomatoes, half a banana and was frantically wrestling a straw donkey that stood in her way of the bread. Clearly alarmed and somewhat shaken by the whole event, the poor middle-aged woman stall-holder started shrieking loudly, arms flailing in a vain effort to restore peace and stop Clare's warpath through her stall.

It was only when I got my hands firmly on Clare's shoulders and ushered her away from the stall did she snap out of her deranged feeding frenzy. She stood there in the street, panting with tomato juice smeared across her face and a broken straw donkey under one arm, eyeing up her next feast. All this commotion had not gone unnoticed by passers-by who had now surrounded the stall in a semi-circle eager to watch what Clare did next. Before it reached boiling point and bloodshed, I plunged my hand into my pocket and produced a fist full of drachma notes, and tentatively offered it to the irate stall holder. A vast amount of money was given over in the name of peace and we left with a couple of carrier bags full of food and a tirade of more Greek abuse. Clare insisted on carrying the food while I lugged our rucksacks the short distance to the church at the end of the street. We sat down on benches with a breath-taking panoramic view of the island and the sea beyond and gorged ourselves silly. Colour returned to Clare's face and, once again, she returned to speaking English. Bellies full and feeling almost normal again, we set about looking for a nights accommodation desperate for a painless night's sleep.

We met an elderly woman who spoke English and told us that she could offer accommodation. She escorted us off the main street to her humble two-up-two-down that had the most stunning outdoor terrace, covered in vines overlooking the ocean. We were shown to our modest

Sunsets, Socrates and sea urchins

yet cosy quarters and joined her on the terrace to enjoy a bottle of local wine and an assortment of locally grown olives and freshly baked bread. We told her, Maria, of our painful stay at the beach and the hours spent waiting for the non-existent ferry to carry us away, at which point she laughed heartedly and told us of the many travellers had gone before us who had also encountered the same problems. It turns out that the ferry docks only once a week, and the beach where we were nearly eaten alive was notorious for its blood-sucking residents. Apparently, the other beaches on the island had been spared and, for some unknown reason, all the hellish creatures had gravitated to that one beach. It actually came as a surprise to Maria that the swarms of jelly fish that usually frequent the shore-line had been absent and assured us that we had been lucky to escape the beach without them leaving their signature scars all over our bodies.

The remaining three days of our stay on Schinoussa were taken up with gentle little jaunts into the village, siestas and general appreciation and thanks that we were still breathing. Finally, the day arrived for us to leave Schinoussa and to say that we were happy to be leaving would be another massive understatement. I had to hold Clare back from jumping in and swimming to the meet the ferry. Once again, we parked ourselves and our luggage on the top deck away from the pissed up, horny teenagers and walking Greek carpets. We needed time to recover and reflect. It felt like we had just escaped from a Vietnamese prison and had jumped on a boat full of American spring breakers. I even wondered how it was possible that the

Lady Luck and Me

same aged people, on the same boat, in the same ocean, were having such completely polar experiences.

Amorgos, our next island, was, by contrast, a popular tourist destination, so being eaten alive and starving to death was unlikely to be an issue. Since it had an impressive monastery that had been cut into the cliff-face, it had made our cultural list of places to visit. It didn't disappoint either. The precarious positioning of the building with the deep blue ocean directly beneath made it an awe-inspiring, humbling experience. Hats off to the ambitious architects who came up with the plan but, more importantly, to the poor, crazy bastards whose job it was to build it. I bet they didn't drink in the same tavernas as the architects.

Amorgos, the island of Jean-Marc Barr's signature film, 'The Big Blue' was just the tonic that Clare and I needed after Schinoussa and the two days we spent there were truly memorable for all the right reasons. Cultural and movie boxes ticked, we headed off to our next island hoping for more of the same.

Our next destination was Santorini, a volcanic island complete with black sand beaches and a reputation for having the most picturesque sunsets in the world. Now I've always been a little wary of such fantastic reputations. From first impressions, Santorini lived up to its billing. The beaches were made up of the finest black sand I had ever seen and sparkled under the gaze of the Greek sun. It was also the hottest sand that I have ever set foot on. Within the first five yards, the novelty of walking on black sand had worn off and been replaced with searing pain and small blisters. It was an island for shoes and, as I looked around,

Sunsets, Socrates and sea urchins

an island for obese Germans to come and turn themselves into pork scratchings.

The following morning, we woke clear headed and with a spritely spring in our step eager to hit the beach. With shoes firmly strapped on, towels under arms and litres of water and sunscreen we found an idyllic spot to spend the day and relax. The first dip in the sea was a welcome relief to the already-hot, rising sun, although negotiating the rocky entry and exit was a little precarious and required careful footing. As the day wore on, the cooling off trips became more frequent and the footing more complacent. By midday, the black sand had reached such a temperature that it could be felt through the soles of my cheap, plastic flip flops, forcing me to run across the sand and flick them off a yard before entering the soothing water.

After several visits, I knew my route well enough not to be burnt by the vicious volcanic sand and no longer saw the journey as a potential danger. All was going well with the casual dipping in and out until the last fateful trip. Three yards from the safety of my flip flops, a rogue wave knocked me off balance, causing me to frantically flounder for footing. Fearful that I would topple and face plant onto the surrounding granite rocks, I hastily planted my naked left foot. Straight away I knew something was wrong. By the time I reached the beach it felt like I had been stabbed with hot knitting needles. Hopping on my right foot, trying my best to keep off the scorching sand, I looked down at my left foot to see five sinister black needles protruding from my sole. Immediately I knew what I had trodden on and squealed to Clare for help.

At this point, I didn't know which was more painful, the sand which was melting my right foot or the

Lady Luck and Me

sea urchin's spines buried in my left. Clare thought I was joking, so giggled, turned over and continued reading her book. By now, my right foot had lost all feeling due to the heat of the sand but there was no mistaking the sensation in my left which was starting to make me feel queasy. As I collapsed on my arse, Clare finally realised that there was a problem and rushed over to help me into the shade.

As Clare took a closer inspection, it was worryingly evident from her gnarled facial expression that it wasn't a pretty sight. All I could see were the end of the fine needles and what appeared to be Moses beckoning me through a tunnel into the light. In our quest to find an undisturbed, perfect spot on the beach we had completely isolated ourselves from any form of possible help and could only just make out what looked like tiny little cherry tomatoes rolling in and out of the sea way down the beach. Without further ado, I instructed Clare to remove as many of the needles as she could and then piss on my foot. Quite rightly, she looked at me blankly, confused at this somewhat strange request. I assured her it really wasn't the appropriate time for me to be asking her to do me a sexual favour and it was purely for medicinal purposes. So, Clare carefully extracted two of the five needles out of my foot and managed to break the remaining three, leaving them buried deep in the sole. Looking around, shifting nervously, she assumed the position over my injured foot, crouching with her hands on the top of her bikini bottoms, ready to whip them down and carry out my absurd request. Nerves momentarily bettered her as she stood up questioning whether this was the right of course of action. As my screams got louder and my insistence more intense, she reluctantly re-positioned herself back over my foot and pulled down her bikini bottoms and pushed hard to relieve herself. Such was the

Sunsets, Socrates and sea urchins

force of her evacuation; it streamed out in all directions, covering my chest, arm, leg, and towel— in fact, everything apart from my wounded, swollen foot.

With no pain relief and saturated in Clare's well-intended urine, she helped me hobble back along the beach. Safely back at our digs, I rested up as Clare hurried out to find a more conventional anaesthetic, only to return with a bottle of ouzo and a packet of paracetamol tablets, on the pharmacist's instructions apparently. With most of the ouzo consumed and half a packet of pills down, I was feeling giddy but much better. Determined not to miss Santorini's epic sunset and off my face on a combination of drugs, alcohol and pain, I harassed Clare into taking me to the island's main vantage point to see its famous sunset.

Sadly, the rest of the island had the same idea and had got there a lot earlier, resulting in us having to stand between two of the tallest buildings on the island and having absolutely no view whatsoever of this so-called magical event. Not only that, dark, grey clouds had gathered so quickly and were rolling in with a threatening presence. As we watched the skies close in all around us, I was expecting the 2000-odd people to hold hands and start singing kumbayah, but, as it happened, the expectant crowd hushed into an eerie silence as if waiting to be abducted.

The mood was punctured by the couple next to us bursting into laughter. What with the day's events and the concoction of different chemicals running through my veins, I was caught up in the twilight atmosphere and this spontaneous laughter was just the interruption that I needed. Spotting that they were holding a bottle of local retsina and feeling my ouzo high was fading, I saw

Lady Luck and Me

them as my ticket to get back to being painless. I initiated conversation. It turned out that they were newly qualified Kiwi doctors on their honeymoon and, seeing as their eyes had developed divergent squints, seemed as though they were having a thoroughly good time. It wasn't long before the bottle of retsina was finished and a new one started — and all four of us had forgotten why we were standing there. Naturally, I was eager to seek their professional advice on the appropriate treatment for my now numb foot. Without hesitation, the husband told me that urine was best at neutralising the pain and drawing out any toxins to which the wife concurred by means of a solemn nod of the head. I looked at Clare, smiled and nodded in a patronisingly smug way. I then went about telling them of Clare's poor aim and my drenching, causing them to erupt with laughter and Clare to withdraw from the conversation embarrassed and humiliated. Once the laughter had subsided, they very kindly offered their services so we left the optimistic crowd and the doomsday sky and headed for the nearest tavern which, as Lady Luck would have it, was only a short distance for me to limp.

Safely inside and away from prying eyes, all four of us bundled into a tiny toilet cubicle. Perched on the toilet seat, I raised my foot to give them the best possible chance of hitting their target and politely looked away as the wife squatted and unloaded a full bladder directly over the damaged area. This, of course, was accompanied by raucous laughter from all parties, except Clare who was urging us to keep down the volume, fearful this bizarre foursome would attract unnecessary attention. Next it was the husbands turn and, even with him supporting himself, his shot was particularly wayward, sprinkling the floor, the walls, my leg (again) and finally with his final squeeze, my

Sunsets, Socrates and sea urchins

foot. I wasn't laughing so hard this time. Mission partly accomplished, we left the toilets and entered the bar where the barman and a dozen people were waiting to shake their heads in a disapproving manner. I desperately wanted to explain and clarify the situation but sadly my Greek and piss-sodden clothes wouldn't be enough to convince them otherwise.

Once outside, Clare and I were immediately forgotten. Without so much as a good-bye or even a final look over their shoulder, they were off in the warm Greek night, arm in arm, ricocheting from one building to the next, giggling hysterically. To this day I don't know whether they were just taking the piss and it was a brilliantly executed plan or whether they genuinely thought that was the best treatment. Either way, I'm hoping they were significantly bladdered to have absolutely no memory of it the following morning. As I hung off Clare's shoulder, in the middle of the deserted street, left foot throbbing and reeking of piss, I decided that it hadn't been the tremendous day I thought it was going to be when I got out of bed that morning, but there was always tomorrow . . .

The next few days spent on Santorini were unsurprisingly dull. Clare became my carer as my foot rendered me immobile, cranky and utterly useless. The urination on the foot served as neither an anaesthetic nor a neutraliser and I watched with morbid interest to see whether my foot might need to be amputated. Thankfully, the swelling had stopped, although the redness and pain were still very much present. Regular doses of retsina and ouzo coupled with the strongest painkiller the island had to offer seemed to be working and allowed me, with help from Clare, to make the short journey to the beach to recuperate and occasionally cry. By the time we had to leave, we had

Lady Luck and Me

successfully seen none of the island's sights and, due to heavy cloud cover, not one of their world-famous sunsets. With Clare serving as a mule carrying both our rucksacks and me hopping along behind her, we were again glad to be stepping onto the ferry and leaving our fourth and final island behind us.

We flew home different people to those we had flown out as. Whilst I carried more physical scars, the look in Clare's eyes suggested she had the more psychological ones. It was our last journey together before we began our university careers and, although it was a mostly silent trip home, we were both aware of the chapter ending. As I sat back reminiscing over the past year, some conclusions were drawn: 1) No good can come from combining alcohol, friends and golf clubs, 2) No good can come from combining alcohol, friends, shiny lights and tattoo parlours, 3) Eastern Europe is a hard place, especially in winter, 4) New Zealand doctors aren't doctors at all, 5) Greece and its islands are barely civilised, and 6) If you ever do watersports, make sure whoever you're doing it with, in whatever capacity, is suitably qualified and has a marksman's aim.

Univershitty

> *'May your university memories last as long as your student loan repayments.'*
> **Anon**

Our return signified the end of our gap year and a parting of ways. The year had been invaluable and I still genuinely think I learnt more in that one year than I had throughout my entire schooling. I now looked forward to university, feeling that the year seeing the world would give me an edge over those who hadn't. The problem was I hadn't yet secured a place at university. Clare had successfully landed a place at her first choice university, Birmingham, whereas I had to scramble through clearing after predictably and monumentally fucking up my exams to such an extent that none of my targeted universities would touch me, forcing me to look for a completely different subject at any university that would accept me.

After two solid days on the phone, I finally managed to convince a university to give me a place on their Sports Studies and Business Management course, starting in September. I had other friends going to Manchester and had only heard good things about the quality of student life. Sadly, it was only upon further scrutiny, that the location of my course meant that actually I wouldn't be anywhere near Manchester, but was to study and live in the beautiful town of Crewe. For those of you who haven't been there, I implore you never to go. For those that have, do you involuntarily shudder every time the word is mentioned like I do? Grey buildings, incessant rain and aggressive locals make it the worst place I've ever been in Britain. I can

Lady Luck and Me

only think the locals' love of their football team must be the only thing preventing them from throwing themselves in front of one of the hundreds of trains that pass through the hell-hole station. I detested every minute I was there and the romantic notion of the university years being the best years in one's life certainly didn't apply to me.

Clare and I drifted apart until we finally admitted defeat and broke up, which contributed to another bout of depression, adding further horror to an already grim situation. It was during these times that I started smoking cigarettes and then weed. I think the first time I tried weed, I was drunk on an empty stomach. I remember having two tokes followed by two hours hugging the canteen toilet with a distinctly unhealthy, grey complexion. The second time I tried it, I was sober. Instead of sending me straight to the toilet again, it temporarily gave me respite from my growing sense of helplessness and failure. It numbed most things, allowing me to withdraw into myself and hide from the world. States of numbness become addictive. Soon I was smoking daily by whatever means, determined to get to a place where simple thought constructions weren't possible. It killed any chance of positive progression but also, and more importantly, eased my anxieties by keeping me in a bubble. It put a buffer between me, everything and everyone.

My mind had been destabilising rapidly since my arrival in Crewe and I had experienced several dark episodes before I lit my first joint. My point is: I don't think marijuana acted as any sort of catalyst or trigger for my mental health problems. Now, with a slightly more educated mind, I can accurately recall each episode of depression I've had, with the earliest being at Holmewood House waiting for the phone call that never came. I was depressed then and knew nothing of it, let alone smoking or marijuana. Although marijuana very occasionally renders me immobile, it does light a creative match, sparking some of the most fascinating conversations with some of the most unlikely people. It takes me down otherwise impossible avenues, usually only concluding when someone has arrived at a fundamental understanding of something that's been bothering them for years.

I'm aware of the health implications associated with smoking weed, especially the psychological ones, and I am in no way encouraging or condoning it but the creativity that it brings can be a very healthy shot in the arm. I have spent many happy hours scribbling down the journeys my imagination has taken me on. I suppose what is key, is finding that balance between me using the drug rather than the drug using me, and that's often easier said than done. Anyhow, let me stub that out, where was I? Oh yes, stuck to the sofa, smoking, eating pot noodles and wondering whether I'd ever get a girlfriend again.

Despite our break up, Clare and I remained friends and so it wasn't the last I saw of Clare or her family. A year after Clare and I had split, I was invited around to celebrate Clare's birthday and found myself having sex in the family bathroom with Clare's flatmate. Drunk, sweaty and wobbly, I slipped off her back and cracked my head on the bathroom sink, splitting my forehead open savagely and spraying blood over all the polished surfaces. The following morning I woke late and was welcomed by Clare's mother in the kitchen, washing bloody cloths. She eyed the leaking gash above my eye as her eyelid flickered in revulsion, before returning to wash my blood out of her towels, shaking her head. I sheepishly said my goodbyes and left Clare's house, too embarrassed to ever return. Incidentally, I tell people

Lady Luck and Me

the scar above my right eye was a nasty elbow I received during my fighting days and not from slipping off my ex-girlfriend's flatmate, in my ex-girlfriend's family home.

When the final exams came along, I was suffering badly. Months had slipped by without me attending lectures. Some days were worse than others but it, the illness, often rendered me mentally useless and unable to leave the house, let alone face dull and complicated accountancy questions. The anxiety of failing the course grew. When I eventually had enough strength, I went and explained to my tutor the reason behind my exam absence hoping to do a resit when fully recovered. She seemed fully supportive, winked and told me not to worry, silencing me when I voiced my concerns about potentially failing the course. When my results came through I was, to say the least, a little bamboozled to have been awarded a Merit in my accountancy module without ever having sat the exam. That spoke volumes about the quality and validity of my eventual qualification.

In the time that I was there, I can vividly remember only two social events, neither of which I am proud of. The first was during my first year in halls, when I got stuck in the toilet having drunken sex with an ugly girl dressed in bondage gear, only managing to escape once the door had been broken down, much to the amusement of the 30 or so people who had gathered around to cheer as I emerged ashamed and with a leather whip mark on my forehead. The second was being followed down a dual carriageway by a police car in the middle of the night. I was convinced that I, and my housemate who I was pushing in a rusty, Morrison's shopping trolley, could outrun them. They patiently drove behind me until my drunken legs and bursting lungs gave out and then escorted me, still pushing my friend in the trolley, all the way back to Morrison's, suggesting we found alternative transport to get us back home.

I have retained absolutely nothing that I was apparently taught but, all these years later, I am still paying back the student loan and, on my current earnings' projection, will have finally paid all of it off by my hundred and fourth birthday. Those monthly deductions from my account serve as a constant reminder of a bleak, unhappy and farcical time, spent in one of the descending levels of Dante's Inferno.

Lady Luck and Me

A Question of Sport . . . Careers

> 'He never fails to hit the target — but that was a miss.'
> **Bobby Robson**

Graduating from university was all a bit anti-climactic. I was so glad to have left Crewe behind me but still had no set career path and, having done Sports Studies with Business Management, I was caught between the graduates who had done a full Sports Studies course and those who had done Business Management. The career most suited to my qualifications would be a sports centre manager but I thought I was destined for greater things, especially after the thousands of pounds that had been invested in my education.

I frequented the Job Centre regularly in the vain hope that something would leap out and show me the way. One of the jobs that did draw my attention was that of a lifestyle consultant working in the prestigious Grand Hotel in Torquay. I fulfilled the required criteria and was optimistic that this could well be my calling. In fact, I convinced myself that this was my dream job. Having applied, I was offered an interview and drove to it feeling confident. I was greeted by the Manager and shown the gym facilities and my potential workplace. Still feeling confident, I sat down for the interview. I had always been advised by both school career advisors and my tutor at university that whatever you offer in interview, you should back up later on in the

Lady Luck and Me

interview to demonstrate your point. 'Good interview technique' they had called it.

The interview was going perfectly and, as we both relaxed, I was convinced I had nailed it and had the job in the bag. He casually asked what else I could offer besides my experience and qualifications to which I answered 'a sense of humour'. More questions came and all the while I was waiting for an opportunity to demonstrate my rapier sharp wit. It finally came when he asked what I liked to do at the weekends. Without hesitation, I slipped into my gay voice and told him I like to dress up as a woman at the weekends and call myself Wendy. This was the point at which he got up, thanked me for my time and left. A dull ache grew in my stomach as the realisation that I had royally fucked up dawned on me. Good interview technique? It couldn't have been better and yet I was still jobless. I cursed the so-called career advisors and left to job search once again.

Having completed my FA Junior Team Managers Award, or 'FA qualification 1' as it's called these days at university, I was somewhat surprised and delighted to find a football coaching vacancy being advertised in the Newton Abbot Job Centre. However perfect the job was, it was in Bristol and, paying a princely £150 a week, was not enough to justify a daily commute of around 100 miles. I phoned the number given and explained my predicament. It was agreed that I could lodge with his other coach and pay a minimal weekly rent with food and transport provided. I was to drive up and meet my host the following afternoon. All the way there, I couldn't help thinking that all this had been far too easy and there must be a catch. I arrived at the specified rendezvous point and was confronted by a battered white Nissan van, the only one in the car park outside the world's roughest pub that garishly advertised

A Question of Sport . . . Careers

two for one lap dances between the afternoon hours of three and five. As agreed, I had arrived right on time, 3p.m. I parked my chariot alongside the van, turned the engine off and stared at the dimly lit pub. Fuck, fuck, fuck! What was I about to walk into?

As expected, the interior of the pub was grim by anyone's standards. The large barman stared at me as I scanned the room, eyes stinging in the thick blue haze of tobacco smoke. In the middle of the room was one solitary figure, his back to me, jeering loudly at the hefty, middle-aged topless woman dancing badly around a greased pole. The numerous empty glasses that cluttered his table suggested he had been there for quite a while. I tentatively approached and introduced myself. He glanced up briefly with reddened, sagging eyes, tapped on the chair next to him and then turned back to the stage yelling at the dancer to dance harder. We both then sat, listening to ABBA and watched the poor woman awkwardly trying to, at best, look average. It wasn't working and all three of us knew it. As she steadily died on that tacky flashing stage, we both watched on, mouths ajar. She didn't make it through the song and toddled off the stage behind a threadbare curtain, quite clearly on the verge of explosive tears. It was all very peculiar and really rather sad.

I was brought out of one the most surreal moments by my companion introducing himself as Gary. He didn't hold out his hand or take his eyes off the stage, he simply said his name in a slurred Bristolian accent, held out a fiver, and told me to get two pints of Stella, glazed eyes still staring dead ahead. I guessed he must have been in his mid-thirties, full head of blond hair and seeing how low he was in his chair, about four foot tall. He was wearing Bristol Rovers shorts and tatty trainers so I assumed he

Lady Luck and Me

must be the right bloke. I got the two Stella's from the mute, solemn barman and rejoined Gary just in time to see the next hideous, middle-age act totter out onto the stage wearing a pink Wicked Weasel thong and feather boa which barely covered her huge, dinner-plate nipples. It was going to be a painful afternoon. No sooner had I sat down with the Stella's, Gary produced another £5 note and pointed towards the stage curtain. 'Make sure you get the two for one,' shouted Gary, concentrating hard on the bouncing breasts of contestant number two who, to be fair, was putting in a far more energetic performance than the last pitiful act.

I made my way over to the curtain and, under Gary's watchful eye, reluctantly called out. Behind the curtain was a make-up room/sex shop with the previous entertainer standing with her hands on hips, still topless, fag in mouth, staring at me through swollen, puffy eyes. Under all the bright lights, she was significantly older and absolutely no way any more attractive. We looked at each other and both knew what Gary had done, the bastard. I held out the fiver and told her not to worry. She grabbed the fiver angrily and stomped towards the curtain. She withdrew the curtain and thrust her right hand out extending her middle finger. From behind the curtain I could just make out Gary and watched him explode with laughter, rocking back in his chair, clapping his hands together like a retarded toddler. She pulled back the curtain loudly muttering 'wanker' under her breath and ordered me to sit down. I sat down surrounded by knickers, dildos and all manner of weird and wonderful accessories.

Perching delicately on the edge of the chair, I tried to avoid contact with everything, fearful I was going to catch gonorrhoea or syphilis any second. I peered up from

A Question of Sport . . . Careers

the limp, flesh-coloured dildo next to me right at the wrong moment. Facing me, the stripper was bent over in her tiny thong trying to unbuckle her 6-inch platforms, cursing loudly between her smoke inhalations. It was a horrid sight that I fear will stay with me for many years to come. She eventually stepped out of her platforms, reducing her height so significantly that she could have been a very convincing extra in the film 'Willow'.

Liam Gallagher had finally screamed himself into silence on the radio at which point she turned, looked, and shot out a finger in the direction of the curtain. 'Don't I get two for one?' I asked, trying to inject some humour into a bizarrely tense situation. She held her pose, eyes widening. As I got up, I knocked the table on my right, sending a glass of water down my grey Nike tracksuit bottoms. Panicking, I reached around for something to rub myself down with and, as Lady Luck would once again have it, the first thing that came to hand was the 10-inch dildo which I had become rather frightened of. She yelled at me to put it down which I couldn't do fast enough, and limped towards the curtain. At the sight of me, Gary, ironically, properly pissed himself and we were both politely told to get the fuck out by the now-very-vocal barman. Gary weaved his way to the door; still laughing like a crazed man, telling John the barman that he would see him tomorrow.

Once Gary was behind the wheel, it was evident that he was utterly arseholed. Following him at a safe distance, I witnessed him narrowly avoid a head-on collision with a young girl on her bike as well as receiving abuse from an elderly man for failing to stop at a zebra crossing. Thankfully for the public, Gary didn't live far away. Having mounted the pavement and rearranged a number of wheelie bins, he finally parked, leaving a third of the van on the road

Lady Luck and Me

and the other two-thirds fully mounted on the pavement. After I had parked conventionally, I followed him in to his ground-floor flat.

Hanging by the door were a selection of baseball bats, golf clubs, hockey sticks, etc. In the tiny, sparse hallway they were the only things worthy of note. When I questioned Gary about them I got a simple grunted word as an answer: 'protection'. Brilliant, I thought, I guess there was a catch after all. Gary lurched his way into the lounge, collapsed on the sofa and fell asleep. I spent the rest of the afternoon sitting watching a shitty, tiny black-and-white telly expecting the front door to get bashed in at any moment, with occasional flashbacks of the stripper undoing her platforms.

I slept on the sofa and food was either Indian takeaway or Dominos delivery, funded in the main by Gary. There was very little consultation and I generally ate what was ordered. Suffice to say, my taste for hot spicy foods progressed rapidly. The football coaching itself was fun. We started work at ten, lunched at midday, more football until half two, then pissed by five. Really it was just a glorified babysitting service for four to eleven-year-olds.

Friday was always the highlight of the week as it was presentation day and Gary was in his element. He was cocky enough to be classed as a confident geezer, but ugly enough to be called . . . ugly and therefore not seen as a threat by any visiting husband. This made Gary a dangerous man on Fridays. He finished his presentation and, when the mothers were milling about talking to other parents, Gary would single out the unattached females and make a bee-line for them, complimenting their child on his/her hard work during the week and the obvious

A Question of Sport . . . Careers

talent the child had. It didn't matter how he had treated the child during the week, he acted like he was their best friend, rubbing their hair or sharing a non-existent private joke with them. It was a polished, well-versed performance that was painfully transparent. He wouldn't spend long on individual women, just long enough to get either a phone number or a rejection and then he was off to the next with the same repertoire. Amazingly, he yielded results and, as we packed up, he would tot up how many numbers he had harvested. If it was any more than none, I was always shocked.

After witnessing Gary's post-presentation spiel one final time, he and the rest of the coaches were to take me out for my send-off drinks. It had been a fun six-week contract and, as we hadn't got into any violent trouble, I was beginning to feel I was running on borrowed time. I was glad to be going. Parking the car just off White Ladies Road, we headed to The Fine Line for an early Friday afternoon beverage. The pints came and went, toilet trips became more frequent and Gary's stories got more and more seedy. There was nothing unusual about any of that; it was when the shots started to appear that the night changed direction. First, it was a pint followed by a shot chaser and then it developed into two shots followed by a pint chaser. I knew I was in trouble when I tried to piss in an empty crisp packet under the table in order to save time going to the toilet. I hadn't thought about what I was going to do with it once I had filled it and still ended up making the journey, but instead of having a full bladder to relieve it was a McCoys packet of piss. Thankfully, my footing was true and I completed the journey without causing a major incident. An hour later, I was in a proper pickle and barely

Lady Luck and Me

able to move. All I could think of was bed and being sick, and not necessarily in that order.

Meanwhile, Gary was on top of his game, inviting some of the county's worst-looking women over to our table. Everyone seemed to be a having a whale of a time apart from me who was barely conscious. Gary announced that it was time he left and, praising the Lord, I struggled to my feet only for Gary to shake his head at me and tell me to sit back down. I giggled and continued to try and make my way around the table only to be stopped and dragged back down onto the sofa by the biggest, hairiest woman I had seen in a long time. I watched Gary smile at me, put 20 quid from the huge bint in his top pocket, turn around and leave.

The bastard; he had actually pimped me out. Unbelievable. I stared drunkenly into the beast's eyes that still had a firm grip on my wrist. 'Don't worry, my lover. I'll make sure you get home,' she purred at me in her Bristolian Barry White voice. I was in no state to try and fight, argue or even walk unaided. My fate was sealed. I don't remember any more of the evening, but I do remember waking up in the morning to her sitting astride me squeezing the air out of my lungs. I left in such a hurry that morning that I made it out wearing only one trainer.

I got a taxi back to Gary's livid and nursing a hellish hangover, only to find my packed bag outside the front door with a note attached. 'Hope you had a good night. It's been fun. G' And that was it. Six weeks living in his flat, teaching with him, him pimping me out and just a note. Now I could understand why he needed that protection inside his front door. I wondered how many times he had done this before and how much money he made pimping

A Question of Sport . . . Careers

off other unsuspecting naive football coaches. I was positive I wasn't the first angry person he had done it to and had no doubt there would be plenty more poor suckers to follow. If any of them have the same experience with the same woman, heaven help them. She should come with a year's free counselling. I solemnly climbed into my car and left Bristol, eager to get home as quickly as possible to shower off the shame of the night before.

Lady Luck and Me

Welcome to the working world

'Success is stumbling from failure to failure with no loss of enthusiasm.'
Winston Churchill

Whilst the universe decided what to do with me, I signed up to an employment agency, willing to do anything to get some money in. One of my first placements was working at Devon Deserts, a huge factory located on an industrial estate on the fringes of Newton Abbot. They provided supermarkets with all manner of desserts ranging from fruit jellies right through to sticky toffee puddings. I was given a white overcoat, wellies and a purple hairnet, and then assigned to the refrigerated blue section which, unsurprisingly, was frigging cold. After wading through a sheep dip-like disinfectant, I was shown to my station. Within the refrigerated blue section was a refrigerated room and in that room was the custard machine for the spotted dick puddings. The puddings passed through the room on a conveyor belt, momentarily stopping underneath the machine so that the custard could be squirted on top. My job was to apply the custard.

After the briefest of instructions, my custard mentor left and I began my work as the custard operative. Despite the bitter temperature, deafening noise, and soul-destroying repetition, all was going well. In fact, it was going so well, complacency kicked in a little and my mind started to wander. I was amusing myself by thinking that because I was operating a custard machine and wearing a purple hairnet, I was by definition a purple-headed, custard chucker. Schoolboy euphemisms were still very

Lady Luck and Me

entertaining to me at the time and I was congratulating myself on a particularly good one when I was abruptly brought back into the freezing room by the coolness of the custard creeping down the insides of my wellies. In the split second that I had taken my mind and eye off the job, the lever had got jammed on, so the custard was spewing out at a rate of knots, covering the conveyor belt, the floor, my overcoat and pretty much everything else in sight. The more I tried to plug the offending nozzle, the more angles I created for the custard, almost as if I was encouraging it to cover parts of the room that had so far escaped the yellow tsunami.

Having exhausted all ways of stemming the flow, I ran out of the room in search of assistance, looking like I was wearing a yellow duvet. Disorientated and overcome by panic and the smell of custard, I unwillingly entered the red section of the factory which was the baking department. Unbeknownst to me, there was a strict colour crossing between department's policy and I, being from the blue section, was very unwelcome in the red section. Before I had the chance to ask for help from anyone, I was confronted by a stocky man wielding a broom shouting at me to get the fuck out. I didn't need asking twice and beat a hasty retreat back into the room which was by now about half a foot under custard. As I stood there like a rabbit in the headlights, watching the custard cascading from the pump, reality dawned that whatever I did now, I would certainly lose my job, get a huge bollocking for breaking the machine, entering the red section and probably have my two hours wages revoked in order to pay for the damage.

After one final look at the increasing mess that I was making, I left the room. Calmly, I strode down the corridor, back through the sheep-dip and to my locker.

Welcome to the working world

Having discarded my soiled clothes, drenched hairnet and full Wellington boots, I left the building and the occupants in it to sooner or later discover that the custard machine had no operator but, instead, a mind of its own and was on a seemingly unstoppable mission to flood the factory. About an hour after I had left, I received a phone call from a very irate agency worker asking me to explain myself and my actions before telling me that I was responsible for causing thousands of pounds worth of damage. Despite my feeble explanation and half-hearted apologies, I couldn't help but smile. I was told, in no uncertain terms, never to contact them again and not to expect any sort of payment for the two disastrous hours I had spent at Devon Desserts. It seemed Lady Luck didn't want me to work in a food factory so slapped me a little then put me back to square one again. She most certainly is a playful mistress.

Having been thrown off the books and barred from one recruitment agency, I took my CV, cap in hand so to speak, to the other Exeter-based agencies, praying that they didn't have some sort of connecting intranet network. If they did then I was essentially on a Pub Watch equivalent, meaning legitimate work would be nigh on impossible to find. Thankfully, at Brook Street Recruitment Agency, they weren't and the blue-eyed, blond consultant welcomed my mainly bogus CV with open arms, clearly impressed by what she read. The standard question of what I would like to do was asked and my response that I didn't care as long as it was well paid, had loads of holiday, was based in the Cayman Islands being surrounded by scantily-clad women, fell on deaf ears.

Funnily enough, the job market always seemed to be flat when I was looking and even the poorly paid, nasty jobs in horrific conditions were scarce. In other words, even

Lady Luck and Me

with my best fictional CV that included voluntary overseas charity work and a double first from Oxford, I would have to be happy and grateful with whatever they could find me. CV scrutinised and bank forms completed, I was led over to a computer terminal. I didn't think this was standard practice as I hadn't had any computer testing in any of my previous agency interviews so all I could think was that this apparent airhead consultant was a lot brighter and shrewder than I had given her credit for and had correctly worked out that the interview, me and my stellar CV didn't quite add up.

'I'm sorry to have to ask you to do this, Mr Dobson, but would you mind doing a quick computer literacy test? I'm sure that with your qualifications and experiences, you'll fly through this in a couple of minutes,' at which point she pulled out the chair for me to sit on and turned on the computer. I was rumbled and we both knew it. I hesitated before sitting down, contemplating how much damage would be done to my pride and potential employment chances if I refused and bolted for the exit. Too much, I decided, and gingerly sat down making sure eye contact was avoided and therefore integrity upheld, for a little longer at least. Computers and I get on like shit and a public swimming pool so it came as no surprise that I understood absolutely nothing of what was on the screen in front of me.

'Ok then, I'll be just over there when you've finished and please don't hesitate to ask if you have any questions or problems.' She hung round the back of my chair as my eyes bore a hole in the screen and my hands dangled tentatively over the keyboard. I'm sure she wanted me to answer or at least acknowledge her so she could laugh at my pain before congratulating herself on her Sherlock Holmes-like skills

Welcome to the working world

of deduction. I didn't do either, I just sat there wishing she would fuck off and die and the ground would swallow me up. The phone forced her back to her desk and I was left trying to decipher the digital language in front of me.

After a couple of minutes of timid key prodding and angry computer noises, I felt the first beads of sweat run down my forehead, along my nose and onto the keyboard below. Another couple of minutes later and still struggling to get off the first page, the sweat was now streaming down my face and neck no doubt much to the delight of the witch who must have spotted my discomfort by now and was very probably revelling in it. The longer I sat there, the more saturated the keyboard became. Using my sleeve as a makeshift handkerchief, I dabbed the keyboard hoping to mop up the moisture before it seeped into the circuit board and released me from this unpleasantness by electrocuting me. Although the computer initially barked at me in protest, the screen suddenly changed, informing me that I had somehow successfully completed stage 1 of 12.

Sensing a reprieve from certain humiliation, I carefully retraced my dabbing with a single digit over the keys until the computer sang with approval rather than grunted with annoyance. F12 was the golden key. Once found, I didn't even try to understand what the questions were asking, I just bashed F12 and watched the stages sail by, each time accompanied by the triumphant bing of success. I giggled and felt like I had just decoded the 'Enigma' machine of World War Two. I would almost go so far as to say I was actually disappointed when the screen eventually flashed up: 'Congratulations. Stage 12 of 12 successfully completed.' I swung round on my swivel chair with considerable cockiness and a grin and looked at the consultant who had serious amounts of disbelief and displeasure etched on her face.

'Right, Mr Dobson,' she said, 'let's see what we can do for you...' and began tapping away, shooting looks at my smug smile across the desk.

'Well, as I said to you earlier, the job market is very slow at the moment, umm . . . Looks like the only position we currently have is a vegetable picker in the same valley as you live, luckily.' My smile fell.

'That's the only job you've got available?' I enquired with utter disbelief.

She sympathetically shook her head, went back to the screen and said, 'I'm afraid so. But it is summer, it pays 160 pounds for a 40-hour week and the hours are nine to five.' I knew she was lying.

'So what was the computer test for? Are you sure there isn't anything else?' she replied sternly, 'that's all there is, Mr Dobson. Now you can take it or go home and wait to hear from us if anything more...suitable comes up...'

We held each other's gaze momentarily, mutual hatred fizzing in the air. Through gritted teeth, I conceded. A job's a job, I thought. Instantly, her face changed as she went back into professional consultant role again. I scratched my way through the necessary documentation, absolutely seething. I didn't mutter a word as I left, fearful my rage might get the better of me. As the door was closing, I heard her shrill, irritating voice: 'I hope you enjoy your job, Mr Dobson.' Bitch. Unfortunately, that was not the

Welcome to the working world

last job my new nemesis gave me. It was the first in a long line of shit jobs.

The vegetable picking job turned out to be mushroom picking which took place in a dark, damp, windowless, black polythene tunnel, whilst the rare summer sun blazed away outside. I shuffled up and down rows of pots of compost on a plastic stool, on my own, plucking the mushrooms off the top, listening to the intermittent radio. I lasted two weeks before deciding it wasn't healthy to spend 40 hours a week on one's own in a dark plastic room doing something you don't give two shits about. I phoned Brook Street hoping she wouldn't pick up the phone. To my joy she didn't, but when I was put on hold, I knew it wouldn't be long before I heard her squawk down the line at me. Sure enough, the next voice was hers. She sounded surprised when I told her I wasn't happy and then did the most insincere cooing noise, blatantly taking the piss.

After putting me on hold for 10 minutes, I could clearly hear her stirring a spoon as she told me I was in luck and a job had come in that very morning and she thought it would be perfect for me. Sensing a possible opportunity that bridges were being rebuilt, I listened keenly to the particulars of the next placement. Extensive travel around the south-west coast, assisting someone in picking up important equipment from elderly care homes was the job description. I was encouraged by her seemingly thoughtful offer, thinking that maybe our little feud was over and enthusiastically agreed, happy in the understanding I was at least doing something worth my while. When I turned up at the address given, it was evident that the job description had been somewhat misleading. The actual job was being a driver's mate to a racist, BNP Leeds football supporter. He would drive from care-home to care-home and sit in

Lady Luck and Me

the van as I ran in picking up dozens of sacks of offensive soiled linen. It wasn't uncommon for the sacks to split open on the way to the van, leaving me having to pick up stained sheets, gloveless. It was windy days I feared the most. It wasn't long before I developed a technique not to dissimilar to a matador teasing a bull in an effort to keep ruined sheet as far from myself as possible. Between the homes, the driver had an insatiable habit of stopping outside every corner shop and takeaway, going in and yelling the most offensive racial abuse imaginable at the proprietors then calmly wandering back to the van to drive to the next one. Unsurprisingly, I didn't last too long in that role either and, much to the delight of my agency nemesis, had to ask her to find me another one.

As 'luck' would have it, a job had appeared only within the last hour that closely matched the skills which I had listed on my CV and was people-orientated. I would be assisting the sales team at a big international motor company, closing deals and introducing new clients. Hourly rate for the first three months of probation and then pay could be negotiated. It was based in Exeter, 20 minutes away, and even sounded like a possible career move. I accepted and immediately went out to buy a new shirt and shiny black shoes. I arrived early to make a good impression and was taken to my desk by the sales team manager. My desk faced the front glass doors, had a computer, multi-coloured Post It notes, a diary and a huge switchboard phone. I was the male receptionist in one of the most alpha male environments you can imagine. As I directed incoming calls to the offices, made them tea, typed up their illiterate reports and proposals, my colleagues constantly took the piss, asking me to wear heels, what size my tits were and whether I had a boyfriend. Initially,

Welcome to the working world

the banter was amusing but when they started texting, asking for naked photos and suggesting I wore a thong more often, I began to feel uncomfortable and hung up my fishnet stockings, vowing never again to be involved in the car sales industry.

The next assignment given to me was a data entry clerk for a department of the NHS, located in Exeter City Centre. The office was open plan, consisting of about 50 desks worked at by middle-aged barnacles, seeing out dull day after dull day, waiting for their retirement and the massive civil servant pension that comes after all those numbing years of service. It was like a working government retirement home. I was the youngest pup in the room. Closest in age was my line manager Matt who, at the age of 39 and married with two kids, had all the markings of a young, pension-driven government care home manager. His saving grace was that he knew it and was already cynical, bitter and embraced any youthful exuberance whenever it came his way. Our regular, illegal cigarette breaks on the stairs out on the fire escape were really only excuses to viciously degrade both the workforce and the job, me playing the enthusiastic puppet and Matt the sinister puppeteer. His arch enemy in the office was a fellow line manager, Sue, and the vast majority of our cigarette break conversations included fictional scenarios of how to bring her down in the most humiliating way.

A few weeks into my tenure, an opportunity arose that was so perfect that neither of us could have imagined it, even in our most ruthless of cigarette break conversations. Sue had left for her hourly lunch break and had left me to complete another typically soul-destroying spreadsheet that she neither wanted nor needed. She used me as a pawn against Matt, knowing any resistance from

Lady Luck and Me

Matt would ensure a meeting with the department head and, owing only to her time served, would threaten Matt and his smooth progress up through the pay bands. I had completed her pointless task, printed out the results and delivered it to her in-tray at her unoccupied desk. In the middle of her desk was her open diary. Impossible to ignore and almost begging to be read, I obligingly cast my eye over her most recent entries. My eyes widened as I read what she was doing during that very lunch break. Matt, noticing my sudden concentration, questioned what I was reading. Sensing potential super stardom in Matt's eyes and a chance for myself to go down in office history, I began to read out Sue's entry:

> 'Nervous about lunch today, haven't seen Steve since telling him it was painful last time. I enjoyed it, the risqué side, but told him he has to use lube next time. Hoping he doesn't mind meeting in the cemetery rather than at the bridge. Dreading talking to him about Dave's 50th. I spoke to Mum this morning and thankfully she doesn't know I'm having affair with my own brother, she would die, and she mustn't know, it will drive the family apart. I'll tell him not to come near me during Dave's birthday. Must be strong.'

Halfway through my reading and with growing confidence, I climbed onto her chair and theatrically finished my reading to the office's stunned stares and to such a silence that Patrick Stewart would have been proud of in any one of his RSC performances. After triumphantly finishing, I bowed to Matt's generous standing ovation and just managed to plant a stabilising hand on the desk before Sue, who had come out of nowhere, pulled the chair from under me, grabbing her diary out of my hand, under a blanket of verbal obscenities. She then man-handled me into the department head's office, demanding I was fired

Welcome to the working world

for an invasion of privacy. Sue was asked to leave the room and, as soon as the door closed behind her, a wry smile crept across his face. He had heard my reading and I knew that he knew that I knew. From that moment, it was all very civil. I told him I'd leave immediately only to be instructed to work until my lunch and he'd sign me off for a full day. He even shook my hand, smiled and thanked me for my services.

I lost a job but, in the process, had given the office more entertainment than they had seen in that stagnant office since the Queen's Coronation. I had also left Matt with never having to worry about ways to humiliate his office nemesis. I'm sure he and all who were present at my reading will take those 30 seconds into their comfortable retirement and hopefully remember it as a highlight in a necessary but truly uneventful vocation.

The next carrot that was dangled in front of me by the agency was characteristically dressed up in the usual transparent bullshit. Opportunity to travel, company benefits, massive potential earnings, blah blah blah, based typically in the same industrial estate where I was almost sodomized in my role as sales team secretary. But, according to bitch face, the potential benefits were worth the risk of being stalked by any of my ex-employers. The job description? 'Sales executive for a progressive, innovative, small team in the exciting and pioneering field of agricultural ball bearings.' After three weeks of sitting in a windowless garage, surrounded by shelves of ball bearings, the only travel that I had done was to the toilet and back. What was even more misleading was the 'Sales' bit of the job description. How I was supposed to sell and hit my targets without a telephone, internet connection

Lady Luck and Me

or any contact at all with the public was going to prove a challenge.

My job wasn't going to be made any easier by sharing the garage with a short, middle-aged, ginger-haired man who happened to be the boss and the only other person to make up the entire workforce. Being a born-again Christian, he insisted on listening only to new-age Christian bands, eight hours a day, every day, except on Wednesdays when he would move his half of the garage furniture and files outside so he and his friends could jam Christian songs at me as I sat opposite them at my desk, staring at a spreadsheet trying to ignore the growing feeling of how uncomfortably weird the whole set-up was.

As if the daily assault on my ears wasn't enough, my boss and space sharer had a clear medical problem with flatulence, both in sound and aroma. The longer I was there, the more regular, potent and less ashamed he became, often filling the windowless, airtight space with such fumes it made my eyes sting and occasionally weep. In hindsight, I actually think the job itself was a rouse and what he was really trying to do was aggressively recruit and convert people by making their life so unbearably miserable that, as a last resort, they would turn to God for salvation. I left the job just before I felt the urge to fill my rucksack with company ball bearings and throw myself into the nearest lake clutching a crucifix.

The last job assigned to me was at the Benefits Agency in Newton Abbot, working in the Social Fund Department, pushing paper around. I got so good at pushing paper around that they promoted me (if you can call it that) to Exeter, handing out the dole cheques. Protected by a two-inch thick, bulletproof screen, I was subjected to the

Welcome to the working world

very worst abuse by drug-addled individuals. Some threats were wholly amusing but most were pretty chilling and, for six quid an hour, it was no wonder that I finished most days passed out on the couch with a bottle of vodka in my hand.

It was during this placement that I became friends with a chap called Al who was of similar age but worked in a different department. One day I was taken off the front desk and asked to drive Al down to Newton Abbot so he could collect some papers. I was given the keys to a souped-up Peugeot 306, complete with Government plates. I saw the Government plates as an untouchable passport to do and go wherever I wanted without reproach. Al didn't have a licence, so I drove. We sped down the A38 at 130 mph feeling that we were part of the Secret Service and parked in the pedestrianised High Street, just because we could. He collected the papers and I stood leaning on the car as people looked at me and the out-of-place car inquisitively. Thinking we should make the very most of the situation, we left the car in the High Street and popped into a nearby pub for a quick pint. It was during the third pint that I agreed to let Al drive. Fearless of the law because of the plates, it seemed to be a great idea.

Al got into the driver's side and bunny-hopped down the High Street, clearing people out of the way. We took a detour via Teignmouth (a good 20 miles off route) with Al growing in confidence and speed. I decided enough was enough when Al drove straight over a mini roundabout, getting the brake pedal and the accelerator pedal confused. With the beer wearing off, we returned to Exeter three hours later than expected and were greeted by a fuming head of department who had received a phone call from the police asking what was so urgent that it

Lady Luck and Me

required 130 mph down a dual carriageway, and where the hell had we been for the past three hours. I bumbled my way through lame excuses saying we got lost and had tried an alternative route in order to avoid heavy roadworks, but they fell on deaf ears and I was told that there might well be an investigation into my actions. Thankfully, nothing came of it apart from a total ban on using the government car again. I worked there for another couple of months, continuing to get abuse from the public and building an admirable tolerance to vodka.

Being only a 20-minute drive from Mum in Trusham, I would make regular journeys back in order to reconnect with the stunning surrounding countryside that we were lucky enough to have on our doorstep and also to see Scott, our dog and my best childhood friend. It was on one of these journeys that I passed a police car. It was after dark and, as our eyes met across the lit road, I knew that a conversation would soon take place. Sure enough, I watched him in my rear view mirror do a U-turn and start following me. I had been pulled over a few times before, probably because I had a short haircut and they were power hungry. He followed me down the country lanes and deep into the Devon countryside, passing neither person nor moving vehicle, just a herd of cows grazing in a field.

In the middle of nowhere his blue lights came on and I obligingly pulled over. He, as they had before, asked me to get out of the car then asked whether I had any needles or blades on my person, before thoroughly frisking me and asking me to get into the back of his car. Again, with full co-operation, I complied. After answering numerous, irrelevant, nonsensical questions accurately and coherently he told me he could smell alcohol on my breath. I assured him that that wasn't possible as I hadn't

Welcome to the working world

had a drink for the past week as I was saving my money and health for Australia. He didn't believe me and insisted I took a breath test which again, I happily did. The result was, of course, negative. He then told me about his time in Australia, his kids, his family and his aspirations to which I politely nodded. With no apology he said I could go and, as I opened my door to leave, he told me that he would have to fine me for having my fog light on and told me to appear at a police station within the next seven days to produce my driving licence, MOT certificate and insurance documents. He then wished me a good time in Australia.

What a prick. That was the straw that broke the camel's back with me and the police. In my experience, the police have only hindered me and my friends' lives and never have they ever been useful. Until that changes, I will continue to view them as sad, lonely, little shits. Oh, and if that copper that pulled me over and fined me ever reads this: 20 minutes after I left you, I was off my tits on mushrooms which were in my pocket, you penis.

Lady Luck and Me

Amsterdamaged

'Of all the things I've ever lost, I miss my mind the most.'
Oscar Wilde

Having barely survived the Benefits Service, I thought I owed it to myself to have a well-deserved break away. So, with two friends, Wee-man and Jimmy, I arranged to fly out to Amsterdam and meet Dingo and Steady, two other friends who were touring Europe in Dingo's Tango orange VW beetle. I'd spent the last couple of years in Trusham living opposite Dingo but, as we went to rival schools, introductions were left far longer than they should have been. In the time that I had known him, I had got to like him and his stubborn ways and still do. Steady, I thought, always looked like he should have been a seventeenth-century swordsman with his well-groomed goatee beard and blond, curly hair bobbing up and down on his shoulders. I found his wit enormously entertaining and so it was to be fortunate then that our paths would cross again, for a little longer, on the other-side of the world.

We were all relatively seasoned smokers, or so we thought, and looked forward to sampling the Grasshopper coffee shop's infamous menu. We decided to look for accommodation after we had caught up with Dingo and Steady which, in hindsight, wasn't the greatest decision. As we waited for Dingo and Steady to arrive, we ploughed through as much of the menu as we possibly could and as quickly as we could. I was the first to feel unwell and sat staring at the toilet at the far end of the room, knowing

Lady Luck and Me

that I couldn't walk but desperately needing to throw up. Instead of even attempting to make it to the toilet, I sat there, turned my head to the right and used the chair next to me as a toilet, much to the disgust of the person sitting on it. I covered her lap, her feet and part of her handbag before Wee-man and Jimmy man-handled me to the real toilet, begging forgiveness on my behalf. Just as I was readying myself for round two in the toilet, the barman burst in demanding we left immediately, ignoring Jimmy and Wee-man's pleas to allow me to continue and that we'd leave when I was done. As I left the toilet and embarked on the staircase leading up onto the street, my stomach leapt again, spraying more vomit on the walls, multiple stairs and all over the back of the barman's trousers as he led us up the steps. Once at street level, Wee-man and Jimmy left me struggling to lean against the wall as they went back in to reclaim our luggage, apologise profusely and generously tip the barman.

An hour had passed since we had arrived in Amsterdam and I already had two people under my arms supporting me as we entered our second coffee shop, still waiting for Dingo and Steady to arrive. The décor was dark and drab with graffiti scribbled on every square inch of everything. It had two old battered sofas, again covered in graffiti that faced out of a large window directly out onto a canal. The music was angry and did nothing to soften the dirty, oppressive environment. I was plonked down on one of the sofas as Wee-man and Jimmy went to the bar to buy sugary drinks, snacks and two of the biggest, ugliest Amazonian mushrooms I had ever seen. Back in the UK, I had partaken in mushroom consumption but they had been tiny brown ones from Dartmoor which you took a small handful of and washed down with local cider. These

Amsterdamaged

bastards stood six inches tall, were a veiny, greeny blue and absolutely terrifying.

Jimmy looked at me, looked at the mushrooms with a quizzical look and then handed one to me. Still not entirely sure of what was going on, I started nibbling at the mushroom as if it was a Magnum ice cream. As I neared the end of it, 20 minutes later, I sat back on the sofa, eyes half closed with a mouthful of what tasted like soil, thinking that I might regret what I'd just done. At that moment, a woman in her early twenties sat down next to me. That, in itself, wasn't the problem; the problem was that she was dressed head to foot in black leathers, wore white foundation with black lipstick, black eye shadow and neatly cropped black hair. Oh, and introduced herself to me as a paranoid schizophrenic. As the marijuana made me more self-conscious with every passing minute, the effects of the hallucinogenic mushrooms began to kick in at exactly the same time that my new friend told me she was a murderer and a detective, she was a horse and its saddle, she was the frost on the ground and the sun in the sky, she wanted to kill me and then bring me back to life, she wanted to eat me and then give birth to me, she wanted . . . and this went on for hours as I watched the walls breathe, the floor move like the sea and a policeman dance on the canal outside the window.

Jimmy and Wee-man had sensed the danger early and were now sitting at the bar giggling and revelling in my misfortune. Eventually, and just when I thought my head was about to explode, she started to slow, close her eyes and then thankfully, fell asleep. Although being aware that this was my best chance of escape, my head was trying to digest all the information that I had just been given and, combined with the drugs, was physically unable to

Lady Luck and Me

co-ordinate my legs long enough to leave. But I had to, I had to get out. As I staggered from the sofa towards the window, I felt freedom from that terrible place was within grasp. For the first time in my life, I welcomed the sight of the dancing policeman and made a bee-line for him. I would tell him about the potential serial killer asleep on the couch and also have a quiet word that the coffee shop was definitely selling illegal drugs. The 30 yards of canal water between him and I didn't seem to be a problem. I thought the quickest way would be to fly over it rather than walk or run across it, so began eyeing up a suitable launch pad. Just as I was about to gracefully swallow dive to the policeman and safety, Jimmy and Wee-man pulled me back into the room, much to my anger. They didn't believe I had the power of flight or the ability to walk on water so thought I should leave with them via the door rather than the window. Like some unfortunate stag on his do, they carried me out of the bar and, seeing I was not fit for man nor beast, booked us in at a hotel/hostel across the road, swiftly putting me to bed and ignoring the foreign tongues which I was now apparently trying to communicate in.

Two days later I surfaced, missing Dingo's and Steady's visit entirely. My brain actually hurt. Trying to make sense of the last 72 hours did nothing to ease the pain, only add to it. Along with the mental trauma, I also had numerous welts over my body, courtesy of the resident bed bugs. On that front, I wasn't alone. Jimmy had been abused properly by them and had developed a John Wayne walk in an effort to sooth his inner thigh bites. Our flight was due to leave that night but, during my unconscious hours, Jimmy and Wee-man had befriended a Dutch barmaid and they were in the throes of a 'who can bed her first' competition. By the time we were supposed to

Amsterdamaged

leave for the airport, neither had won and, due to both of them being too stubborn and pig-headed to admit defeat, decided to stay until there was a clear victor. Two days later and with me following them around sheepishly still having paranoid schizophrenic flashbacks, Wee-man finally made the break through and we could leave.

For the entire flight home, Wee-man was a pain in the arse as he strutted around like a doubled dicked peacock rubbing his victory in Jimmy's face. His victory swagger was short-lived though as Jimmy would have the last laugh. Three young men returning from Amsterdam is every Customs and Excise officer's dream, so it didn't come as a surprise when we were pulled over and led into an interview room. Our interviewer was a big, middle-aged lady who was utterly resistant to any of Wee-man's banter and, as he tried his best to raise a smile, Jimmy, who was usually so chirpy in such situations, remained strangely quiet. After the standard questions were satisfactorily answered, she turned to our bags. Wee-man continued his ineffectual charm offensive until his bag was zipped open. Full to the brim were the most filthy bestiality-based porn magazines and DVDs known to man.

For the first time, the officer's face changed from 'seen and heard it all before' serenity to 'take him outside and shoot him' outrage. Wee-man, for the first time since leaving 'the Dam', said nothing and stared hopelessly at the contents of his bag. Jimmy turned away giggling. I looked on vacantly, not really aware what was going on. After further inspection of the bag, it seemed that Jimmy had replaced all of Wee-man's belongings with the most offensive porn you can buy outside the black market. Jimmy and I were allowed to leave while Wee-man had to stay to answer more questions. On exiting the room, Jimmy jokingly suggested

Lady Luck and Me

to the Customs officer that maybe a cavity search might be necessary. Fifteen minutes later, a visibly subdued Weeman joined us, unable to look us in the eyes and wanting to get out of the airport as quickly as possible. In the short journey back to Bristol, Jimmy's questioning of what happened in the interview room went unanswered, much to Jimmy's delight. Once the taxi pulled up, we all went our separate ways, trying to digest the last few days and then trying to erase the memories. I haven't been back to Amsterdam since and, whenever I hear the word now, a little bit of wee comes out.

Australia

'I have to choose between this world, the next world and Australia.'
Oscar Wilde

Despite my best efforts, it seemed that the UK wasn't ready for me to find employment or any happiness for that matter, so I did what comes most naturally to me and ran away, thinking anywhere away from the UK would give me a better chance to find that elusive inner peace. As my sister had recently settled in Australia with her boyfriend, Lynden, and as it was an English-speaking country, with sun and pretty much as far away as I could possibly go, it was the obvious choice. Visa acquired, ticket bought and bags packed, I boarded the long-haul flight to Sydney and a year of adventure.

Jet-lagged, dehydrated and seriously over-tired, I was less than happy when customs pulled me to one side to inspect the entire contents of one of my bags but not the other (which bamboozled me a little), apparently looking for alien flora and fauna that might destabilise their carefully balanced ecosystem. The concept is noble and wise and, quite rightfully, they are doing their best to preserve a unique country but the attitude and the suspicion with which people are treated by these eco-warriors is way over the top. War criminals are treated with more respect. The poor person ahead of me had a dandelion seed embedded in the tread of her shoe and I've never seen so many heavily armed policemen swoop on her, handcuff her and lead her away to a private interview room, to no doubt cavity search her for lemon pips or old potato peelings. I, thankfully, was

Lady Luck and Me

only given a stern look and told to be on my way. Head down and feeling unnecessarily guilty like everyone does, I emerged through the sliding glass doors into the arrivals terminal and onto Australian soil, so to speak. Emma was there waiting with a beaming smile, along with her husband-to-be, Lynden.

Emma and I had been close during childhood, sharing schools and holidays together at Grandma and Grandpa's when dickhead took the rest of the family to Spain for a three-week holiday. Out of the three siblings Emma had always been the most ambitious, regularly driving herself into the ground in her efforts to succeed. Once she had graduated from Cardiff University, she headed off overseas, coming back briefly to spend time in Bristol before she was off again. She never really came back, eventually deciding to lay roots in Australia. No matter how strong relationships are, geography will always ram an almighty wedge in them. Before she had started her adventures we had made a pact that if either of us was in real trouble, contact must be made. Now that she was on the other side of the world, distance and time difference created such a huge obstacle that the pact could no longer be relevant. Don't get me wrong, I love Emma dearly and would still contact her if that doomsday ever comes, but she's not top of the list anymore. Anyway, given the time we had spent apart, I very much looked forward to seeing her, meeting her Yorkshire fiancé and working out what made Ems finally drop anchor thousands of miles away in Australia.

So once a very solemn handshake had taken place, Lynden shot ahead with my rucksack, leaving Emma and I to reconnect. It was whilst I was making my way through the terminal to the car park that I became more and more aware of the colourful characters I was passing and the attention I was receiving. At first, I thought the natural English charm had been spotted in my gait but the more notice I took, the more I realised the attention I was receiving was exclusively from men. The conversation between Emma and I began to falter as I became more and more self-conscious until, unable to take any more of the unwanted attention, I asked Emma whether I was dressed appropriately and why all the male interest. She informed me that the Sydney Mardi Gras had just finished and the most likely reason for why men were staring at me was the unmissable rainbow luggage strap I was proudly displaying. Everything then fell into place. The immigration officials hadn't touched my rainbow bag, probably in fear of catching some disease from the multitude of sex toys I had in there. Lynden, the proud, straight, Yorkshireman had bolted ahead so he wouldn't be seen to be my gay lover and the passing airport gays probably saw me as one of their own, fresh off the plane and maybe looking for some action. I got to the car and removed the strap, hiding it under the spare wheel in the hopes that one day Lynden suffered a puncture on Oxford Street and the strap would act as a gay AA card. To my knowledge that never happened, but the thought and gesture was there. You are welcome, Lynden.

They very kindly let me stay with them and their flatmate, John, in their flat in Bondi Junction until I found my feet. It was a two-bedroom, open-plan flat so I had to make a rudimentary camp much like you do when you're six years old, in one corner of the lounge. Sheets hung on washing lines that stretched the width and length the room in an attempt to give me a little privacy which I was grateful for but, in reality, they served only as an eyesore and gave the impression that I was protesting against

Lady Luck and Me

conventional sleeping arrangements. Honestly speaking, I did nothing around the house. Emma and Lynden would work, come home, take it in turns to cook for all of us, wash up and barely make it to nine o'clock before retiring to bed exhausted. My daily routine for the first couple of months was very different. I would wake around ten in the morning, feeling aggrieved at being woken too early by the rising temperature, fix myself some breakfast and dump myself in front of the television, regularly checking the fashion channel in the hope the gazelle-like women were modelling transparent lingerie. I remember feeling robbed if I had to leave the couch and walk the ten yards to relieve myself. Even though one of the most famous beaches in the world was within spitting distance, it was still far enough away and involved leaving the flat which I had absolutely no intention of doing. Besides, it wasn't going anywhere and I had plenty of time to get sand in my nether regions.

By the time Emma and Lynden returned home from work, the local papers were strewn across the living room table and I was reclining once again in front of the television in an effort to appear that I was exhausted from a solid day's job hunting. Eventually, I got bored of being shouted at by aggressive car salesmen on television and made away across town to take evening classes in Wing Chun kung fu. I knew that Wee-man had an interest in it and had always promoted its many health benefits. Not only did the instructors teach the class Wing Chun moves but also other dirty street fighting moves, much to the class's delight. I did enjoy it and persevered with it until the class were asked to wear the club's flak jackets for photos of the instructors coming up to a student with a knife. I quietly slipped out of the door as instructions for the disclaimer forms were being handed out. As bad photo shoots go that one had the potential to be one of the very worst. Two ambulances passed me on my way to the underground, sirens screaming as they headed to where I had just come from. I shivered, quickened my pace and didn't look back.

Being out of money and back in front of the TV again prompted me to get a much-needed job. I was a bum. My laziness and self-pitying had to change and change it did by finding a job. Actually, strictly speaking, I just took up an opportunity which had been offered weeks ago by one of Emma's friends to work for his removal company based in North Sydney. It couldn't have been made easier for me. I was to be picked up from outside the flat, driven to the job, driven back to the flat again and then get paid cash in hand at the end of the week. Logistically, the job was simple; physically, it was a different story. Long days, sometimes 12–14 hours, under the Australian sun, without breaks and nearly always undermanned, meant bed was looking attractive from about an hour after starting.

We were made up of a motley international crew that constantly changed, never having the same personnel from one day to the next; either the long hours broke people or the sheer physicality of the job. For the couple of months that I stuck it out, there was only one other person who stayed the distance and he was a four-foot tall Ukrainian ex-body builder who signed his name with a cross and often viewed road kill as a free meal. He was the kind of bloke who wouldn't think twice about trying to single-handedly carry a grand piano to a fifth-storey flat and would burst blood vessels screaming at people if they dared stop to take a drink. By the end of our time working together, we had built a mutual respect for each other; his for me was simply time served where so many others hadn't and mine for him was a combination of fear of him ripping

Lady Luck and Me

me to pieces and his determination to get the job done as quickly as possible. Conversation between us was limited as he spoke in one syllable words or incoherent grunts but it was enough communication for us to get through the day unscathed.

By the end of the shift, I returned to the flat knackered, usually just in time to wish Emma and Lynden a good night and thank them for the meal which they put aside for me. John the flatmate went to bed later which gave us the opportunity to sit out on the balcony and smoke. He didn't smoke cigarettes but was more than happy to smoke tobacco in spliffs and that suited me just fine. If you didn't have a regular dealer, Kings Cross was the place you bought 20-dollar bags of weed off dubious characters who hung around dimly lit corners or outside the numerous sex shops. As you passed them by they would quietly whisper in your ear which drug they were peddling, assuring you it was the finest, highest quality in Sydney (if you've ever been to Amsterdam or Brixton you'll know exactly what I mean).

The decision of which dealer to approach was usually made based on appearance, with the fuller faced, more rotund variety being favoured over the skinny gaunt kind on the assumption that healthier looking ones might not be looking for their next heroine hit quite as quickly and might give you a better deal (this unfortunately is still a theory as I didn't sample enough to present this as fact, although one day I intend to return and conclude my studies). Once the 20 dollars were handed over, they would wander away and pluck the small bags from random places such as tree trunks or cracks in building walls in an effort not to be caught dealing and, therefore, avoid arrest and possible incarceration. Trips to Kings Cross were a last

Australia

resort and were always resisted as, every time I drove away, I had the inescapable feeling that I had just been bent over a barrel and shafted.

Back at the flat, John had fully embraced the New South Wales policy of two marijuana plants per household and had grown both plants from seedlings. By the time I had arrived, they were standing about two-feet tall, lanky, very green and far too young to do anything with but such was our appetite/desperation to smoke I'd take nail scissors, cut off bits here and there and microwave them in a feeble attempt to dry it out so it would smoke. The microwave actually made the weed worse and wet, and within a week of my arrival John was the not-so-proud owner of two, three-inch, dead stalks.

Just as my body had become accustomed to the rigours of removals, Lady Luck played her hand again. It was another day, another house to move and another driver who I'd never met. The loading part of the job had been done without a hitch and I was getting on well with the long-haired, slightly peculiar, 40-year-old, skinny Australian when he decided to take a detour via his bedsit on the way to our unloading destination. On entering his bedsit, it was clear and a little unsettling to see that he had, to put it mildly, a passion for Second World War model soldiers. There were hundreds of them everywhere. On top of the wardrobe, there were half a dozen two inch German snipers lying down taking aim at an American patrol which were on their way from his sock drawer to his pants drawer and two more American paratroopers hanging from the stained lampshade over his bed. As I sat nervously on the edge of his bed wondering what the hell I was doing there and what the hell was about to happen, he rummaged around under his dirty laundry and produced an enormous

Lady Luck and Me

bong. Before I knew it, he'd loaded the bong (or bowl, as the Aussies call it) and thrust it under my nose, offering me a lighter in his other hand. Not being one to turn away such opportunities, I dutifully lit the bong and took a huge hit. As I passed it back, it began to kick in and I became even more aware of the model soldiers that surrounded me, making me feel like I'd stumbled into a weird *Gulliver's Travels* version of 'Saving Private Ryan'. As panic set in, I excused myself in order to get some fresh air before I lost my mind.

Soon after, he wandered out and asked for a hand getting his broken fridge into the van. Not really knowing what was going on, I obliged and found myself at one end of the oldest, biggest industrial fridges I'd ever seen, let alone carried. By this point I was in auto pilot, sweating profusely and trying to negotiate the ramp that led up into the van. Just when I thought I had made it, I tripped on the end of the ramp and fell. Absurdly thinking that I couldn't drop the fridge, I cushioned its fall with my fingers. As I lay there, battered, with fuzzy vision, I watched as a pool of blood started escaping from beneath the fridge. Due to my drug-addled state of mind no pain was registered, so I calmly watched as the floor of the van began to change colour. My colleague dropped his end and rushed around to me swearing and panicking. At the sight of my blood, he fainted and landed on the fridge on my fingers and then rolled off, leaving me trapped under the fridge looking at an unconscious person and an ever-growing puddle of blood.

Thankfully, he came round after a few minutes, at about the same time that my nervous system registered that I had hurt myself. Doing his best not to look at the blood, he managed to lift the fridge enough for me to withdraw my hand and see what damage had been done. Initially it was difficult to tell exactly what had been injured and to what extent but, after plunging my hand into a bucket of water that he had kindly fetched, it seemed that the ring finger on my right hand had taken the full brunt of the fridge and was now severed through to the bone with layers of fat, muscle and nerve endings all clearly visible. And, for the second time in 10 minutes, he went down like a sack of spuds leaving me staring at my hand and at him, trying to work out which I should treat first. A sharp slap to the face sorted him out and first aid bandages in the van sufficed to stem the flow of blood.

Unable to do the unloading and with a huge rogue fridge covered in blood, we returned to the boss's house to explain why we weren't able to finish the job. I sat in the passenger's seat, nursing my limp finger and peering through heavily blood-shot eyes whilst he told the boss of my accident. Initially he was concerned for me but, after looking into my red eyes and hearing my slurred sporadic speech, his concern was replaced by polite annoyance. He told my Aussie friend to take me home and told me to get my finger looked at then find another job. Still heavily under the influence of the pot and, by then, the searing pain radiating from my finger, I didn't put up any argument but just sat, nodded my head and gazed forlornly out of the window. I guess the moral of this story is never lift incredibly heavy objects with razor-sharp edges directly after taking a monster hit from one of the largest bongs known to man, off a stranger who's obsessed with military toys and can't handle the sight of blood.

I didn't see anyone about my finger and did my best to dress it myself, letting the body heal in its own time. My recuperation was spent where my journey had begun, on the couch, in front of the television, frequently

Lady Luck and Me

flicking back to the fashion channel. Three or four weeks later I was ready to return to work and set about finding it wherever possible. The local papers offered very little so I signed up with agencies to help with the search. Ironically, the only job they could offer with an immediate start was working for a Chinese removal company. Reluctantly I agreed and was soon working with a father and son that spoke no English. Not only was I their dog's body but also their translator, contract negotiator and navigator. The pay, however, didn't reflect the extra services I was providing, and although at times it was hilarious, it wasn't worth the money. Arguments in two different languages about how we were going to carry a four-poster, wrought-iron, double bed up three flights of narrow spiral staircase must have seemed like a Monty Python sketch to onlookers. I decided to hang up my removal overalls for good and, although I've been involved in many house moves since, I haven't worn overalls in a professional capacity since.

Coinciding with my removal retirement was the arrival of one of my dearest friends, Wee-Man. I hadn't been abroad with him since the fateful Amsterdam trip and hoped our upcoming Australian exploits would be a little more memorable and a little less mind-bending. Small in stature, but enormous in personality, he was a trained lawyer, good-looking, confident and with a velvet tongue. He had turned his back on his law training and had begun pursuing a more spiritual path, finding out about himself, the world around him and how he fitted into it. The timing of his arrival was perfect for me. I had saved enough to take a few weeks off and was itching to get out of Sydney. Also, Emma, Lynden and John were starting to tire of my makeshift bedroom in their lounge, my hours lounging in front of the television and generally being a lazy bastard around the flat for far longer than anyone had expected me to.

The decision was made to take a road-trip up the east coast to stay in Wee-Man's friend's summer house on a beach just outside a little town called Rollingstone in Queensland. After investigating the extortionate prices of rental cars we decided that I should approach John and ask about the possibility of borrowing his pride and joy, a 1974 yellow Ford Falcon that comfortably slept at least two and was built specifically for a journey like ours. John had restored this mechanical beast to all its former glory and was seen most Sunday mornings lovingly waxing it before strapping his surfboard to the roof and cruising along the sea front, stereo turned up, to his favoured surfing spot. Not surprisingly, John viewed my request with a certain amount of trepidation since it had only taken me a couple of weeks to decimate his two 'green children' on the balcony. But, being the generous, kind-hearted soul that he was, he eventually and foolishly agreed.

Lady Luck and Me

The weird, the wonderful; the Australian East Coast

'The Australian Book of Etiquette is a very slim volume.'
Paul Theroux

The day of our road-trip departure dawned and, like giddy schoolchildren on the final day of term, we said our goodbyes to Emma and Lynden, got one final car maintenance lesson/warning from John and headed off. Before we left Sydney, we picked up one of Wee-Man's friends from England, Jimbo, who had flown in a couple of days prior to join us on our epic adventure. After stopping to fill the tank and buy suitable driving music, we were on the open road, windows down, sunglasses on and Willie Nelson blaring out of the stereo. We took turns to drive and the first few hours went without a hitch.

As night began to fall on the first day, thoughts turned to accommodation and, after consulting the map, decided that Coffs Harbour would be our best bet. Unfortunately, as soon as the decision had been made, we felt the awkward wobble of a puncture. Pulling over in the middle of nowhere, we discovered that despite John's diligent maintenance, he hadn't included a tyre wrench in the spare tyre kit, leaving us stranded with no form of communication, with 12 slices of processed cheese, half a can of Lilt and the prospect of being murdered, raped or both by some Australian hillbilly. We had all seen Wolf Creek. With the three of us lying in the back, the word cosy would be an understatement. It would have been a

Lady Luck and Me

bittersweet moment if anyone had stopped to see whether we were all right. On one hand we would have probably been able to change tyres but on the other, our potential saviour most certainly would have got the wrong idea. As it happened, no-one passed during the night and none of us got much sleep.

At the break of day we were horrified to see a massive neon sign that read '24 hour service station. Repairs. Spare parts', not 300 yards further down the road from where we had spent the night. How none of us had seen the sign the night before remains a mystery but, half an hour later, we were back on the open road, puncture repaired and the newly acquired tyre wrench safely stowed away.

The point of the road trip was to get out of Sydney and spend some days on a private beach in a comfortable summer house, so sightseeing was done very much from the car windows. The reasons for stopping were fuel, food and toilets, although it turned out that Jimbo didn't think the third reason was a good enough one to stop, much to my dismay as I uncapped a bottle of warm Mountain Dew and took a swig.

It was on the second day that we came a little unstuck with the law. We had made good time in the morning and our expected time of arrival at Byron Bay had been reduced by a couple of hours simply by Wee-man driving ridiculously quickly. All three of us were oblivious to the speed he was doing as we were too preoccupied with hitting Lionel Ritchie's higher notes on his 'Back to Front' album. The policeman behind us though was acutely aware of how fast we were travelling. What made matters worse was that Wee-Man didn't see the flashing lights in the rear-view mirror or hear the siren and was somewhat surprised

The weird, the wonderful; the Australian East Coast

when he saw the police car alongside him, signalling us to pull over. My experiences with British police have never been good so, after thinking we had done well avoiding getting raped on the side of the road the night before, dodging the same bullet in prison would be considerably more difficult. As Wee-Man wound down the window to talk to the policeman, clouds of marijuana smoke escaped, seemingly sealing our fate behind bars and playing paper, scissors, rock to see who would pick up the soap in the showers.

Amazingly, the policeman was remarkably laid back about the whole situation. He spoke to us like adults, swearing repeatedly and casually wiping the sweat from his brow with his sleeve. Since Jimbo was the only one with a driver's licence on his person, he was asked to take over the driving duties from Wee-Man. The problem with that was that Jimbo was so stoned he was white as a sheet and started throwing up as soon as he tried to get up from the back seat. The policeman shook his head, exasperated, and told Wee-Man to carry on driving warning him to watch his speed and advising him that if he was stopped for any further offences, it was likely to cause him future Visa problems. As Wee-Man buckled back up, started the engine and peered through the gap between the steering wheel and the dashboard, the policeman wished us a safe journey and returned to his vehicle. None of us spoke, mainly in disbelief at his leniency but also because we were shit scared of how badly wrong it could all have gone. For the policeman, it was probably just another day and I doubt whether we were the first or the last battered tourists he stopped on that stretch of road for exactly the same offence. Soon enough though, Lionel was wooing us again

Lady Luck and Me

with his dulcet tones, Wee-Man was speeding again and the whole episode forgotten.

Our next overnight stop was to be the hippy town of Byron Bay, made famous for its spiritual vibe and laid back attitude. We arrived just after dark and were greeted by bar after bar, all promising 'magic space shakes' in 'Byron's most chilled bar'. Teenagers dancing on tables absolutely wasted did not strike me as a chilled bar, but that was the disappointing reality. Every bar we passed offering sanctuary from the hectic modern world was crammed full of youths dancing to the loudest electronica music you could imagine. Now and then we saw old men and women who were still trying to live the free-loving sixties lifestyle with their CND T-shirts, long hair, sandals and John Lennon pink glasses, preaching that aliens had landed and the end of the world was nigh, whilst popping another acid tab into their mouths. It was an eclectic mix of the young trying to lose their minds in any way possible and the old who had long lost theirs and were now trying to find it again.

We continued on past the bars until we found a quiet place to leave the car and wandered into town in search of the real soul of Byron Bay. An hour later, we still hadn't found a genuinely relaxing place to hang out so we gave in and settled for the quietest bar we could find. It was more of an open-air beer tent full of plastic tables and chairs that served schooners in plastic cups. The revellers seemed to be middle-aged Australians of both sexes, sporting ill-fitting T-shirts over bulging bellies and tiny shorts that their arses were chewing rather than wearing. We sat down, ordered our beers and did our best not to draw any attention to ourselves, despite being a good 20 years younger than anyone else there. During the second beer a lady in her

The weird, the wonderful; the Australian East Coast

forties approached our table and asked whether she could join us. Wee-Man, sensing some entertainment, pulled out the chair next to him and offered her a drink. By the time we were finishing our second, she was half way through her third and holding it together admirably well. She was wearing a long black backless dress, high heels and, out of everyone in the tent, was comfortably the most attractive. A couple of minutes later, a small boy, about five or six years old, came to the table and tugged on the woman's arm, 'Mummy, can we go home now?'

'No, Mitchell, go and play with the dog,' she replied violently moving her arm away from his tiny hand. Behind us in the road, a large mangy dog was rifling through bins, clearly a stray, and most probably disease-ridden. At that, Mitchell wandered off, weaving his way through the tables and out of sight. After a brief, awkward pause, the conversation started up again. Wee-Man and his silk tongue were working overtime, impressing her with his Queen's English and risqué innuendos whilst Jimbo and I buried our heads in our beers as Wee-Man's conversation went from flirting to outright filth. Feeling thoroughly embarrassed, I did my best to bring the conversation back to some sort of civility by enquiring about the tattoo on the base of her back. Being in Byron Bay and still hoping for some spiritual evidence, I thought my question was well founded, 'That's an interesting tattoo on your back, is that the eye of Ra?' She lowered her gaze, looked at Wee-Man and in her strong Queensland accent replied, 'No. That's so I can see who's fucking me in the arse.' I dropped my beer; Jimbo choked and spat his mouthful of beer over the table while Wee-Man just grinned.

At that, she got up from the table, took Wee-Man by the hand and led him away to the toilets. Gobsmacked,

Lady Luck and Me

Jimbo and I looked at each other in disbelief and ordered another beer. Five minutes later, our table was approached again by Mitchell who asked the whereabouts of his Mum. Jimbo, without thinking told him that she had gone to the toilet and so off he went, to the toilets. I gave Jimbo a rollicking for not thinking it through and very probably sending the poor boy off to get scarred for life when he found his mum in a compromising position with a total stranger, in the toilets. A couple of minutes later, Wee-Man, red faced and perspiring, the woman and Mitchell all returned to the table. Wee-Man sat whilst the woman grabbed the boy's hand roughly and said, 'Come on then Mitchell, let's go, I've got to get up early for a *Readers Wives* photo shoot. Ok . . . well . . . nice to meet you then boys.' At that she left, pulling Mitchell behind her and whistling to the mangy dog which duly followed. Wee-Man looked visibly shaken by the whole experience and immediately finished his beer in one and ordered another. The rest of the night was a bit of a blur, but I do remember insisting that Wee-Man wore his trousers to sleep in, just in case he had picked up some highly contagious venereal disease.

The following morning we were woken by the police and asked to move on, thankfully no names were taken. Driving out of Byron Bay, we passed numerous people still struggling from the night before and continued north, through Brisbane and on to Mackay. After sleeping again in the car, we were dying to get to the summer house so that we could enjoy a proper bed and a break from each other's body odours. Three days in a car without a shower begins to test even the most hardened of noses.

Finally, we arrived at Rollingstone and turned off down a dirt track to where the summer house and its private beach were located. As we emerged from the bush

The weird, the wonderful; the Australian East Coast

into a clearing, we saw a small ramshackle house on our right and a much larger, wooden house with an enormous veranda on our left, with the sea directly ahead of us. Not being entirely sure we had found the right place, we warily left the car, calling out in the hope that if we were in the wrong place, we wouldn't be mistaken for common thieves and shot by a house proud hillbilly. Climbing the stairs to the front door of the larger house, we were startled by a loud 'G'day' from behind us. Swivelling round expecting to be looking down the barrel of a shotgun, we were unpleasantly surprised to see a bald, fat, sixty-year-old man walking towards us, naked as the day he was born.

'Hello, fellas, I've been expecting you. I'm Neville, or Nev if you like.' We shook hands and introduced ourselves, still expecting an explanation of his nakedness to come at any time. It didn't. Turns out that Nev was the caretaker who lived alone in the house on the left and, judging by his beaming grin and enthusiastic handshake, he hadn't seen anyone in a while. He passed us on the stairs and began an unstoppable running commentary on the house, surrounding area, wildlife and his life story, but still no explanation as to why he was starkers. He was, I suppose, an aging Stig of the Dump, who could, so he claimed, read auras. Maybe the years of solitude had got to him but it was evident from his ramblings that he was lonely, eccentric, slightly unbalanced but a really nice chap. The house consisted of three bedrooms, an open-plan lounge/dining room and an amazing library, full of weird and wonderful books ranging from spiritual philosophy to teach-yourself-Russian. It was in this library that I found a dusty old book on ancient traditional Chinese medicine which immediately struck a chord with me and, little did I

Lady Luck and Me

know at the time, would have a profound influence on me and my life.

The days at the summer house were spent reading on the beach whilst smoking Nev's home-grown weed. Nev pottered around, tidying as he went, still naked, more to make the point that he was working so that when we returned to Sydney we could give the owners a glowing report on Nev's unwavering work ethic. In the evenings, we would sit on the veranda drinking beer, smoking more weed and letting Nev read our auras. I apparently had a very purple aura and, according to Nev, was destined for great things. Sometimes, Nev would whisper his stories, why, I have no idea since the nearest person apart from us was at least two kilometres away, but it meant we had to lean in close to hear and, on more than one occasion, resulted in a brief but definite encounter with his freely swinging, wrinkly cock. In such an event, excuses to leave the group were made and the unfortunate person hurried in to wash the touched-upon part, always thankfully without Nev's knowledge.

He had some tales though, most of them I fear were bogus such as the time he swam from Australia to New Zealand because he couldn't afford the flight or the time he turned down Marilyn Monroe's sexual advances because he didn't like the shade of her lipstick. All in all, the week spent at the summer house with Nev was a delight and certainly worth the journey. I don't know why, but we never did find out why Nev was always naked; the most logical explanation was simply that there was no need to wear clothes. It seemed that the surrounding vegetation and wildlife was trying to somehow reclaim him, embracing

The weird, the wonderful; the Australian East Coast

him to be one of theirs, at one with his environment. Chances are, Nev died there, alone and still naked.

We decided to take the same route home, but stopping at places we hadn't stopped at on the journey up. The first night back on the road was to be spent in Rockhampton, about halfway between Rollingstone and Brisbane, and had nothing, as far as we were concerned, of any interest. A lay-by sufficed for our overnight stay and we were back on the highway, shortly after the sun had risen, to our next destination, the town of Bundaberg, famous for its magnificent rum. An hour or so away from Bundaberg, the car started to make peculiar noises. Turning up the power ballads CD we hoped to drown out the strange rumblings and pretend everything was fine but, alas, the noises got louder and louder and the car eventually ground to a halt three or four kilometres short of Bundaberg, spewing steam from under the bonnet. None of us knew the first thing about engines but that didn't stop us prodding around in the hope it would miraculously stop steaming and start up again. Ten minutes and three nasty burns later, we admitted defeat and stood at the side of the road waiting to be rescued. As Lady Luck would have it, we didn't have to wait long and, what's more, our saviour had a pick-up truck with a tow rope. He also had a speculative poke around under the bonnet and, like us, was burnt for his troubles, before giving and offering to tow us the short distance to Bundaberg.

Thanking and waving him goodbye, we went into the garage that he had dropped us off at and went to speak to the mechanic. From the outset, the mechanic's body language didn't look good. As he re-appeared from under the car, he looked at us and solemnly shook his head. He then reeled off a list of words that only a Formula One

Lady Luck and Me

team would understand, finishing with 'it's fucked', which we all understood. By his estimation, it would take a couple of days to fix and would cost anything from 3000 to 4000 dollars, depending on the extent of the damage, which he would only know after working on it for a few hours. Between us, we could probably have raised about half of it but that would have left us penniless for food and accommodation, so repairing it looked completely out of the question. He then added insult to injury by telling us that we would have to pay 500 dollars to have it scrapped. The three of us stood there looking at each other, hoping that one of us would come up with a genius plan to salvage the dire situation. Nothing came and, as we stood there in silence, the mechanic piped up, 'Tell you what fellas, look, the engine's fucked, you aren't going anywhere in it, but I'll tell you what I'll do, as you look like nice fellas, I might be able to use some of it for spares, so how about I give you each a four pack of Bundy and coke and enough for a train to get you back to Sydney. That's the best I can do. I really am doing you fellas a favour.'

The bastard had us over a barrel, and he knew it. Without being able to consult anyone else who knew anything about cars and with no mobile to phone John, we were out of options and took the collective decision to take the bastard up on his offer. As he left to go and get the Bundy and cokes out of the fridge, he had the audacity to repeat his last sentence again, 'I really am doing you fellas a favour'. Wee-Man did his best to make light of the situation, telling us that at least there was no way we could be stopped by the police again. Unsurprisingly, I didn't find it funny in the slightest and tried to explain that it wasn't them who would have to tell John that his baby had been exchanged for some booze and a train ticket. With one final

The weird, the wonderful; the Australian East Coast

look at the car and clutching the four-pack to my chest and a hundred dollars in my hand, I was consumed with guilt and started preparing myself for a stint in hospital as soon as I returned to Sydney.

The Bundy and cokes didn't touch the sides on their way down and did little to ease the growing anguish. The closer to Sydney we got, the quieter the conversation became. It was agreed that all three of us would tell John in the hope that one of us got away to tell the story.

When we arrived at the flat, head down and tail between our legs, Emma and Lynden informed us that John had flown back to the UK for a family emergency. This was received with mixed emotions. I shouldn't have been elated to hear that John was attending a family crisis but it meant it gave us a stay of execution for the time being. My next thought though was the epitome of cowardice and I'm still thoroughly ashamed of thinking it and, worse still, acting on it. Using the excuse that I was conscious that I had overstayed my welcome at their flat, I packed up my belongings and told Emma that I was moving to a hostel in Kings Cross. The real, terrible reason was that I wouldn't have to face John and tell him directly, probably using a phone call or a text to break the news. When Emma quizzed me about telling John of what had become of his beloved car, I insisted I had every intention of telling him face to face, but would first be considerate and let him recover from what I imagined would have been a traumatic UK ordeal. With the help of Jimbo and Wee-Man, I quickly gathered my belongings and left the flat in search of accommodation in Kings Cross, vowing to return when John had settled back in again.

Lady Luck and Me

One job, many professions

'Lead me not into temptation — I can find it myself.'
John Bernal

The hostel that I booked into, The Pink House, comprised a multi-cultural mix of people, some of whom had been there for months. There was a courtyard that captured the sun all day long and was the place where it all happened. Good quality weed was dealt by numerous people and boxes of cheap wine started flowing way too early in the day to be healthy. The combination of drugs, alcohol and a fierce sun took its toll on many, especially the off-the-boat, fresh-faced, over-enthusiastic Brits, who we began running sweep stakes on as soon as they had arrived. It wasn't uncommon that one of us would deliberately sabotage the mark in order to win the sweepstake, much to our opponent's annoyance.

It was in this courtyard, after another bruising session, that I met Phil, a thirty-odd-year-old from Newcastle who had been residing in the Pink House for a couple of months but, more importantly, had been working nights as a handyman/dog's body for the flagship David Jones store (the equivalent of 'House of Fraser'), in the city centre. In his addled state, he swore to me he would get me a job working with him and, as he could barely walk, I took this oath with a mighty barrow load of salt, not at all expecting anything to transpire.

To my amazement, Phil remembered AND got me the job, starting the following Monday night on 20 dollars

Lady Luck and Me

an hour. No questions, no CVs, no interview, just Phil's word had got me the job. I tried to remember what bullshit I had fed him during our six-hour bender, or now, looking back on it, our six-hour interview, and came up with a horrible, nagging feeling I might have told him I had hand-built the sixteenth-century manor house my mum lived in. How and why I said that escapes me but, even more worrying, was that Phil, the handyman, accepted it and probably gave that as my qualification to work in one of the most prestigious shops in Australia.

Monday night came and I was shitting myself. What was expected of me, I had no idea, but if they were hoping for me to rebuild the shop, they would be sorely disappointed when I asked them which end of the hammer you use to cut wood with. Thankfully, I had nothing to worry about, since the job consisted of occasionally pushing clothes rails around in order for contractors to do their work and tidying forgotten, unused rooms on the top floors. We had access all areas and Phil's previous months of working there had given him a unique and intimate knowledge of all the shop floors, camera positions, the locals in the pub opposite and, best of all, the two security guards by the back door. Phil was equipped with a two-way radio so that if any problems arose, or more clothes rails needed to be pushed a few yards, we could be contacted. Apart from that, we were left to our own devices under the instruction to clear away anything that might hinder the shop's ability to make the most amount of money as possible during trading hours. The operational distance of the two-ways had already been tested to the pub opposite and, according to the security guards, had a range of at least a kilometre. From the outset, it was clear Phil was there for the money alone and certainly didn't see this as

One job, many professions

any sort of career move. Within an hour, we were reclining comfortably in the pub opposite with our second beer in hand and the two-way safely tucked deep within Phil's overall's pocket. I was more arseholed after my first day working at David Jones than I've ever been at any wedding.

Sitting in the courtyard during the day and working/pubbing during the night actually became quite punishing. After a couple of weeks suffering with a throbbing liver and hallucinations from sleep deprivation, I decided to do my best to try and get sleep during the day. That was easier said than done. As I was trying to catch some shut eye, my fellow dorm mates were soaking up the sun and cheap wine in the courtyard, occasionally coming up in varying states of inebriation to remind me of what I was missing. By the time I got up to start my night's work, I had to pick my path around and over dozens of motionless bodies. Although everyone had perfectly reasonable beds to sleep in, most ignored them and woke to find themselves on a floor, slumped over the table or tangled in the banisters on the stairs. Every evening it was as if a crazed gunman had wandered into the hostel during the day and had mown down everyone indiscriminately.

After a couple of months of the same routine, Phil and I got bored of being professional drinkers and decided to branch out. Our first mission was to establish exactly how far the two-way radios could operate, as this would determine how far afield we could venture. Sydney's Oxford Street is the city's gay road and, like most other gay roads in the world, is one of the best places for entertainment. Not only are there hundreds of bars, drag-queens and bewildered Japanese tourists, there are also more porn shops than you could shake an erect penis at. As Oxford Street was well within the two-ways expected range, Phil

Lady Luck and Me

and I came up with a plan. We guesstimated there were roughly 20 porn shops along Oxford Street, all with their own individual theme, catering for all sexual preferences from the straight porn shop right through to those who had a penchant for the farmyard animal. As Phil and I weren't the least bit attracted to animals or wearing black rubber suits whilst choking on a snooker ball, we opted to check out the straight porn shops first and then go from there.

For anyone who isn't familiar with a porn shop set-up, let me briefly explain. Usually, there are tight doorways or staircases into the shop in an attempt to shield any poor unwitting person from eye-watering dildos, then there are the hundreds of DVDs, usually showing both sexes of all ages in all positions (their parents would be so proud), then the costumes, toys, and other bizarre contraptions that I have no idea what or where they're for. Then there's the fat hairy bloke with a pony tail and thick glasses behind the desk, watching porn on TV and then past the fat bloke, cubicles or, as they're known in the industry, 'gloryholes'. I had been to my fair share of porn shops over the years, always as a bit of a giggle with the boys, and never as a serious paying customer but I had never come across these 'gloryholes' before. The idea is, you enter the cubicle, put a dollar into the slot and choose what kind of porn you want to jerk off to. In both walls at crotch level, there are holes through to the adjoining cubicle. In the straight porn shops you're more likely to get women sticking their hands, tongue, etc. through to help get you off or in gay porn shops, men. It seemed Phil hadn't experienced these before either and, sensing his excitement, he was keen to try it out.

After a brief discussion in the middle of the shop, it was decided that we would go to as many straight

One job, many professions

'gloryholes' as possible, therefore effectively making us not only professional drinkers but also professional wankers. The first one was a bit of a novelty and, with no help on offer, we emerged from our individual cubicles, flushed, giggling with embarrassment and hurriedly left the shop with adrenaline pulsing through our veins. On we went to the next shop and, like seasoned pros, made a bee-line for the 'gloryholes', ignoring all the porn paraphernalia on the way. Again, no help was forthcoming so we left, spent. The third shop, Phil thought it would be a good idea to buy some poppers and, at the point of 'release', inhale. He assured me it would be the best orgasm I had ever had. I took his word for it and bought some of my own and headed to our respective 'gloryholes'.

All was going well and the poppers certainly made me giddy, albeit heavy on the lungs, and I began to look forward to my 'moment'. Just as I was about to arrive, a hand came through the hole to my right. Knowing that Phil was on my left, it was clearly a stranger's hand and noticing the hairy fingers, signet ring and the aggression at which it was trying to get me, was not a woman's. Having just inhaled a massive amount of poppers thinking I was about to experience nirvana, my vision, balance and co-ordination were fucked. I shot up, stumbled and, with my trousers and pants around my ankles, fell out of the cubicle knocking over a stand of DVDs in the middle of the busy shop. With the poppers still fucking my head up, I thrashed around on the DVDs not knowing where I was or what the hell was going on, still exposed for all and sundry to see. In the end, I had to be helped up by the fat, pony-tailed shop keeper, by which time I was able to focus enough to pull my pants and trousers up and see everyone else in the shop pissing themselves. Head down and buckling up my

Lady Luck and Me

belt, I bolted out of the shop and down the stairs to see Phil sitting on the curb, rocking, chain smoking. It seemed that Phil had experienced the same rogue hand before me and had managed to escape without causing a scene that will live long in the memories of those who saw me flailing around like a fish on the bottom of a boat. We came to the mutual decision that our professional wanking days, brief but fun, were definitely over.

With the poppers in our pocket, we returned to the pub and began drinking heavily in an attempt to erase the porn shop memory. Not long into the session, we were summoned on the radio to see our boss. Our next job was to box up bits of the old wooden David Jones staircase into little plastic boxes which were to be presented to the employees. We found another abandoned room and painstakingly began the dullest job in the world. Not long into it, Phil thought that taking poppers would lighten the job and help the time go more quickly and so, after every five boxes, we would take a huge sniff of the poppers, giggle hysterically and then hope our hearts didn't explode.

It was after one of these huge hits that the door opened and in walked our boss, the Managing Director and five or so very well-dressed people. I hadn't taken my hit but Phil had double-nostrilled his and, with his head going bright red and eyes all over the shop, he pointed at the boss and his guests and began laughing uncontrollably before falling backwards off his chair. Four or five seconds passed with Phil out of sight but still howling with laughter before he went silent, stood up, corrected his chair and then began boxing up again as if nothing had happened, seemingly oblivious to the fact that we had company. The suits stood there staring at Phil and then turned and left the room. Our boss hung back, closed the door and then

One job, many professions

told Phil to see him in his office in an hour. When Phil returned, he had been given an almighty bollocking and told he could see out the rest of the week due to his, up to this point, exemplary service and then he would have to find another job.

This put Phil and his devious mind into overdrive. We completed the boxing up and headed straight for the pub so Phil could tell me of his master plan. It was simple, yet brilliant. Phil hadn't got to know the door security out of politeness or the kindness of his heart but because he knew this day would eventually come. Phil's regular outings to the pub were not just for drink, they were necessary for the security staff to get used to Phil coming and going as he pleased, without them having to stop and search him every time, or even question where or what he was doing. Without further ado and with only three employment days left, Operation Trojan Horse was put into action.

We left the pub and headed straight for the Paul Smith suit level. Carrying on as normal under the security cameras, we hung the suits on a clothes rail and casually wheeled them out the back away from the cameras, just like we had many times before. Behind closed doors, the overalls came off, the Paul Smith suit went on and the overalls back over the top, before wheeling the rail back on to the shop floor. From there, we left via the back door, bantering with security staff, then over the road to the pub toilets to undress, hiding the suits in an open store cupboard before sitting down to have a drink and a much-needed cigarette. On the first day, Phil managed the two most expensive Paul Smiths suits and I, after wrestling with my conscience, escaped with the most beautiful woollen Paul Smith cardigan which, months later, Lady Luck (in the guise of a washing machine) reduced it to something

Lady Luck and Me

more befitting of an upmarket Mothercare garment. Phil's rampage continued over the next couple of days whereas I, still intending to keep my job and myself criminal record-free, resisted the temptation to revamp my entire wardrobe.

With Phil gone and no questions asked about the missing stock, I was promoted to head up our new little team. The thieving and poppers stopped only to be replaced with extended pub outings and indoor cricket matches in the forgotten rooms. Soon though, the refurbishment at David Jones was complete and I was forced to look for a new job, getting a piece of the boxed wooden staircase as a thanks and a memento for my services, which still raises a smile every time I come across it. My finishing at David Jones also coincided with me moving out of the Pink House and into a flat with two friends just off Bondi Beach. The flat itself was a hole and was used as a party house, with the tradition of cheap wine and marijuana smoking continuing. My job hunt led me to a café on the beach front which had an advert in the window looking for a kitchen porter and, as I had experience working as a KP at the golf club, the Iranian owner took me on. I was straightaway thrust into working with a young, utterly mental, Russian chef who handled a butcher's knife like it was a stick of celery, not caring where it landed and what it cut. In a kitchen roughly the same size as a portaloo, it was terrifying. After six straight hours washing, preparing veg and staying as far away from the Russian maniac as I possibly could, I asked the Iranian about my pay, to which he answered, 'One dollar an hour until I think you're worth more'. Fearful of the Russian with his knife and the Iranian owner's moustache, I nodded, dropped my potato and peeler and excused myself, never to return again. Walking home fuming, I wandered how many previous fools had

One job, many professions

fallen for the same stunt. I bet if I go back now the same ad will still be in the same window. Bastard.

As the money dwindled and the job situation became more desperate, the decision was made to leave Australia. Bidding my farewells to my Pink House friends and flatmates, it was time to head over to Bondi Junction and say goodbye to my sister, Lynden and, with a beating heart, John. I remember getting off the bus outside their flat, standing behind a bush gulping in big breaths, thumbing my chest and slapping my face in preparation for the beating that was surely coming my way. As it happened, I left with my face intact and no broken bones as John unfortunately had to once again return to the UK. Before I die, I'm determined to find John and at least buy him a six pack of Bundy and coke as my thumb hovers over the speed dial button for the emergency services.

Lady Luck and Me

The elusive spirit

'Massage is the study of anatomy in braille.'
Jack Meagher

As I mentioned earlier, the time I had spent with naked Nev and in the summer house's library had left two very different lasting impressions on me. Back in sleepy Devon, I began my research into the vast and complex world of alternative therapies and complementary health and soon became excited at the prospect that maybe, just maybe, I had found my calling.

Ideally, I wanted to learn something that had the potential to take me anywhere in the world without needing expensive equipment. A keyword search on the internet yielded some interesting results such as tea leaf clairvoyance and buttock manipulation specialist, which both fitted what I was after, although I thought I needed something which was a little more scientifically based and less likely to get me committed. Having dismissed hundreds of weird, wonderful and some downright outrageous therapies, I stumbled across shiatsu. If you don't know what shiatsu is then, simply put, and according to the ever reliable Wikipedia, 'shiatsu is Japanese for "finger pressure"; it is a type of alternative medicine consisting of finger and palm pressure, stretches and other massage techniques. There is no scientific evidence for any medical efficacy of shiatsu, but some shiatsu practitioners promote it as a way to help people relax and cope with issues such as stress, muscle pain, nausea, anxiety and depression . . . shiatsu is usually performed on a futon mat, with clients fully clothed. It is also performed on horses.'(I would just like to add that

Lady Luck and Me

shiatsu can be given to horses rather than, as suggested, the practitioner giving shiatsu whilst seated upon a horse.)

This treatment seemed perfect and, on further investigation, I was convinced my stars were aligning since there just happened to be a local shiatsu school hosting an open day the very following day in Totnes, a town no more than 20 minutes away. So, with another spring in my step and hopeful belief, I went along to the open day.

On entering the venue, it seemed that either word of the open day hadn't got around or there genuinely wasn't much of an interest to learn this ancient therapy. In the room there must have been 10 students with their mats laid down on the floor, milling around, waiting for people like me to come through the doors. On seeing how animated they suddenly became, it had clearly been a very slow day. They were offering a 20 minute taster session for a donation and would be happy to answer any questions relating to the course and the therapy. When I agreed to have a treatment, they all lined up as if I were a high-ranking military officer about to inspect squadies. I was asked by who appeared to be the main man to pick one and, as I walked up and down the line, I could feel their eyes pleading with me to pick them. In the end, I went for a middle-aged woman, hoping her years of maturity combined with a womanly touch would hopefully produce a better introductory massage.

As soon as I had made my decision, the rest of the students dispersed outside, leaving me, my therapist and the enigmatic main man in the room. As requested, I laid face down on the mat, and readied myself for my first shiatsu session. Initially, it was very soothing just to lie there and be worked on by trained healing hands and soon I was drifting off into a relaxing meditative state. My relaxation, however,

The elusive spirit

was short-lived as she proceeded to dig her thumbs harder and harder into my spine, forcing me to tap the mat in much the same way a wrestler does just before he passes out. What with it being my first-ever treatment, I thought this technique and the pain I was experiencing was all part of it, so allowed her to continue, hoping she would soon ease off. She didn't and, as her thumb pressure increased, so did the speed at which I slapped the mat until, unable to stifle it any longer, I let out a yelp of pain. The main man who had been peering out of the window, swung round and hurriedly made his way across the room to us. 'Oh no, Mary . . . Not again!' and then started grappling with her to try and separate her from me. Once he had rolled Mary off me and onto the mat next to us, I shuffled along the mat and sat against the wall, in pain, in shock and in an effort to protect my aching spine from any more damage that might be inflicted by Mary's vicious thumbs. The main man helped the visibly shaken Mary to her feet, and then gently ushered her to the door, kindly asking her to drink a glass of water and a take a deep breath of fresh air.

Closing the door behind him, the main man now introduced himself as the head of the school and began profusely apologising for Mary's behaviour. He informed me that Mary had just been released from a domestic violence programme and her counsellor had thought it would be a good idea for her to try and immerse herself in the spiritual world by studying a massage course. According to Mr Wispy hair, Mary occasionally relapsed and thought her male patients were her ex-husband and subconsciously went about inflicting what pain she could until she was physically wrestled off. He tried to lighten the situation by telling me I was lucky that I was lying on my back. Apparently, the last poor unfortunate fellow

Lady Luck and Me

that Mary had relapsed with needed assistance leaving the room after Mary had lost her mind and touch on his groin region. Sensing my lack of amusement, he sincerely assured me that Mary would no longer be taking any part in the course, and that this one incident should not be taken as a reflection of the school or its students.

Awkward pleadings over, he instructed me not to encourage Mary by giving her a donation (like I was going to) and offered me an extended session with him as a way of an apology. Despite having been there for 30 minutes, I still had no understanding of what shiatsu was, how it was done or what it felt like. Determined not to be hasty and write this career off prematurely, I agreed to his offer and nervously reassumed my prone position on the mat, alert and ever watchful to any movement around my still tender spine. I was glad I stayed. Once again, I drifted off into a semi-conscious state as he silently moved around working my body. I was brought rudely back into the room by Mary poking her head around the door and asking whether she could finish the massage that she had started, now that she was feeling better. Mr Wispy hair sighed, hung his head and again escorted her back out the door, quietly enquiring as to the whereabouts of her medication and the last time she had taken it. As the door closed behind them, I was left sitting on the mat, trying to focus on the benefits of the second massage and forget the pain from the first.

It had been a bizarre hour and, in it, I had found a health practice that I was sure I wanted to pursue. I also had the realisation that not all middle-aged women were harmless, loving beings of tender wisdom. I left the room feeling considerably lighter on my feet and yet still slightly paranoid that Mary would leap from somewhere and attempt one final assault. Thankfully, I made it to the car

The elusive spirit

unscathed and, as I left, saw Mary sitting on the car park wall tucking into a small bottle of vodka. On each exhale of her cigarette, she abused passers-by, verbally and, if they got too close, physically. As I drove past, I smiled at her, hoping a familiar face and a smile would go some way in pacifying her mood. When she ran down the road, vodka bottle in hand, cigarette dangling from her lips, trying to rip off my rear window wiper, much like the chimps do at Longleat, I realised she required a lot more than a stranger's smile.

The school was set in a tranquil valley, deep in the Devonshire countryside and was the perfect location to learn shiatsu. My fellow students ranged greatly in age and profession, all seemingly jaded with the rigours of the rat race. From the off, it was a lot more theoretical than I thought it would be and, with no solid scientific evidence to back up the theory, I preferred to learn by way of sensation and intuition. We were expected to carry out 100 treatments in the first year, practising what we had learnt in the weekend classes, making detailed notes and recommendations to each individual on how to improve their health and well-being.

As the first year progressed, spiritual competition between students went from the sublime to the ridiculous. One pupil announced he had turned vegan that week due to him feeling the anguish of the animals on death row, while another piped up that he had also become vegan and would only eat food given to him by the forest, as he had become one with all living things. It got to a point where the teacher had to interject and prevent one member of the class coming to the practical classes naked as he felt that clothes stifled his spiritual, healing energy. The crazy thing about all this was that as soon as the day was over they

Lady Luck and Me

climbed into their V8 four wheel drives, put the air-con on high and drove two hours home.

The first year drew to an end and, after revising for the un-necessarily difficult exam on all things theoretical including how star signs influence our dietary requirements, we retired for the end-of-year break. Halfway through the holidays, the school phoned looking for the next years tuition fees upfront and, after explaining that I hadn't had the results for the first year and therefore didn't know whether I had been accepted into the second year, the school's secretary told me to pay the money and, if for any reason I wasn't accepted onto the second year, the money would be refunded. I began to think and worry the school was more interested in money than teaching, but carried out her wishes and duly paid the second year's tuition fees.

Thankfully though, I passed the first year, just, and embarked on the second year with considerably more cynicism. The second year carried on in much the same vein as the first with students continually trying to out-do each other with tales of enlightenment all the while driving home in the latest gas-guzzling machines. I wasn't immune to trying to become more spiritual myself. I was spending longer and longer in the countryside meditating and, in particular, trying to rid myself of my ego. At the height of my meditating, I was sitting and watching my thoughts pass for up to five hours a day and started to convince myself that I was making good progress. As shiatsu's main ingredient is 'intention', I thought I would give a better treatment if I could clear my mind at will and feel what

The elusive spirit

my client needed and then, through purity of intention, heal them.

One weekend at the school it all came to a head. I was working on another student when all of a sudden, everything went blank and I mean everything. I didn't know where I was, how I had got there, what I was doing, who I was working on and the most alarming bit of all, couldn't understand a word that was being spoken to me. It was as if the teacher and the person I was working on had suddenly begun speaking in Chinese. I was helped to my feet and led out of the room to a bench in the courtyard. I sat there, trying to make sense of trees, the ground beneath my feet and the glass of water that was thrust in my hand. Two hours passed and I still sat like a frightened rabbit, jumping at the wind as it passed through the leaves. Seeing I wasn't fit to continue that day, the 'caring, healing, understanding teacher' put me in my car and told me to go home. I sat there as if I was at the controls of a spaceship, wondering what I was expected to do next. Another hour passed and I can only imagine an auto pilot set in for before I knew it, I was home, sitting and staring at the garage door, still unable to comprehend what my mother was saying.

Two days later I was still sat staring at the garage door, in a vegetative state, unable to think, function or feel. Finally, something in my brain snapped and I was back, spurred on by the one single thought that only I had the power to change the situation. I gradually came around, frightened and not knowing where or what I had been doing. In the weeks that followed I wrestled with the idea that I had spurned a chance of enlightenment and that my ego had been stripped away to such an extent I had been looking at the world with such purity that I hadn't

Lady Luck and Me

been able to embrace it and had returned to see the world through the same eyes that I had since birth.

I returned to the school a couple more times but, after the lack of empathy, support and care these so-called spiritual teachers had shown, combined with their impatience to get my money, I seriously questioned their motives. I had learnt enough and had given enough treatments to be able to charge clients and soon started to build up a regular, reliable client base. In spite of my many suspicions of the school, I found shiatsu did indeed benefit people and had many positive results, improving such symptoms as asthma, back pain and stress but put it solely down to the body healing itself, all without the need to consult the lunar cycles, being naked or eating moss off a rotting tree stump.

That wasn't the end of my shiatsu tuition though. Encouraged with the progress I had made with my clients, I enrolled a few years later onto a more liberal course of shiatsu called Zen shiatsu, which allows the practitioner to be guided by intuition and not as classical shiatsu suggests, by theory.

Once again, I was shocked by how much the course cost, seeing that the point of this treatment is to heal people with a caring, drug-free philosophy that requires only the use of the fingers, hands and elbows as equipment. Anyway, I paid the fees and went along to the three-day course, excited that maybe I had finally found the right school. The 12-person group consisted predominantly of women, bringing back the painful memories of Mary. Our teacher was a man in his late forties with a chiselled jaw, tanned face and a mischievous glint in his eye. He was, for his age, good looking and had an abundance of energy,

The elusive spirit

which after introductions he displayed by getting everyone in the group to dance with him, not to music but to the rhythm of the universe. Hmmm . . . my suspicions were aroused again but, trying to be as open minded as possible, I went along with it, awkwardly trying to fit in by throwing my limbs around as if I was having some sort of fit. Then followed his teachings which were simply, free your mind and massage wherever the universe directed you on the person's body. He picked the most attractive woman in the group and then set about basically groping them all the while asking in a seedy, husky voice whether it felt good. At times, I didn't know where to look and, as he told us to partner up and go with our instincts, he continued his intimate massage.

By the end of the three days, he had worked on all the women, thoroughly, and had started his rounds again, deciding for some unknown reason not to work on me. At the end of each day, he asked a different woman to stay behind so that he could improve their technique with one-on-one tuition. As our certificates were handed out qualifying us to go fourth and charge extortionate amounts for this bogus practice, he held up his self-published book on tantric shiatsu sex which, because we had attended his class, was available to purchase at a discounted price. I was out of the door before I had the chance to see whether anybody took him up on his generous offer.

That, to date, was my last shiatsu tutorial and, although I'm sure the vast majority of teachers and practitioners alike are genuinely practising with the very best intentions of helping their students and clients, I will forever more regard these spiritual, healing, so-called professionals with an unsavoury whiff of suspicion.

Lady Luck and Me

Sorry seas

> *'It is always so simple, and so complicating, to accept an apology.'*
> Michael Chabon

It was during this time of 'spiritual' self-discovery that I was inspired by Wee-Man's belief that in order to spiritually evolve you have to make amends with the past and, in particular, the people who have given you mental baggage. One of the biggest problems I had had since childhood was the blame I attached to my father. As chance would have it, without any prompting from me, Dad called one day out of the blue and invited me to join him, my half-sister, Bex and his wife on a hired yacht for two weeks in Antigua. The cynical side of me thought that my invitation was solely based on Dad needing a bit more brawn to help him sail the yacht but, with understandable trepidation, I accepted his offer and jetted off to the Caribbean for the New Year.

For the first few hours after our arrival, things were a little tense but, having eaten and consumed numerous cocktails and bottles of wine in one of the islands most expensive restaurants, the atmosphere eased. When Jo, his wife, and Bex, who was about 12 at the time, retired back to the yacht, I had my long-awaited moment alone with Dad. With my heart racing and my balls feeling a little bit bigger than usual, I asked him the question which had been burnt on my mind for years. I looked him in the eye and asked, 'Why is it that everyone thinks you're a cunt?' His reaction surprised me. As expected his fists closed and knuckles went white but, instead of leaping

Lady Luck and Me

over the table and ripping my head off, he calmly said. 'I'm sorry. We were adults and adults make mistakes.' And that was it. I looked at him and he looked at me. Now I wanted to leap across the table and tear his head off. His honesty and straight-forwardness had caught me unawares. I was expecting long, drawn-out excuses that dodged the question, like politicians do, but was now left without any wind in my sails, frantically thinking of a question which would make him squirm and shift uncomfortably.

As the seconds ticked away, no questions came and the intensity of the situation slowly evaporated, leaving me being the one shifting uncomfortably, frustrated at the ease at which he had slipped off the hook. I drank more hoping to become irrational and irritating until his anger got the better of him so I could justify screaming the torrents of bile that had accumulated over the years. Instead of causing the wanted showdown, the alcohol actually went some distance in healing the wounds rather than deepening them, highlighting our shared mannerisms and sense of humour. There was no way he was forgiven that evening, but, tiny bricks had been laid to rebuild the very big bridge. As the holiday went on, Dad and I became more comfortable being around each other, respectfully and consciously sidestepping potentially flammable situations in the name of peace, occasionally leaving a disgruntled Jo and Rebecca on the boat as we went ashore to top up on rum and swap stories from the many missing years.

It was New Year and we decided to see the next year in at Shirley Heights, the old fortification that overlooked English Harbour along with what seemed like the rest of the island. As the samba band played, Dad and I took regular trips to the bar for our rum and cokes and it wasn't long before my inhibitions were lost, allowing me to spark

Sorry seas

up conversation with anyone and everyone. A particularly friendly native islander dropped in to our conversation that he was selling cocaine for US$50 and, being in the party mood, I thought that this would be the perfect time to stuff it up my nose. So I obediently followed him to the toilet where he said he would leave the wrap after he had taken my money. I was a little upset to find the wrap that he had left me contained not cocaine but the words 'Fuck you' written in black felt tip pen. There was no chance that I would find the bastard again and even if I did what was I going to do? Take him to the police? Demand my money back? I put it down to foolish naivety not to be repeated again and went back to the bar to drink myself into oblivion.

The next conversation I struck up was with a young Dutch couple who had sailed a catamaran from Croatia to English Harbour and, as the conversation went so well, they invited me around the back of one of the stone towers to share a joint with them. The combination of rum and cokes and marijuana on an empty stomach left me considerably worse for wear and, as I mumbled my thanks and goodbyes and stumbled back to the party, I knew I was in trouble. I bounced off several people and inanimate objects in an effort to find Dad and co. but to no avail. I eventually came to the conclusion that I'd been gone for so long that they must have left and gone back to the boat. My plight hadn't gone unnoticed by one 'caring' individual who offered me a lift back down to the harbour in his boat's minibus. I gladly accepted his kind, generous offer and slumped in the back seat as he told me that he was a crew member on a large Saudi-owned yacht.

We pulled up on the pier, alongside the yacht and I followed the procession of other crew members onto the enormous boat, holding on to whatever I could as I

Lady Luck and Me

went. It was only when I saw a bed in front of me that I realised the gravity of the situation. My 'friend' insisted I stay as, at this time of night, my personal safety would be at risk if I tried to get back alone. Summoning what strength I had left, I pushed him aside and wobbled out into the narrow corridor. Twenty minutes later, sweating and breathless, I was still wandering through the maze of corridors, desperate to find my way off the gigantic gin palace. Finally and gratefully, I stumbled back onto the pier and into the New Year's night. I ricocheted my way back to our yacht incident free and collapsed face down on my pillow, knowing that I had narrowly avoided having my anal virginity taken from me.

For the remainder of the trip, I did my best to keep my feet on our yacht, only daring to venture off in the company of dad, fearful I would land myself into an irretrievable situation. On the whole, I enjoyed the trip tremendously but the most important thing that I took away from the whole experience was my dad's simple apology and, since then, whenever we see each other it's always fun, light and enjoyable, as it should be with old friends. Sure the questions and blame still linger but without the burning fury they once had.

I returned home, swapping the crystal clear, Caribbean blue skies for a deep, grey, cheerless blanket, having learnt three further truths: I had gained a friend, I had the zest to travel again, and not to trust a gay stranger to help you to a yacht when you're utterly arseholed.

As the British winter worsened, so did my mental state. Short, sunless hours and long, damp, dead nights seem to have a profound effect on my achieving any sort of happiness. I know I'm not alone there but, instead of

Sorry seas

investing in a light lamp to ease the S.A.D symptoms, I convinced myself it wasn't only the cripplingly depressing days and nights but also the gnawing feeling of not belonging; not belonging within the family, of course, but also not belonging in Surrey society. It seemed society's expectations of me and my expectations of society differed dramatically.

Wee-man had been emailing regularly with his foreign adventures and had finally settled on the shores of Koh Phangan, the infamous Thai party island. He was holed up in the hills off a small bay, practising veganism, and mind expansion with a 24-year-old German ex-gymnast. He had assured me that I might be more at peace with myself if I joined him on his little island paradise. For the previous year he had been living in Brazil and studying Wing Chun kung fu with one of the country's most respected masters. What with my brief stint in Sydney practising the same form, I was intrigued to see what he had learnt.

At the time I had very little money, if any at all for that matter and at the rate I was earning would have to wait until 2034 to make the journey. I think it must have been the lack of money due to lack of direction, motivation and self-worth that began another episode of deteriorating mental health. It was the fear of me declining again that forced my loving Mum's hand. She was to sponsor me to find inner peace, or at least a more positive mind-set. Since my last serious depressive episode occurred whilst I was trying to learn the 'the spirit path' I was hesitant to throw myself back into it and had consciously flipped, now regarding it with cynicism and scepticism. I had become far more interested in the darker side of Yang rather than the previously sought after light side of Yin. I had somehow

Lady Luck and Me

justified it to myself that if I was able to heal with my hands I must be able to harm with them.

I told myself that countless generations had used martial artistry for spiritual advancement and, seeing as the hours I'd spent sitting meditating had been somewhat inconclusive, I decided to try to reach the same end goal using a different, more aggressive approach. What better place to search for that spirit physically than in South-east Asia, home to Buddhists and, more importantly to me, home of Muay Thai or Thai kickboxing, all under warm, blue skies.

After more heartfelt thanks to my mother for her love and faith in me, I said my tearful goodbyes determined to return home more rounded and more at peace with myself.

I'm coming for you, Mr Palin

'Some of the worst mistakes in my life were haircuts.'
Jim Morrison

Instead of heading straight to Wee-man, Muay Thai and certain carnage, I decided to head north and experience a morsel of south-east Asia before getting holed up on a tropical island. Numerous travellers that I had met had given glowing reports of the tranquility and sleepiness of Laos, which sounded like the perfect environment to start searching for my inner peace and what could be better than two days in a slow boat down the legendary Mekong, taking in all the sights and sounds of rural Laos.

My boat bubble was swiftly burst within the first hour after being woken by a blotted, rotting pig's snout gently banging against my head as it rested on the low slung sides of the boat. Apart from the dozen or so dead pigs that floated by, logs the size of steam roller wheels regularly knocked us off course resulting in ear piercing anguish from the female passengers. If I thought we were having a rough ride, I could still manage significant sympathy for the poor, impatient fools that had decided to take the fast boat. Imagine a bobsleigh, complete with four, and on occasion five, helmeted passengers hunched in crash position directly in front of an engine that Rolls-Royce would be proud of, hurtling down the same debris strewn river. Twice I saw boats collide with logs, launching them like V2 rockets into the over-hanging rain forest canopies and twice I didn't see what became of the passengers, only what became of the boat, or what used to be parts of a boat.

Lady Luck and Me

For the remainder of the journey, I was grateful for the occasional stench of decaying pork.

Arriving in the ex-French colonial town of Luang Prabang in Laos, the first thing on my mind was to shower, shave and generally feel human again. Two days on the Mekong River and a night on opium acquired from one of the many natives on board who had their pockets lined with the stuff, had reduced me to a mere shadow of my former self. The mid-range hotel just outside the city centre provided a godly hot shower and conventional porcelain toilet, satisfying two of my immediate needs. I donned the bright pink/purple Duffer St George T-shirt and headed out in search of a barber. I had seen Michael Palin on television, when he was in India, receive his best shave from a blind man on the side of the street and was hoping to have a similar experience here.

I wandered the streets eyeing every corner and makeshift market stall hoping to see a withered old man holding a cut-throat razor beckoning me over. Alas, after two hours in the midday sun with a humidity factor of a 100 percent and the stench of the Mekong oozing through my pores, I settled on a small barber's shop down a quiet alley. On entering I was greeted by a hunched, gnarled old woman. It was a sparse, dilapidated shop, with a single blue plastic chair facing a heavily scarred mirror. The shop itself was unremarkable; the most interesting feature was a woman in her twenties lying fast asleep across four plastic chairs along the back wall.

Before I had time to question the old lady I was ushered, or rather, pushed into the solitary plastic chair in front of the mirror. It soon became worryingly clear that the old woman spoke no word of English. Even in

I'm coming for you, Mr Palin

my slowest Queen's English I got the same smile, the same nod and the same incoherent Laos babble. Just when I was beginning to question Michael Palin's authenticity, an old man, presumably the old lady's husband, appeared from a back room. I eyed his painstakingly slow journey towards me suspiciously, not quite sure what to make of this hairdressing relic and his erratic movements until he was at the back of my chair. Then it became blindingly obvious. He was clearly in an advanced stage of Parkinson's disease and vibrated at such a rate I was sure that he must have been mains powered. It was then that the thought crossed my mind that, actually, I would quite like that third box to remain un-ticked and would find it considerably more reassuring if he could see. He draped a faded, floral shower curtain, complete with mildew and the acrylic fastening rings, around my neck and rested his trembling hands on my shoulders, exhausted after all the exertion.

The two worked in partnership with the old woman assisting, directing and, although I didn't understand the language, abusing her husband and his technique. He did his best to ignore her, now and then shouting back whilst tentatively fingering my head. All the time, the young woman slept. My request for a grade-three clip fell on deaf, drooping ears as the old man proceeded to take a used, disposable, rusty razor off the shelf from under the mirror and scrape it right down the middle of my unprepared head. No shaving foam, no gel, no nothing. I cursed myself. How many indications did I need to tell me that I shouldn't have had my long-awaited shave here?

By the time first blood had been drawn, it was too late to beat a hasty retreat. The damage had been done. I looked at the bald, naked white strip down the centre of my head and the blood leaking from it and wondered

Lady Luck and Me

whether I had just contracted HIV. The arguing and the world's most painful haircut continued and I watched as my head became progressively bloodier. By the end of the haircut, the top half of my head shone white, interspersed with tiny bits of white tissue paper in a vain attempt to stem the blood from the many bleeding nicks. The contrast of the newly shaven whiteness to my suntanned, stubbled face gave me a convincing gay biker look. The potential hazards of walking through the capital of a communist country looking like a raving homosexual had not been mentioned in any of the travel guides that I had read. Funny that, I guess they didn't think anybody would be that stupid.

As the old man turned to wash his hands, I saw my chance of freedom. I quietly withdrew my hands from beneath the shower curtain and attempted to rise only to be put firmly back into place by the old woman's muscular hands on my shoulders, who had seamlessly replaced the old man behind my chair. The shower curtain was tucked back in as my angst and their arguing started up again. After a quick flick of the hands, the old man picked the razor back up and repositioned himself once again behind my chair. With short, rough, unforgiving strokes he hacked away at my facial hair and raw skin. For a grown man who has always had the softest, sensitive skin, the assault was truly damaging. By the end of the 'treatment' it was more difficult to establish where he hadn't cut. He washed my face down with a once white damp cloth and dried it roughly with a scratchy brillo pad-like face towel.

My face was screaming. As always seems the case, just when I thought he couldn't damage me anymore he produced, from nowhere, an ancient bottle of Old Spice with which he liberally covered my face and neck, perfectly completing the homosexual image. If he had woken up

I'm coming for you, Mr Palin

that morning and decided he was going to make his next customer a queen, his eyes must have lit up when I walked in. I doubt that he had but, if he had, it was impeccable and that old bastard was a genius.

Rising from the chair, I was giddy with pain and humiliation. Knowing that I had yet to walk through town and stay holed up in the hotel until both my wounds and my hair improved, made me despair even more. Palin was back on my hit-list. Husband and wife lined up at the door smiling at me, seemingly overjoyed with the service they had provided and the depths of despair that they had plunged me into. The wife produced a calculator from her pocket and tapped away. The sum escapes me now, but what is for sure is that the roles should have been reversed and they should have been paying me compensation. Handing over the money felt more like buying my freedom from Sweeney Todd than paying for a professional haircut. At last though, I was at the door and almost out of their clutches. As the door was opened for me, the husband mumbled something to his wife and immediately the door was closed again. The wife turned to the girl sleeping on the plastic chairs and shook her roughly, waking her and her temper. Angry words were exchanged before the husband took over the shaking role, eventually rousing the girl enough for her to sit up and squint at me through tired eyes. She wasn't unattractive. I put her at 18 tops and quite clearly constituted the third family member.

The wife produced the calculator and proceeded to tap away again, deleted it and re-entered a smaller amount, much to the husband's and the daughter's obvious displeasure. From their grumblings, it was clearly evident who wore the trousers in the family. With a sharp silencing comment, both father and daughter fell silent as the wife

Lady Luck and Me

smiled, showed me the figure on the calculator and pointed at her daughter. If my maths was right, she was trying to sell her to me for about 150 pounds. Politely, I smiled at the young woman, the father and then at the mother whilst shaking my head, now getting really quite desperate to leave. Turning towards the door sparked another family conversation, with the mother hurriedly amending the figure on the calculator. The daughter was clearly infuriated over how little her mother now thought she was worth. I exited the shop with a horror-movie head but still single and with the family in a heated dispute. I kept my head down the entire journey back, too ashamed to look up and see what kind of reaction my bloody Mardi Gras impression was getting. Back at the hotel, I drew the curtains, found out about room service and collapsed on the bed watching Laos TV, and there I stayed for the next two weeks as my body and soul did their best to forget and recover.

Having healed and hidden the pink T-shirt, I emerged hesitantly from the hotel for the first time in a fortnight, eager to see what Luang Prabang had to offer apart from its barbaric barber shops. 'Lonely Planet' had listed the Buddhist garden, 10 km outside the capital, as a must-see for any traveller, so off I went. I expected the gardens to be sacred places of running waterfalls, lotus flowers and areas of vibrant vegetation to sit, meditate and self-reflect. The gardens themselves really weren't at all impressive, a mowed, farmed, ankle-breaking field. What was impressive was the imagination of the creators of the statues that were dotted throughout. The best were unbelievably amateur, looking as if they had been the work of an angry heroin user, whilst the worst had all the hallmarks of blind, deaf and dumb toddlers. Despite the surrealism of the place, it was nice to be out and not to be drawing attention from

I'm coming for you, Mr Palin

people thinking I was a gay man with a rare, unsightly skin condition.

With the photos taken and a healthy amount of sunshine received, it was time to taxi back to the sanctuary of my hotel room once more. As no car taxis were available, the only decision left to me was to take a tuk-tuk back. Once the price had been negotiated, I sat back to take in the pleasant, green paddy fields and the warmth of the dying sun on my newly repaired head. It was due to the relaxing nature of the journey that my mind decided that a joint on my hotel balcony would be the perfect way to end the day. My experiences of tuk tuk drivers throughout South-east Asia had taught me that they were the wheeler-dealer, Arthur Daley kind that could get or knew people who could get pretty much anything you wanted, from working girls to cheap jade Elvis figurines.

As the tuk-tuk came to a halt at lights on the outskirts of the capital, I saw my chance to enquire about the possibility of acquiring a small amount of Mary Jane. Surprisingly, my driver spoke reasonable English and, without the need to repeat myself, he lifted up his cushion and revealed a transparent pillow absolutely stuffed with weed. At exactly the same time, a police car drew up alongside us and stopped. I had read *Bangkok Hilton* and *Damage Done* and, as both were horrific accounts of tourists being caught with drugs in Thailand, I shuddered at the idea of how a communist country in South-east Asia might treat a tourist caught with drugs. Somewhere I had read that the one thing the Laos police take more seriously than someone breaking the midnight curfew was tourists in possession of drugs, with convictions carrying death

Lady Luck and Me

sentences or, at the very least, long hard-labour sentences in some truly horrendous hell holes.

The lights changed but neither vehicle moved. Slowly, the blacked out window of the police car was lowered and a sun-glassed copper craned his head to take a long look at me. My driver replaced the bag of weed under his cushion as the copper opened dialogue with him. The conversation seemed brief, although I can't be sure as my attention was on my impending sentence and my ever-loosening bowels. The officer looked at me again, wound up the window and sped off, blue lights flashing. Amazed that I had not been bundled out of the tuk-tuk and into the police car there and then, I was convinced the policeman had given the driver strict instructions to deliver me to the closest police station immediately. Fearing the worst and convinced that I was now being driven to my death, the tuk-tuk gently pulled away but instead of following the police car, continued on our journey until we reached the entrance of my hotel. Confused and suspicious, I asked what was going on and what had been said to the police. He simply replied, 'They make sure I get good price.' With that he reached back under his cushion and took the weed back out. I could have made love to that man; I think I even tried to. Such was my relief, I bought twice the amount of weed I wanted, or needed, and at double the price he had asked.

Alive and temporarily kicking

'Every knee will bend before me, and every tongue shall give glory to God.'
Jesus Christ

The 18-hour train journey from Bangkok to Chiang Mai was mostly spent hovering over a hole or, as the Thais like to call it, the toilet, as both my stomach and bowels did their best to rid whatever poison I had ingested. Eventually, when my body's evacuation and train journey came to an end, I bustled around the old, walled city looking for somewhere to rest my weary bones. After dismissing the first two hostels for cockroaches and blood-stained walls respectively, I found a quiet cheap hostel to lie low and recover for a day or so. 'Lonely Planet' had sung the praises of a nerve touch massage course and, being a shiatsu practitioner, I thought it best if I added another string to my bow by booking a place on the five-day course.

The school was a five generation-old family business and was now in the hands of Mother Pek, who must have been 80 years old and sat in the corner of the room occasionally waving her bamboo stick at the Thai teachers if she thought the technique wasn't being adhered to. There were 10 of us in the class, all Western foreigners with a large contingent being American and, one in particular, being vastly overweight. We paired up and watched as the Thai instructors bent and contorted each other before we attempted the same. Four days in and I was sceptical of its healing and relaxation qualities as most of us had experienced serious pain and few after effects of wellbeing. This thinking wasn't helped when the small Swedish partner

Lady Luck and Me

of the large American, under the watchful eye of Mother Pek herself, tried to repeat what we had just been shown by the instructors and, with one almighty pop, dislocated her partner's knee, leaving him writhing around on the floor in agony, addressing and blaming God, Buddha and all other holy beings in the Devil's blasphemous tongue. Five of the group were instantly sick when they saw the injury and, on seeing the poor Swede's face as she ran out in tears, some were left with serious psychological scarring. Only three of us returned the following day to complete the course and, when the certificates were handed out, we hurried away, thankful all our limbs were still intact and vowing not to use any of the techniques we had been taught unless we were in a wrestling death-match.

Another highlight of Chiang Mai was the Tiger Temple, situated a short journey outside the town. It was a strange place where all kinds of animals roamed free, sometimes with disastrous results. The keepers of this temple/animal sanctuary were small in number and young in age with a rotund, bald, Buddhist monk keeping them and the animals in check with a two-yard twig. The tigers themselves were apparently wild, coming and going at will from the surrounding jungle. After paying a donation, punters were invited to carefully wander up and stroke the tigers, escorted by one of the helpers. As I awaited my turn, I wondered if the baseball cap in the helper's hand would be a strong enough deterrent if the tiger suddenly decided it didn't want to play. My turn came and, as I approached the mighty beast, all the worst scenarios flashed before my eyes. My fully grown male tiger eyed me coming and fixed its gaze. My escort, clearly acting on self-preservation, stopped, whispered to me to stand still and then he proceeded to slowly walk backwards until he was safely behind the

Alive and temporarily kicking

barrier, warning me of no sudden movements. My heart and sphincter were working overtime but, thankfully, it seemed the tiger had already eaten and had little interest in me. It lazily stretched, closed its eyes and sighed heavily, much to my relief.

As I began to retrace my steps, the escort, still behind the barrier and loving my discomfort, told me not to walk away but approach it as the tiger now respected me. I doubted that, I doubted that very much. Gingerly I approached and, as quietly as I could, knelt down beside it, sinking my hand inches into its soft fur on its gigantic, untamed head as I pulled the most insincere smile for my photo to be taken. It was easy to see how, with just one lazy swipe of its paw, a man's head could be cleanly severed and, as this realisation dawned on me, I decided I had ridden my luck far enough and began to slowly retreat, much against my evil, escort's wishes. Back behind the barrier and feeling invincible, my escort looked me up and down, looked back at the tiger and dismissively blurted out, 'Pussy'.

A week later, I read a report on the internet that a school teacher had had a similar encounter but had lost the top of her head and, who could be seen smiling in the corner of the aftermath photo? Yep, you guessed it.

Lady Luck and Me

Contemplating the life of Pai

'A 20-stone woman with buckling ankles smelt as if something had died in her creases.'
A.A. Gill

From Chiang Mai I took an overcrowded bus to the traveller's Mecca, Pai, along with loose chickens, drunken businessmen and schoolchildren all sitting on the smallest, hardest wooden seats the Devil's carpenter could muster. The longer the journey went on, the more the driver seemed determined to beat some imaginary 'what percentage of northern Thailand can you get on your bus?' record. At one point, there were people hanging off both the inside and the outside of the windows and, as the terrain steadily deteriorated, so did the people on the outside. Most of the young men clinging to the sides of the bus seemed to see the journey as some sort of Russian roulette, gambling on how far they can get before being shaken off or dislodged by on-coming traffic. Twice I saw a dusty ball of limbs roll down the road behind us and twice my fellow passengers failed to show any compassion whatsoever towards their fallen countrymen. Perhaps it was a daily occurrence and they had become numb to it or maybe, like me, they were concentrating hard on getting any kind of feeling back into their bruised and battered buttocks.

Two hours in and only internal passengers and their livestock left, I drifted off, tired after failing to nullify the arse pain which had by then migrated halfway up my spine. I was woken not by the chicken dozing in my lap or by the drunken businessman who had fallen asleep snoring and was now dribbling on my shoulder, but when the bus

Lady Luck and Me

came to an abrupt halt at our destination. After carefully handing the chicken back to its suspicious owner and peeling the businessman off my shoulder, I realised I only had my head and arms functioning, none of the rest of my body moved or even had the slightest sensation in it. As the bus emptied, I was left in the back corner thumping my body, trying to get life back into it. Nothing. If somebody had shot my lower half repeatedly with a nail gun there and then, I would have laughed at them.

With no feeling coming back to my legs and, seeing my rucksack, lying alone in the dust just waiting to be picked up by a passing opportunist, I knew I had to stir my body into action. Manually, I lifted one leg and placed it in the aisle and then did the same with the other much as a wheelchair bound person would do. Shuffling to the edge of the world's worst seat, I heaved myself up and stood in the aisle, with my weight entirely on my hands. As I lurched down the aisle, seat to seat, my legs still hadn't joined the party and were dragging behind me. Just at that point, the driver came back on board, no doubt assuming all his passengers had long gone, to see me sweating, groaning, and slowly dragging my legs down the bus towards him. To him, it must have seemed as if he was in some real-life zombie horror movie as he shrieked, turned and jumped back out of the bus, closing the doors behind him.

I pulled my redundant legs along, eventually reaching the front of the bus to be welcomed by about 10 squashed, terrified faces at the door. Thankfully, by then, enough blood had returned to my lower half and I was able to stand, although a little wobbly. Still a little unsure, the driver watched me and my legs return fully before hesitantly opening the bus doors and allowing me down the stairs to the onlookers' hushed silence. Smiling as much as I could

Contemplating the life of Pai

and mumbling what I thought were reassuring noises, I picked my way through the small crowd and retrieved my rucksack. Dusting it off, I strapped it to my back, nodded to the crowd and slowly backed away into the streets of Pai.

It was easy to see why Pai had become a magnet to travellers. With its quaint streets, bamboo river crossings and colourful meadows, it was a perfect place to read books, contemplate and just, well . . . be. Low prices and an abundance of good, well-priced accommodation meant that many of its foreign inhabitants were there illegally, knowingly overstaying their visas in order to stay in the Shangri-La surroundings, occasionally having to hide in the shadows whenever there was talk of visiting police. If Thai immigration had decided to pay a surprise visit, they could have hit their annual target in just one day.

Since it seemed to be a place of contemplation, my thinking was to find a remote spot where I could spend a couple of weeks in nature just doing that. At the very back of the town, I found a pod of tiny bungalows sharing communal toilets and showers and, for an absolute pittance, it was perfect. I paid the rent upfront for a bungalow set back from the rest and the furthest from human interruption. With paddy fields stretching indefinitely behind the bungalow and a curtain of small trees at the front, it really did feel like I was in my own little kingdom.

The first couple of days were spent sitting on the small veranda at the back, smoking joints, watching small birds dart between fields, all the while unaware of my legs turning an angry, sunburnt pink or the armies of mosquitos that almost bled me dry. With my food supplies running low and my imagination starting to play tricks on me, I headed into town on the third day in search of tobacco and strangely enough, fish, which I had been craving the

Lady Luck and Me

last two days. To this day I still don't know why; I detest fish and they detest me, always have and always will. I never found any fish and, thankfully, the cravings subsided over the next three days. Supplies replenished, I began my journey back to the bungalow, having only interacted with an aged, semi-naked Thai shopkeeper.

Nearing the track that led away into the wilderness and, eventually, my bungalow, the last shop window caught my attention. Advertised was a four-day hike through some of the hill villages that bordered Burma. It included overnight accommodation in the tribal villages, elephant trekking, traditional river boating and a guarantee that no other tour group or tourist would be seen during the entire four days. It also stipulated that anyone interested should be of reasonable to good fitness due to the mileage covered and the terrain encountered. After successful price haggling with the consultant, I booked myself on for the following day, excited at the prospect of, apart from the two other bookings and the guide, not seeing another Western face for four days. The elephant trekking also sounded fun. I had visions of myself as a modern-day Mowgli, living on the back of my elephant, roaming aimlessly around, speaking only the language of the jungle and growing the most spectacular beard, long and thick enough to trap the native wild boars so I could eat like a king.

My fellow hikers were a Dutch couple in their late forties and could in no way be deemed to be of reasonable to good fitness. With the new-day sun barely on the horizon, their thin, sweat-saturated, white cotton T-shirts gave the impression that they had just been in a fierce 20-plus stone wet T-shirt competition. Their open-toed sandals and knee-high white socks only reinforced the idea that they were poorly prepared and clueless as to what the four-day hike entailed. I was intrigued to see what munitions they had packed into their one and only tiny fanny pack

Contemplating the life of Pai

which, on the husband's over-hanging, sodden stomach, resembled more of an eye patch. I didn't have to wait long as after the brief introductions were made the wife undid the pack and pulled out a half empty can of coke which was generously passed around, consumed and then safely tucked away again.

Thank goodness they were amicable as I was sure this would make the certain future resuscitation attempts so much easier to deal with. Our guide, Mit, was a Burmese gentleman, also in his early to mid-forties, but couldn't have been more different in his physique to the Dutch couple. Sinewy, lithe and with sharp, darting eyes, he regarded the couple with obvious fitness concerns. Thankfully, this was missed by the couple who immediately began peppering him with irrelevant questions like two over-excited schoolchildren embarking on an annual field trip. Within a couple of minutes of us setting off, the questions dried up as their huge frames heaved up and down as they tried to suck in enough air to keep their legs moving forward on the perfectly flat tarmacked road.

Mit spoke reasonable English and had been living as a political refugee in the hills we were on our way to visit since he was a small boy. Like many of the men from the hill tribes, he had been a hunter in the jungles surrounding Pai before tourists with wads of cash began arriving. For him, the career change was a no-brainer. Why walk the jungle hunting for food and living off the land when tourists were willing to give vast sums of money to just be guided around the trails he had known since he could walk. The flip side of this was that many of the traditions and the way of life of the tribes were slowly being polluted and worn away by Western influence. Mit didn't wear his village's colours

Lady Luck and Me

anymore; he preferred to wear Levi's, a Paul Smith T-shirt and play games on his Blackberry.

We entered the jungle with the Dutch couple already lagging behind, struggling for breath. We had been walking for an hour before Mit had to start sharing his water with them. The plan was to walk a couple of hours, stop, have lunch and then continue on for another couple of hours to the first village where we would be spending the night. After the first hour, Mit had to revise this plan as it was clear there was no way the necessary mileage would be covered in time. An hour after starting and barely out of sight of Pai, we stopped and had lunch, much to the relief of the visibly pained couple. Mit didn't sit down but dutifully gave out the pre-prepared lunches which consisted of processed cheese and a bright pink spam-like substance sandwiched between sweet white bread. In the time it had taken me to inspect mine, the couple had finished theirs and were poking around in the arid earth for anything that might have been remotely edible to shove in their eager mouths. Mit, sensing their dissatisfaction and rumbling tums pointed out large green ants that were milling about around our feet and jokingly suggested they tried a couple. Before he managed to finish his sentence, the wife had taken off her damp sandal and was beating the ground hoping to capture some on the sole.

The afternoon hike was revised and shortened twice so that we arrived at our first night's accommodation to an unprepared Burmese family of six, all wearing traditional dress in a wooden house, on stilts that barely had room to house all of them let alone us. As the mother cooked rice over the open fire in the middle, the four children, ranging in age from four to eight, sat in silence, mouths slightly ajar, staring at me and the Dutch couple's stomachs. In a darkened corner, Mit was handing over cash, all the while gesturing apologies for what I can only imagine was our unexpected and seemingly unwelcome intrusion into their

Contemplating the life of Pai

home. Like anywhere in the world, cold hard cash seemed to pacify the situation and, after another bundle was passed, Mit joined us, hands clasped together, respectfully bowing to each family member before sitting down and staring aimlessly into the flames.

After the Dutch couple had almost eaten the family's entire rice reserves, we all bedded down around the dying fire. I was sandwiched between the youngest child and the mother and felt truly uncomfortable about the whole affair, twitching nervously, desperate to avoid any contact either side of me. With the combination of the Dutch couple snoring raucously and the family of pigs that constantly squealed directly below, it wasn't the most rewarding of sleeps.

Blurry eyed and stiff as a board, I sat upright to once again join everyone else, staring into the fire. During the night, I had learnt that loosely bound bamboo poles over a pig sty and a thin threadbare woollen rug was how not to make the perfect bedroom. My comment that I didn't expect to see this lay-out on 'Grand Designs' anytime soon was received with quizzical looks. Apart from the obvious sleep deprivation in everyone's eyes, nothing had changed for the last 10 hours, everybody as motionless and expressionless as a well-gone corpse.

Everybody except the Dutch couple, who were fresh faced and doing their clumsy best not to knock over the family's shrine to Buddha on their way to the door. It was like watching deer on ice as they clung on to each other tentatively negotiating their way over the creaking bamboo. If one had gone, the other would be certain to follow and, without question, they would have ended up with the pigs below and Mit would have to hand over substantially more cash for repairs. As Lady Luck would have it, they made it out of the house unscathed. Just as I was sighing with relief, the unmistakeable crack of splintering wood was heard

Lady Luck and Me

followed by a high-pitched female squeal. Mit was first up and shot to the door, closely followed by me. I'll never forget the sight that greeted me: wedged, halfway down the nine-foot ladder with her feet dangling not a foot from the inquisitive snouts below, the woman had broken two rungs and had very securely fastened herself at the waist, inside the ladder, and was now pleading hysterically to her husband to rescue her. He was frantically trying to reach her outstretched hand whilst balancing precariously on the bamboo platform. Without hesitation or a second thought, Mit shoved the husband back into the house and replaced him, trying to grasp the wife's sausage fingered hand. Having been enveloped by her meaty digits, Mit pulled with all his might to release her from the most peculiar of prisons.

The combination of Mit heaving, the woman crying out, the husband swearing and the pigs getting audibly more excited was, like the sight, a sound I'll never forget. The hosting family meanwhile hadn't moved a muscle and continued staring at the now cooking rice, seemingly oblivious to the commotion directly outside their front door.

After about three minutes and 15 attempts of trying to pull her free, it was abundantly clear that she wasn't going to budge and that the pigs weren't going to lose interest. With Mit struggling to free her, he told the husband to get down below and try to help. The husband flatly and simply absolutely refused before breaking down and quietly sobbing. Exasperated, Mit turned and yelled at me to go down and push her from beneath. This, of course, involved me getting friendly with the giant sow and her six almost fully grown piglets and this immediately conjured up images of Bricktop from 'Snatch': 'Pigs go through human bones like a knife through butter.' I realised, through Mit's fruity language and the wife's increasing desperation, the seriousness of the situation. Despite now

Contemplating the life of Pai

having a responsibility bestowed upon me to be part of the rescue operation, the surrealistic comedy value of the moment was not lost, making me work hard to suppress the raucous laughter that was bursting to get out.

Armed with a sturdy stick, I entered the sty with my heart beating unhealthily quickly. A couple of wallops on the most ambitious pig's arse soon had them all retreating into a corner. Foolishly, in my haste, I hadn't thought about footwear and had leapt off the platform barefooted. As heroic as I thought it was, this was sheer stupidity. Not only was there a splinter in my sole from the landing but, since entering the pig enclosure, my feet were covered in pig shit, human shit and all other random bits of shit to the ankles and all the while Bricktop kept repeating in my head, 'Like a knife through butter'.

The view of the wife from below was far worse than it had been from the top. There was far more chance of Mit pulling off her arms than dislodging her body. Her barely covered arse spilt over the bamboo ladder rung with what remained of her torn, black thong serving very little purpose indeed. As I positioned myself beneath her, the dilemma of where I was to place my hands began to vex me. The only feasible placement was on her exposed arse which was directly at my head height. This also put my groin in direct firing line of her flailing feet. My requests to stop kicking me in the bollocks seemed to encourage her to kick more frantically, forcing me to take evasive action by way of doing a weird kind of Mick Jagger dance.

So with my hands disappearing into her fleshy buttocks, feet ankle deep in shit and hips gyrating to an imaginary Rolling Stones number, I began to push up, hoping that maybe the force from me below and the strength

Lady Luck and Me

of Mit from above might be enough to wriggle her free. Alas, it was in vain, leaving us with no option but pulling her from below. Although I tried making my intentions as clear as I could to Mit, I wasn't entirely sure that he had fully understood. I reached up and grasped her around her middle, desperately trying to avoid being sucked headfirst into her lily-white bottom; Mit repositioned himself above her steadying himself for the big push. As I pulled down from below, he pulled her arms from above, unwittingly turning her into the victim of a rudimentary human rack, which in turn resulted in an ear-piercing scream. Clearly something had been lost in translation. Realising our error after the second big heave, Mit finally began pushing her down from above. It wasn't long until the same splintering noise could be heard coming from the third rung which her arse, by now, had nearly completely engulfed. All of a sudden the rung gave way and sent her straight down on top of me.

Right then and there, I was convinced that this was how I was going to go, drowning in pig shit with a fat woman on my face. I got one more face full of arse before she managed to scrabble to her feet, not giving one thought to her saviour. As I looked up, all I could see against the white cloud cover were the silhouettes of six pig heads moving closer and closer. I thought it was all over when something grabbed my right wrist and tugged, which, to my relief was Mit's hand. He was using my stick to good use with the other and soon had the pigs retreating to the corner once more, allowing me to turn and crawl my way out, kicking the sty gate closed. The ordeal was over and as

Contemplating the life of Pai

I lay there on my back filling my lungs with shit smelling air, I felt sure I had just used up one of my lives.

It was only when I got to my feet that I saw that the entire village had gathered around, quietly talking and chuckling. Having decided there would be no fatalities, they dispersed as quietly as they had come, leaving the Dutch couple hugging and whimpering, Mit splayed out exhausted and me next to him covered head to foot in shit. Our hosting family still hadn't left the house but were craning their heads around the front door, expressionless, almost as if they had seen it all before. Four bucket loads of stagnant, larvae infested water later, most of the physical filth had been washed away leaving only the stubborn, offensive stench behind. The remainder of the hike would be spent battling with nausea and the uncomfortable thought of what I had been rolling around in and the health implications of my heroic deed.

The Dutch couple ate their breakfast on terra firma, away from the pig sty and away from any bamboo ladders, whilst Mit and I ate with the family, in silence. The longer I sat there, the more visibly agitated the mother next to me became until, unable to contain herself any further, she fired angry words at Mit, who, nodding respectfully, leaned over and quietly asked me to finish my breakfast on the bamboo platform outside. Embarrassed, self-conscious and wishing I was soaking myself in a hot bubble bath, I shamefully crept out of the house and ate the remainder of my rice on my own, watching the Dutch couple and cursing them my under my breath.

With breakfast and my humiliation complete, Mit handed over more cash before we left the village, much to everyone's relief. The front door of the family's home

Lady Luck and Me

was abruptly shut without even so much as a wave, well before Mit had fully descended the broken ladder. Wisely, the Dutch couple kept their distance behind us, sheepishly staring at the ground whenever they were asked a question. Over the next three days, whenever we had climbed a rise, I would purposefully hang back and stand as close as possible to them, making sure they shared lungfuls of the foul odour that continuously clung to me like an unwanted companion. Mit remained mute for the majority of the following days, doing his duties but certainly not over extending himself or offering any friendly nuggets of native information. On one occasion, he stopped dead in the middle of a jungle trail staring at a large tree. From afar, it looked as if the tree's trunk was vibrating. On closer inspection, it became clear that actually it was thousand's upon thousand's of hairy, hand-sized spiders crawling all over one another. The Dutch couple and I crept closer, carefully raising our camera's to our eyes, hoping to capture one of nature's most skin crawling events. From behind the camera's eyepiece, I saw a stick crash into the middle of the swarm and then heard Mit who was standing behind us, run off. As the stick fell, it pulled down with it a moving mass of brown legs. Dropping my camera, I watched in horror as the mass became one large, arachnid transformer swiss balll and started rolling straight for us. I was off down the path like a greased greyhound, slightly in fear of the spiders but mainly terrified of being trampled to death by the screaming and wheezing Dutch couple who were hot on my heels. After a hundred or so metres, the spiders gave up the chase and melted away into the jungle undergrowth, allowing the three of us to breathe in what oxygen there

Contemplating the life of Pai

was in the humid air. Mit sprang out from behind a large tree, grinning from ear to ear.

Having unanimously voted to boycott the danger of river rafting, we entered the elephant riding village. Thus far, I had come through Mit's and the jungle's best efforts unscathed and this being our last activity, was confident I might just make it all the way to the end. The Dutch couple weren't faring so well and, having been inseparable since the ladder break fiasco, were mortified to learn that, due to their weight, the Mahout insisted they rode separately. Even then, the unlucky elephants didn't look entirely comfortable with their cargo and vocally expressed it. Mit stayed behind, waiting and scheming for our return.

We left the village on the back of our beasts, seated in a wicker basket-like cradle that was covered with old, tatty rugs. The Mahout at the front had no such luxuries and sat on the crown of his elephant's head, steering it by digging his heels into the back of the animal's ears. Some elephants we passed had some terrible injuries, ranging from bloody damage on the head caused by its 'carers' hatchet to weeping sores on legs from the over use of the bamboo whip. The four elephants we were using seemed to be injury free, in good condition, and shared a mutual respect with their young carer.

Sadly for me, if anyone was to be Mowgli that day, or any other day, it was him. He was the real-life reincarnation of the Disney character, complete with the hair, loin cloth and animal language skills. As he bolted off through the undergrowth, the Dutch couple and their struggling mounts were once again lagging behind and, hearing their frequent yelps, were not getting much protection from the elephant's prominent spine. I smiled.

Lady Luck and Me

At first, I found the whole experience delightful. I was away from the dangers of Mit and the jungle floor, still within ear shot of the troubled couple and being gently swayed into a meditative state by one of the animal kingdom's finest.

Just as I was beginning to relax for the first time in four days, a knife-like sensation shot through my stomach followed by salivating and the involuntary spasms that inevitably come before vomiting. Taking a large swig of water and a big breath, I concentrated hard on the horizon hoping that it was nothing more sinister than motion sickness. Initially, I thought I had quelled it and, once again, settled back onto my rug, watchful but confident it had passed. There was no warning the second time and at the same time I had registered that I was being sick, my elephant must have felt it on top of his head. Before I had managed to get my head over the side of the animal's enormous back, I had covered its head, its ears, both its sides, most of my top and nearly my entire wicker seat. After two more similarly ferocious bouts, I was thinking there couldn't be much left in me to get out. I was wrong. With the Mahout miles ahead and the Dutch couple miles behind, I was left spraying the elephant with each lurch forward. As sweat cascaded down my face and my stomach cramped, my bowels gave way, completing the worst elephant ride in history. The poor wicker seat was being filled from both of my ends, much to the curiosity of my animal and its muscular, inquisitive trunk which I was feebly trying to beat away.

Eventually, the Mahout re-joined us and saw the horror. Without muttering a word but with the same fearful expression that Mit had had thinking one of the couple was about to die, he turned around and hurried us back down the path to the village. Mit was predictably unsympathetic.

Contemplating the life of Pai

If anything he was slightly irritated by our early return, throwing his cigarette down and waving his arms around as he set about collecting his belongings for the final leg. The Dutch couple were slightly more compassionate, having seen me being thrown around like a rag doll on top of my now multi-coloured elephant. Lady Luck also played her hand as the Mahout made us walk in single file, putting the Dutch couple directly down-wind of my loosening bowels and rebellious stomach.

After being poured out of my wicker seat, I sat on the dusty ground covered in my own mess, head spinning and stomach churning as they took my elephant away for a thorough hosing down. With a stern shake of the head, Mit handed over more money before promptly setting off with the Dutch couple in pursuit and me struggling not only with my rucksack but also to walk in a straight line. The humidity, stench in my nostrils, chaffing and deepening feeling of disorientation started to make me think that I wasn't going to last the distance. Mit had pretty much washed his hands of the three of us, not turning back once to see whether we were in tow and it was still touch and go whether the Dutch couple were going to make it. After what seemed like an eternity and having lost stones of weight in fluids, we reached the outskirts of Pai. Without turning, Mit waved his hand in the air and was off into the town, not to be seen again. The Dutch couple followed suit soon after, again without so much as a farewell or a thanks. Despite them being entirely responsible for the dysfunctional last four days, I was a little sorry to see them go. We had survived what Mit and the jungle had thrown at us and they had, against all the odds, physically managed to cross the finish line, albeit many pounds lighter. Psychologically, it was another story. Ever since laddergate,

Lady Luck and Me

they had barely spoken a word to Mit and I, and had held on to each other like two frightened orphans.

I limped back to my bungalow as dusk began to fall, desperate to be on my own. As much as I wanted to shower, I didn't have the physical strength or the mental capacity and just wanted to lie down and die. I barely made it through the door before collapsing on the thin mattress still sweating and still leaking from both ends. I can't be sure how long I laid there; all I vividly remember were the hallucinations of an army marching towards me, getting louder and louder, nearer and nearer and in their hands, big shiny hunting knives. The other odd thing that I remember is a short-haired white woman, I'm guessing in her mid to late thirties, average in appearance, sitting beside me, gently feeding me mango slices and pineapple chunks. She didn't speak, she just smiled, lovingly feeding me fruit. She departed as discretely as she had arrived, leaving me to the soldiers and the knives.

Eventually, my fever broke and I remerged back into the world of the living and to the aftermath of a truly awful experience. The state of the bungalow was unimaginable in every sense of the word. To this day, I still have no idea how long I flirted with death but my rucksack, the floor, the walls and even some of the ceiling had all paid dearly. If hell has a prison cell, it can't be any worse than how I had decorated my bungalow. Amid all the muck and flies, two empty polythene fruit packets stood out, clear as day, untouched by any of the surrounding filth.

What troubled me most about the whole episode was not what illness had taken hold of me or the mammoth cleaning operation ahead of me or even that I could now clearly see all of my ribs, it was who was the short-haired

Contemplating the life of Pai

woman? I went over in my mind all the people I had had contact with whilst in Pai. Apart from Mit, the Dutch couple, the half-naked shop keeper, the tour agent and the old man who I had rented the bungalow from, I had not spoken to another soul and out of those few people, only the old man knew of my bungalow. How did she find me? How did she know I was in serious trouble? Why didn't she talk or tell me her name? Why did she appear with fruit? When it comes to serious illnesses, this was the worst and the closest I've been to meeting my maker and without her intervention, I would have probably died alone, forgotten, in the back of beyond and not found until my rent had expired. Possible theories include that she wasn't ever there and I had myself wandered into town and bought the fruit, hallucinating her presence or that she had seen me stumbling into my bungalow in the twilight hours and had, after a few days, perfectly timed her visit with fruit, never to return. To this day I am still none the wiser and still question whether she was a figment of my fevered imaginings or whether she had somehow been sent to me.

Having woken from hell, the first shower could only be described as heaven. It turns out that I had been holed-up, fighting the Grim Reaper for a week and, as I stood looking at myself in the shower block's full length mirror, I was reminded of the Auschwitz prisoner photographs. There were no scales, but I didn't need them to know that I had lost a substantial amount of weight. My skin was a dull grey colour and my cheekbones were sharp enough to be used as weapons. Most of the stench was removed with the help of the industrial strength shower gel/bleach I had found by the sink, although as the flies still hovered above me, it was clear that some of the putrid scent still lingered. Only after I had dried myself did the exhaustion

Lady Luck and Me

and humidity hit and all I wanted to do was to lie down and sleep, not that that was likely with the carnage that awaited me back at my lodgings.

And so began the grim task of cleaning my bungalow. I disrobed in an attempt to get the fresh air to my naked, sallow, stinking body and started throwing all of my soiled belongings onto the mini veranda. Once everything had been laid out and I had successfully attracted all the flies in Northern Thailand, I went on an optimistic search for a hose. Now that everything moveable had been removed from the interior, I could see the true extent of my illness. The walls were made of a rattan-like weave on to which my bodily fluids had dried. On second thoughts, the hose wasn't going to cut it, so I went on an even more ambitious mission of hunting down a high powered pressure washer. Ten minutes in and with the midday sun and my weakness taking their toll, I surrendered to the fact that neither were going to be found and reluctantly returned to the bungalow with a bucket of shower water and an ancient scrubbing brush knowing there was a very real possibility of throwing up again. In hindsight, I should have waited until dusk. The combination of effluent flicking all over me, gathering in puddles beneath my feet, all in a seven by five foot south-east Asian sweatbox in mid-summer, was not ideal recovery from a serious illness. Finally, I finished one of the worst clean-up operations of my life and sat back on the veranda; exhausted, watching the flies pick off what I'd missed.

The following day my rent ran out and so had my patience with Pai. My so-called time of contemplation and self-reflection had turned out to be anything but. I slowly made my way back to the same coach park and took my seat amongst the farmers, tourists and goats and started

Contemplating the life of Pai

to make mental preparations for the painful journey back to Chiang Mai. However, not far out of Pai, Lady Luck smiled on me. My increasingly uncomfortable neighbour left her seat and crammed herself into the corner of the coach amongst the goats, gesturing to other passengers that I was foul-smelling and leaving me, for the rest of the journey, to sprawl myself out over the wooden bench. As I settled myself for a much needed snooze, I smiled and thought to myself, ahh . . . an enormous cloud with now a paper-thin silver lining.

If any lessons had been learnt from those strange couple of weeks, they were: do not hike with morbidly obese people, do not wade through pig and human slurry in bare feet, do not have rattan walls in your bathroom, ever, and, just in case, keep an open mind to the possibility that, just maybe, something or someone is watching over you.

Next stop, Chiang Mai train station and Bangkok, then a flight to Koh Samui to hook up with Wee-man again. 'Surely my luck must change, it's got to, hasn't it?' I foolishly thought.

Lady Luck and Me

Rest, relaxation, angry wildlife and organ extractions

'I don't do well with snakes and I can't dance'
Robin Williams

I took the short internal flight from Bangkok to Koh Samui and then a boat to Koh Phangan and, finally, to Haad Tien Bay. Exhausted, and seemingly unexpected, I entered Wee-man's bungalow to find a blond, blue-eyed beauty not a foot from myself, sitting naked on top of a very surprised Wee-man. I greeted them, apologised and backed my way out of the bungalow, leaving my rucksack on his balcony as I went in search of a very cold, very long alcoholic beverage.

I rented a bungalow from Eden Garden Restaurant, not far from Wee-man for 100 baht (£1.50) a day. For that money, I got four walls, a roof, mattress, mosquito net and a fan that didn't work. I also got one of the most spectacular views overlooking the ocean and Haad Yuan Bay whilst being within earshot of the dulcet reggae tones that 'Eden Garden' endlessly played. The positioning was perfect. Eden Gardens was perched on huge rocks that the ocean gently lapped against. It was constructed entirely of bamboo and was basic yet practical in design. It was a long open-sided room with a bar at one end and a stunning view over the ocean at the other. Small, knee-high tables with cushions underneath ran along each raised side with the middle being left clear for late night revelling underneath the psychedelic Bob Marley flags that covered the ceiling. For me, it was the most tranquil and peaceful of all the

Lady Luck and Me

restaurants in both bays and attracted other like-minded travellers from all corners of the globe. It was the kind of restaurant and location where people would go out of their way to say hello to strangers at the bar and invite them to sit at their table to exchange travelling tales, cultural advice and joint-rolling techniques. Weed was readily available under the code name BBQ as were mushroom shakes and, on weekend nights, MDMA in powder or liquid form could also be purchased if a relationship had been forged with the bar staff.

For the holiday-makers, it might have been perceived as cliquey, with the same people whiling away the hours with the same conversation. For the long-termers like me, the familiar faces represented family and provided a sense of unity as we had all found ourselves, for whatever reason, in this remote, beautiful sanctuary, thousands of miles from our homelands, all on a quest to find reason and ourselves. The conversation did regularly become repetitive, but that wasn't due to ideas or subjects being exhausted but more like the hours and hours consuming different varieties of drugs and copious amounts of the quality uncontrolled Chang beer. My fellow long-termers ranged greatly in nationality, age and background but all shared the common interest of self-realisation and mind expansion. From the spiritual, yin-yang tattooed, ex-Israeli army commander to the millionaire Californian Hollywood movie story-boarder, we were all there to escape a life that hadn't made sense. There were about six of us that met up daily for months, eating, drinking, smoking and theorising about the world and also keeping Eden Garden in business during the off-season's quieter months.

Sleeping and eating in the one place naturally helps to build a rapport with the staff and at Eden Garden the

Rest, relaxation, angry wildlife and organ extractions

staff were the owners. Joe and Geng were Thai brothers in their late twenties who spoke little English but greeted me with open arms every time I saw them. Trust and respect was quickly established and, within a month, I had keys to the bar fridge and was free to help myself when I wanted, marking down what I had taken on my tab behind the bar. Both brothers were front-of-house specialists with Joe being the resident DJ and Geng being the sleazy, smiley and ever-hopeful ladies' barman. Unfortunately for Geng, Joe was tall, softly spoken, with long dark hair and attracted women like moths to a flame. Geng was short, almost toothless and manic in his mannerisms, making him the very opposite of Joe. It was like a Thai version of 'Twins' with Joe playing Arnie and Geng playing Danny De Vito. What Geng did have on his side though was unrelenting perseverance and a skin as thick as a rhino's. With sheer tenacity and the help of lethal cocktails and the odd MDMA hit, the weaker willed younger women would often ignore his obvious physical flaws and surrender to his horny charms, more in the hope they would be left alone the next time they visited the restaurant.

The longer I spent at Eden Gardens and the better I got to know Joe and Geng, the more I understood about the local politics and local culture. On the surface, Koh Phangan was a relaxed, laid-back island almost exclusively catering for the tourist industry and the infamous Full Moon Party. Billed as the biggest beach party in the world, scores of all nationalities come to get off their tits on buckets of Samsong whiskey and coke and partake in whatever drugs they can get their hands on, all in a seemingly liberal environment. Regardless of the numerous anti-drug warning signs all over the place, party-goers had a 'safety in numbers' mentality, disbelieving the signs to be true. Uniformed police were scarce but undercover police, who were more abundant, mingled amongst the tourists offering

Lady Luck and Me

drugs in an attempt to entrap them. For the seasoned full moon party-goer, these incognito cops stuck out like sore thumbs. Not only did they dance unbelievably badly but their shell suits, well-groomed hair and shiny black leather shoes could be spotted a mile away. It was only the already wasted and incoherent tourists that fell for their patter and were immediately frog marched off the beach and into an episode of 'Brits Banged up Abroad'.

For the thousands of people who danced and vomited the night away, police numbers and arrests were staggeringly low, considering the Thais' zero tolerance to drugs. One of the reasons for this was the influence of the Thai mafia. Like many places around the world, cartels and organised crime were far more powerful than the local authorities and Koh Phangan was no exception. Many bars all over Koh Phangan sold a variety of drugs which were controlled by the local mafia. The bars took a small cut with the mafia taking the lion's share and paying off the police to turn a blind eye. Only a certain number of arrests were allowed to be made each month, a quota if you like, and they were highly publicised in order for the police to be seen upholding the zero-tolerance drug policy. Not only did the bars pay a percentage for the drugs, they also had to pay the mafia rent just to operate. If these rules weren't adhered to, punishments such as burning down the offending bar were not uncommon and sent a powerful message out to the other bar owners. Naturally, locals didn't speak of any of this to the *farang* (foreigner) in fear of repercussions and it was only through time spent at bars and whisperings in corners that I understood the true extent of the mafia's control over the local economy.

As well as the mafia's influence in the drug and real estate market on Koh Phangan, they also had a far darker interest in the Full Moon Party. Of the thousands of international teenagers who journeyed monthly for the world's best-known party, some were still too young to

Rest, relaxation, angry wildlife and organ extractions

know their limits and drank themselves into a coma, often collapsing on the way back to their rented accommodation. In the dawn light of the following day, it was not unusual to see lifeless bodies scattered all over the beach, lying where they had fallen, much like the aftermath of the D-day landings, I imagine, waves gently lapping against them. These were the lucky ones. These were the ones who the mafia left alone. The unlucky ones were the ones who had keeled over off the beaten track, in the shadows and in the undergrowth. Many of these unfortunates never woke; the ones who did often woke to discover large, painful, crude stitching on their bodies, having been a victim to the lucrative black market demand for body organs. Most had had their organs harvested for a specific buyer, whilst others had their organs extracted just to auction off to the highest bidder. The majority of the ones who lived were too scared or confused to report it to the authorities who would, in any case, be reluctant to help and returned back to their homeland nursing a very probable life-threatening infection and missing a vital organ.

The fourth and final time I took the boat from Haad Yuan to Haad Rin, the Full Moon Party beach, I vowed there wouldn't be a fifth visit. Having just left the shore, the over-crowded long tail boat capsized in the rough seas throwing all of its passengers and their belongings overboard. In the darkness, screams of panic filled the air as terrified people desperately tried to clamber ashore while the waves continued to bear down on them. I have no idea whether everybody made it back, safety was not the skipper's concern, his wallet was and he began rounding people up for a second attempt. The majority of his passengers refused to board again and their requests for a refund fell on deaf ears as he still intended to fulfil his part of the contract. I was meeting a friend at the party and, since I had no other way of communicating with him, hesitantly climbed aboard, alone, hoping this wouldn't be the last journey I made. Thankfully, once around the point,

Lady Luck and Me

the sea subsided and, as we drew closer to the beach, the familiar battle of the bars' sound systems and rows upon rows of people, peeing in the sea amid drunken swimmers, greeted us. Once there, the fourth time was much the same as the previous three except, this time, I was much more aware of the seedier, darker goings on and, as a result, was a lot more restrained and observant than I had been before. For the remainder of the time I was on Koh Phangan, I steered well clear of the Full Moon Parties, determined not to appear on TV behind bars or be the subject of an aspiring amateur surgeon.

You didn't have to be at THE Full Moon Party to enjoy the full moon festivities. Every secluded bay and bar seemed to have their own version and all the ones that I visited were significantly more civilised, safer and enjoyable than the supposed 'world's best beach party'. Having seen enough of the others, I was more than happy to celebrate the month's lunar cycle at Eden Garden with my surrogate family. It was at one of these monthly shin digs, with Eden Garden's dance floor packed, that their generator suddenly failed. I had been enjoying myself for several hours and was, honestly speaking, a little worse for wear yet feeling invincible so offered my services to help Geng get it started again. As I struggled to get my flip flops on, I should have realised that I really wasn't in any fit state to traipse through the night jungle to where the generator was housed. Swaying from side to side and trying to focus by means of one eye, I desperately tried to keep up with the sober Geng and follow his torch's beam through the dark, unfamiliar environment.

The other unnerving thing about this particular journey was that in Geng's other hand was an ancient, rusty pistol. When I enquired as to how and why he was

Rest, relaxation, angry wildlife and organ extractions

holding a pistol, he informed me it was common practice for most bar owners on Koh Phangan to have a gun under the bar to, apparently, protect them against stray, rabid dogs. At the time I thought it was a little unusual but was too arseholed to think about both that and where I was placing my feet.

The generator seemed miles from anywhere and, since it wasn't powering any of the lights in Eden Garden, was in complete darkness. I stood, leaning against a tree watching Geng circle it, scratching his head, torch in one hand, pistol in the other. It was clear Geng didn't know the first thing about generators as he started randomly kicking it. By some miracle, he managed to kick it back to life, startling me enough to lose balance and fall awkwardly into the undergrowth. With the restaurant lights and back on, the generator and surrounding area lit up like a Christmas tree. As I got back to my feet, Geng squealed. Wrapped around the generator was the biggest snake I've ever seen. Its head was the size of a rugby ball with ten-pence pieces for eyes. Its body was the width and texture of a 70-year-old oak tree. It was almost mythical.

Geng, without a second thought, lifted the pistol and, instead of shooting it, hurled it at the legless reptile, turned and bolted back through the jungle and back to the safety of the revived party, arms in the air, screaming like a three-year-old girl, leaving me to face the agitated beast alone. At that moment, I discovered the very best sobriety cure. My eyes had never been sharper or wider, or my bladder weaker. The gun had struck the monster on the side of its head which was now rearing and slowly hissing its way towards me. As it began to unfurl its massive trunk, some power took control of my right hand and, to my horror, began moving it towards my left foot. I, as a conscious

Lady Luck and Me

mind, still had no control whatsoever when it removed my flip-flop from my foot and followed Geng's lead in throwing it at the advancing serpent. Not so thankfully, the years of playing cricket had honed my throwing arm and, as the flip-flop struck the animal directly in the middle of its head, I cursed those once-blessed Saturday afternoons.

The flip-flop did nothing but antagonise it further as it quickened its unfurling, getting closer and closer to what I assumed would be its striking distance. Turning on my bare left foot, I ran towards the music and lights, taking several thick branches in the face as I went. Within a few yards of restaurant safety, adrenaline pumping, I overshot my braking. The force of the necessary emergency stop broke my flip-flop, causing the sole of it to bend double under my foot, catapulting me the final three yards to land in a crumpled mess at the foot of the bar with a bloody face and broken flip-flop that was now half way up my shin. Geng, the little shit, pissed himself laughing whilst the rest of the gathering crowd looked on bemused.

The remainder of the night was spent recounting the man versus beast tale and, as the night got later and later, the snake got bigger and the heroism greater, earning me alpha male points with the men and lustful looks from the women. As my confidence with the evolving story grew, so did the exaggeration, finally landing me in an argument with a huge man from Florida who, ironically, kept several snakes as pets. He couldn't believe I had escaped a 40-foot snake by biting it. I maintained my defence for as long as possible, even quoting Steve Irwin and Crocodile Dundee at one point but, as my epic victory tale swiftly began to

Rest, relaxation, angry wildlife and organ extractions

unravel, I hastily retreated with what little dignity I had left, actively avoiding the American for the rest of the night.

Alas, that wasn't the last I heard of the snake as, two days later, a snake fitting the same gigantic profile raided a neighbouring restaurant in broad daylight, wriggling through terrified customers to the kitchen, snatching a live cat and disappearing down the path with the kitchen staff and their machetes in hot pursuit. They finally caught up with it on the beach and, in full view of horrified sunbathers, hacked it to pieces. From the carcass, they extracted the unfortunate cat, dead, and a single, half-digested flip-flop.

Lady Luck and Me

You wanna fight? Fight me

'I know the human-being and fish can co-exist peacefully.'
George W Bush

Spending time with Wee-man is never time wasted and, as I began to relax in my environment, my sense of belonging strengthened. With Wee-man continually beating me in wing chun rounds and being reassuringly Zen-like with it, my need to study a disciplined martial art was only reinforced. The Muay Thai camp at the summit of a steep hill seemed the sensible place to start.

The open-air gym was perched on the very top of the hill and had stunning panoramic views over both the Haad Tien and Haad Yuan bays. It was a modest set-up, comprising a blood-stained canvas ring, a couple of punch bags and some old rusty barbells but had dedicated and passionate instructors who cared little for *farangs* complaints of exhaustion. Training was split into two sessions per day, with the morning session starting at 7 a.m. with a run through the sand on the beach below followed by technical one-on-one training. By 11 o'clock the heat of the sun made training unbearable so a four-hour lunch was taken where pupils were expected to eat, sleep and be fully rested and prepared for the afternoon session. For me however, it meant an amble back down to the restaurant, a big fat joint and four hours staring at the ocean, prodding bits of my body to see where it didn't hurt.

The afternoon session was sparring and conditioning and it was brutal, especially for the first hour as all my

Lady Luck and Me

body and mind wanted to do was lie down and enjoy the marijuana that was coursing through my veins. Believe me, nothing sobers you up more than being repeatedly punched and kicked in the head. Once my high had been properly beaten out of me, the sparring which is really a game of physical chess became very enjoyable. By six, the armies of mosquitoes, attracted by the scent of sweat, covered any naked torso like a cheap jumper, making any further training futile due to wild arms swinging in all directions in a vain attempt to keep the skin intact.

This routine was followed for six days a week (Sunday being a rest day) for several months. With my past Wing Chun training, wiry body and sports knowledge it seemed I was a natural Muay Thai fighter, so much so that as the months passed, gym-owner Eck was getting more and more excited that he had found a potential world champion on his books, I kid you not. Eck waived my tuition fees, telling me I could pay him back with my winnings further down the line and began intensifying my training. As he was no longer able to compete in sparring with me, he began inviting other fighters to come and spar with me, including a former national heavyweight Thai champion who pummelled me and a Canadian UFC fighter who was by trade a wrestler, a man mountain and terrifying. After a week of handing me my arse the Canadian invited me over to Canada to train in his gym and be part of the Canadian UFC circuit.

As much as I was enjoying these new challenges, I wasn't sharing Eck's vision of Muay Thai world domination and had to put Eck off several times from entering me into shady, unlicensed fights which he called match practice, knowing full well would make a healthy profit whether I won or lost. Eventually, my conscience of training for free

You wanna fight? Fight me

got the better of me and I agreed to fight for money. The first fight was cancelled due to me sustaining a broken foot during training, which only encouraged Eck to train me harder on my upper body strength and fitness by means of working the punch bag for hours on end. By the time my foot had healed, my right elbow had begun to discolour. Eck put it down to the thousands of strikes I had put into the punch bag, reassuring me it was nothing to worry about and I should be getting mentally focussed on the forthcoming bout.

Fight day arrived and, after a brief warm up, my team and I took a chartered boat to the stadium at Haad Rin. Word had got around that there was a promising *farang* fighting against the southern champion and the locals had turned out in force. I was shocked by the sheer numbers and, as I was led through the crowd, Thais clawed at me, bundles of notes exchanging hands with feverish excitement once they saw my height and physique. I was the headline fight and, as I was being rubbed down by my team, I could hear the thousands behind the curtain cheering every fist, elbow, knee and foot that was landed in the warm-up fights. Once the boxing ointment had been applied to my warming muscles I stood up and poked my head through the curtain just in time to see a fighter receive a reverse spinning elbow to his throat, sending him straight to the canvas, convulsing. His bloodied opponent stood over him, obviously concerned as the fallen fighter's trainer clambered over the ring ropes with a biro in his hand. The crowd was going nuts. Even from my distance I could see that his throat had collapsed and he was struggling to breath. To my horror, the trainer removed the ink nib from the biro and plunged the empty plastic casing into the gasping fighter's throat. There was a hush from the crowd

Lady Luck and Me

as they looked on expectantly. Blood spilled down the side of the neck of the now still fighter and then cheers went up as the trainer gave a thumbs up to the referee, signifying the fighter was breathing again. The victor thrust his gloves in the air, much to the delight of the blood-thirsty crowd, as the referee announced him as the winner.

I watched as the downed, unconscious but breathing fighter was carried out of the ring through the inquisitive crowd and past me. I shat myself. I was expecting to get hit a few times but hadn't imagined I would at any stage be fighting for my life. Eck sat me down without saying a word and began massaging my shoulders. As I was wondering whether it was too late to bail, I glanced to my right where my opponent was being prepared by his team. He politely nodded to me and then looked down at his hands which were being wrapped. I noticed that under his wraps, he had a two inch metal strip protruding over his knuckles. My concern was spotted by Eck who smiled at me, and produced a three-inch coconut husk that he strapped over my knuckles. He then reminded me of my training. Always strike down and where possible over or in the eyes. The cut from the husk would split the skin and gush blood over the eyes, therefore blinding my opponent long enough for a fatal strike to be landed to finish the fight. He had taught me that, but at no point had he mentioned that crude knuckle dusters would be worn under the tissue paper-thin boxing gloves.

Thinking it was now a fight to the death rather than a man's game of chess, I wasn't feeling that invincible when the MC introduced me to the crowd. Despite getting rapturous applause and stray hands all over body, I couldn't get the image of the biro sticking out of the previous fighter's throat out of my head. As I entered the ring to

You wanna fight? Fight me

attempt the traditional ritual Wai Khru, I spotted my sister, Charmian with her then-boyfriend seated in the front row. Through email I was aware she was on the same continent but it came as a genuine surprise to see her unmistakable grin beaming back at me. It was a bitter-sweet moment. Great to have family support, but fearful that she might be witness to a tragic family event. Although I did kind of hope that she had been taking careful notes from the fight before, if anyone had to plunge a biro into my throat, I'd prefer it to be my sister rather than an over-excited local.

After getting the crowd into a frenzied state, the bell went and I began dancing around the ring desperately trying to remember the months of training and trying to forget the fate of the previous fighter. My left jab, which Eck told me was world class, landed squarely on my opponent's nose, sending him into the corner, blood spraying everywhere. As I stood over him, watching his eyes glaze over, I heard Eck in the corner shouting 'finish him, finish him'. I hadn't spent six brutal hours a day, six days a week for months for my debut to finish with one punch so I stepped away, not fearing for my life anymore but once again seeing it as a game of chess which I could control and finish at any time I wanted. I chased him around the ring, cheered on by the baying crowd, kicking and punching to devastating effect. My fitness, reach, power and discipline were too much for this so-called 'southern champion' and, as the fourth round bell went, I was happy I had displayed enough skill to finish him that round and walk away unscathed and with a following.

I intended to finish the fight as I had started and manoeuvred myself into a position where I could throw my left jab, and leave him cold on the canvas. I saw his guard drop and threw my biggest left, just as he threw a stray left

Lady Luck and Me

hook, missing my head but catching my over-extended left shoulder. With the adrenaline rushing through my body I didn't feel the impact and carried on, dancing around the ring looking for my next opportunity to finish the fight. Out the corner of my eye, I could see people in the crowd putting their hands to their mouths and heard the vocal support wane. My once-reliable left jab didn't seem to be working, regardless of how many times I tried to throw it, nothing happened causing me to look down and see I no longer had a left arm, just a bony end with my hand slapping my knee. I turned away and parried my opponent's punches and kicks as my mind tried to make sense of what I had just seen.

A towel was thrown in from my corner and the referee positioned himself between me and my opponent, ending the fight, to the crowd's dismay and my opponent's pleasure. Eck and my sister helped me out of the ring and back through the poking and prodding crowd back behind the curtain and waited for the on-site doctor to arrive whilst I was given smelling salts to keep my mind active and the pain at bay. The doctor appeared through the curtains, absolutely arseholed and tried bending my arm back into position before Eck pushed him aside, swearing loudly at him, wrapped me in a towel and bundled me through the disgruntled punters to a waiting car.

With my sister by my side, whispering soothing words in my ear, we drove over rutted roads, down a jungle track arriving at a wooden shack and were welcomed by an elderly Thai man no more than five feet tall. We were ushered into his sparse sitting room and he asked me to sit as he calmly examined my dangling arm, tentatively prodding my exposed shoulder socket. By now the adrenaline had drained from me and a nauseating pain had set in, making

You wanna fight? Fight me

me feel queasy, to put it lightly. He then asked me to stand as he placed his shoulder directly under my armpit, took my dangling hand in his and jumped up and down in a vain attempt to pop my arm back into the shoulder socket. Despite my complaints of pain, he continued bouncing up and down. His or my size was the problem, so he placed a couple of thick books under his feet and tried again, bouncing up and down until finally a click was heard and the pain subsided, not fully but to a bearable level.

Satisfied that the injury had been dealt with, Eck paid him and we made our way back to the beach for the most uncomfortable boat journey of my life. Once back on dry land, arm in a sling, Eck got me drunk, telling me that I had more than enough to make world champion, I just lacked that killing edge which, after a couple more fights, I would have in abundance. He handed me bundles of cash which included my fight fee, side bets and sponsorship money, courtesy of Red Bull, and sent me down the unpaved, tree-rooted track, drunk, wishing I was returning to the arms of a loved one rather than a dark, ant-infested bamboo shack with a severely injured shoulder, the extent of which I was to find out later. My first professional bout hadn't gone the way that those of previous potential world champions had gone but, thank the Lord, I wasn't breathing with the aid of a biro in my throat.

Those who had seen my fight and resulting injury treated me like a rock star and those who hadn't soon heard about it, earning me a legendary reputation in both bays. Even being stoned, drunk or usually both, nothing seemed to take away the dull pain in my left shoulder and as there was no qualified doctor to consult, I bumbled on thinking all it needed was time. A couple of weeks passed with no improvement, and the shoulder pain now came secondary

Lady Luck and Me

to my right elbow. Eck's early diagnosis of severe bruising seemed to be way off the mark, as my entire right arm had inflated to twice the size of my left. The constant throbbing pain made it unbearable to touch but, more alarming, was the unmistakeable stench of rotting flesh. The initial angry red discolouration had now spread from the elbow and was steadily creeping up to my shoulder and down to my fingers. People no longer questioned my arm being in a sling but politely enquired whether I was aware of the colour and the horrific odour that seemed to be exuding from it. I assured them that I was aware of it and, in an attempt to prove that I had it under-control, regularly administered antiseptic iodine along the length of it.

It was clear that it was badly infected but with what no-one knew. Somebody suggested that salt water would help neutralise the pain so, driven by desperation for pain relief, disregarded well intended warnings about the cleanliness of the sea and promptly headed down to the shore, carefully removing my sling before gingerly wading into the water. With my left arm held tightly across my chest and my inflamed, stinking right arm dangling by my side, I laid down on my back, faced the sky and began kicking my legs, trying to forget the pain in both my upper limbs. It seemed to work. Encouraged by the pain relief for the first time in days, I began kicking harder, enjoying the painless freedom and the warm sun on my face. The first time I raised my head to see how far from the shore I was, the most implausible event occurred. A shoal of flying fish, which wasn't uncommon, passed me by, and, as I was admiring just how close they had come, a rogue stray one emerged a foot from me, flying headfirst into my forehead. I kid you not. From the ensuing shock, I consumed a large mouthful of salty sea water which in

You wanna fight? Fight me

turn panicked me further; causing both arms to come away from their moorings as I tried to regain buoyancy, sending searing pain through the rest of my body.

As I attempted the 180 degree turn back to shore, I felt a small tug on my flailing right foot. The sensation was the equivalent to a hand shake but, as my right foot went immediately cold, I knew it was more sinister than a savage piece of seaweed. My mind went into overdrive, irrationally thinking I had been attacked by a shark and that the blood in the water would attract other sharks, giving me, in my mind, seconds before getting ripped apart. By now, both arms and both legs worked frantically to get me back to the shore as quickly as possible, not thinking or feeling the damage in either of my top two limbs. I clambered out of the water, onto the shore and looked down at my right foot. My toes were barely visible beneath the heavy tide of blood and, whilst the pain had returned to my arm and shoulder in spades, my foot remained ominously pain free. The rapidly darkening sand around my foot indicated I was losing blood, fast. I knew I was in trouble.

With my arms stationed in their original pre-ocean positions, I hobbled up the beach and along the rickety, wooden walkway, hoping I would make it back to Eden Gardens before the combination of the three injuries got the better of me. Roughly 40 yards from the restaurant, I was spotted by Geng who, on seeing the blood staining everything around me, came rushing down just in time for me to collapse in front of him. With the help of another waiter, I was carried into the restaurant where they crudely bandaged my foot with an industrial-sized plastic bin-bag. Shock must have set in by then, as the 15-minute boat journey around to Haad Rin seemed to take seconds. I was carried by Geng and an equally concerned taxi driver to his

Lady Luck and Me

car and then driven a short distance to the nearest health clinic.

On entering, I was quickly ushered through to a plastic-covered table in a back room. The plastic bag was removed with its bloody contents cascading over the tiled floor. As the female proprietor's hand covered her mouth in horror and Geng gagged, I knew it wasn't good. After a brief conversation in Thai, Geng turned and told me there wasn't time to get to a doctor at the hospital in Thong Sala and she would have to stitch it then and there before more blood was lost. I was told to lie back, not look and given a bit of old rope to bite down on. The local anaesthetic which was injected into my foot sprayed everywhere rendering it absolutely useless. Two attempts later and with puddles of blood now forming under the table, Geng pulled up a chair next to the table, held my hand and informed me the wound required stitches inside the foot before the skin covering it could be stitched. For the next 30 minutes, as the needle weaved in and out of the exposed tissue, tears rolled down my cheeks. I vaguely remember hearing Geng yelp a couple of times as I crushed his hand whilst he was holding me down. By the end of it, I was exhausted and a little delirious and walked out on crutches and in the possession of weapons-grade pain-killers. Geng walked out with a blood-soaked T-shirt and a bandaged hand. Payment for the medic's services was paid by Geng to be put on my tab at Eden Garden. Now, the dull ache in my shoulder had become tertiary to my right foot and right arm.

It was only after several conversations with local fisherman and experienced scuba-divers that I learnt that an aggressive, territorial Trigger fish was the most probable explanation for my injury. Although rare and extremely unlucky that suggestion has yet to be bettered. To this day,

You wanna fight? Fight me

I actively avoid large bodies of water, including the bath, and even refuse to eat any sea-dwelling creatures, such is my suspicion of them.

Lady Luck and Me

The Man from Uncle

*'Just as a a candle cannot burn without fire,
men cannot live without a spiritual life'*
Buddha

I didn't accompany Geng to the generator again and spent the rest of my time at Eden Gardens just as a patron. The weeks passed and my surrogate family of long-termers became fewer and fewer until I was spending time either training at the gym or talking to people who were only staying a night or two. Just when I was thinking it was time to move on, Joe and Geng's uncle moved in to one of the bungalows. Immediately we connected. He was a small, wiry but incredibly youthful 50-odd-year-old man who had bags of energy and wisdom to spare. He had spent several years serving as a travelling Buddhist monk, living off the occasional alms in order to meditate for hours on end, deep within Thailand's jungles. But, along with his insightful wisdom and spiritual awareness, he had a hardness about him. Since he had left his spiritual path he had successfully set up and run a couple of businesses but had run into problems with the local mafia, forcing him to flee to the islands and stay incognito with his nieces.

The time I wasn't training, I was with Uncle, staring at the stunning view, talking until the early hours about spiritual laws, the ego and realisation of the self. Despite these fascinating and formative conversations, I'm still not entirely sure that Uncle was indeed Joe and Geng's authentic uncle or whether that was a generic word used for elders. What is for sure though is that when Uncle told Joe or Geng to do something, they did it, no questions asked.

Lady Luck and Me

The second uneasy detail is that Uncle knew a disturbing amount about the local mafia and how they operated. His voice became harsh and authoritative if he thought anyone was misbehaving or disrespecting and, although he didn't drink and only chain-smoked weed, it did nothing to quell his volatile temper.

Prior to meeting and spending time with Uncle, I had always questioned how realistic it was to be spiritually minded without being alienated and ostracised by society. Uncle managed it simply by respecting himself and respecting the code by which he lived and to hell with anyone who disagreed with his choice of path. It sounds so simple and obvious but it was one of the most understated yet powerful lessons I have learnt with regards to judging others and their choices. To this day, I'm sure Lady Luck delayed my departure from Koh Phangan just so I could spend valuable time with Uncle. The timing and relevance of our conversations had a profound effect on me understanding the practicality of living more spiritually in an ever-increasingly materialistic world.

Not long before I left, Uncle offered to teach and show me what he had learnt by accompanying him back into mother nature serving, as he called it, 'an informal apprenticeship'. As much as I was tempted, I had plans and other dreams to fulfil so politely declined. I still get emails from Uncle and he did return to the Thai jungles not long after I left and, still, he continues to enlighten and inspire. I have written this because I have always vowed to myself that, if I ever did write a memoir, I would acknowledge the impact Uncle had in my spiritual development and write about it, in recognition of its importance.

Oh no you're not . . .

'You shall not pass!'
Gandalf

It was clear that the Gods wanted me to move on from Koh Phangan which, thankfully, I had arranged prior to my shoulder injury. I had had an email interview with the head monk at a Shaolin monastery in eastern China and he had accepted me on the condition that I was there to spiritually evolve through martial arts discipline. I intended to spend a year learning practical kung fu, traditional Chinese medicine and meditation. In spite of the recent physical set-backs, I had my visa in my passport and was looking forward to the Chinese challenge ahead of me. My slinged left arm, infected, poisoned right arm and bandaged right foot, were not going to stand in the way of my determined spiritual and physical progression. A week after my aquatic attack and with the help of both legal and illegal painkillers, I made my preparations to finally leave the 'quartz island'.

With only one of my limbs working at full capacity, the ordeal of packing my belongings into my trusty rucksack was truly exhausting and, even in the early morning sun, left me saturated in sweat and in need of a final shower. I put a waterproof plastic bag over my bandaged foot and hopped to the shower. Again, the challenge of showering without causing further damage took its toll and, after the shower had been turned off, I lent on the ceramic basin to recover and regain composure before hauling my rucksack down to the beach and waiting taxi boat. All of a sudden, the basin gave way, crashing on to my bagged, injured foot beneath,

Lady Luck and Me

causing me more pain but, more importantly, splitting the basin lengthways in two. Having already paid my bill and fighting against the clock, I decided to reattach the broken sink back onto its failing fittings and email Eden Gardens at a future date, explaining what had happened.

Satisfied it was as secure as possible; I pirouetted to get my shower gel and caught my buttock millimetres from my arsehole on the exposed razor-sharp ceramic corner, ripping a deep, two-inch gash which immediately began spurting blood on the white-tiled walls. The painful memory of my trip to the medical clinic a couple of days earlier was still fresh in my mind and I was not about to let another complete stranger lie me down, open up my arse cheeks and stitch me back together. Just imagine if they stitched the wrong hole! The image was enough to make me feel queasy, let alone actually making it a reality, so tentatively and painfully stuffed my new wound with bundles of toilet paper. By the time I had washed the blood off the surrounding tiles, a red, crimson stain had already seeped through my khaki shorts.

The boat journey around the point on choppy seas was horribly awkward and as my arse wound got pounded by the unforgiving wooden bench on which I was seated, I did my best to keep my mind off the several areas of pain by reflecting on the week. There was little doubt that Lady Luck had punished me for overstaying my welcome by exponentially increasing my injury list. To China I was to take, a still swollen dislocated/broken shoulder, a bruised forehead, an infected right arm, a heavily stitched right foot and now a worryingly deep laceration next to my arsehole. I was sure I had lost weight but was unable to determine whether that was through lack of food intake or significant

Oh no you're not . . .

blood loss. Hardly the best preparation for what was sure to be a gruelling experience in China.

I left the aeroplane's cleaner with his work cut out and limped through the airport to get a taxi to Koh San Road and my one night's accommodation. Maybe the altitude was to blame but, by the time I had dumped my rucksack in an overpriced dingy hotel, the pain in my inflamed right arm was driving me to distraction and, after enquiring at the front desk, I followed directions to seek professional medical advice. I must have been a sorry sight when I staggered into the whitewashed medical clinic; they must have wondered where to start on me. I refused help for my foot and shoulder and neglected to tell them about my leaking arse, making my right arm the priority and purpose of my visit.

The stench hit the two of them like an aromatic kosh making them recoil and quickly reach for masks which they placed over their nose and mouth. They prodded the length of my arm, gauging my howls as they went. They had a brief discussion in Thai and turned to tell me I had two tropical abscesses on my arm that needed cutting out immediately otherwise there would be a strong chance I would succumb to septicaemia which, they assured me, could be fatal in the humid climate. Not caring what they did as long as it alleviated the pain, I granted them permission to do whatever was necessary.

This time, a cork was placed between my teeth as they injected me at several points along my arm in what seemed like a haphazard fashion, numbing the arm and thankfully the pain. I watched as they went about their work, carving out yellowy green pus which seemed to go right down to the bone. When blood started to run freely, they

Lady Luck and Me

were happy they had extracted the infection. Half an hour later and with dozens of blood soaked gauzes scattered all around the place, they packed the two holes with antiseptic wadding and bandaged my arm. For a small extra fee they asked whether I would like the bacteria to be sent away for analysis. I agreed, curious to discover what had caused the excruciating pain that I had endured for weeks and jotted down my email address. After wholeheartedly thanking them, I paid the extortionate bill and left with two weeks' worth of antibiotics and more weapons-grade painkillers. It was over and I felt I had been born again, returning to my hotel on a high, and to a long, much-needed sleep.

The following day, the swelling and stench in my arm had subsided, although my shoulder, foot and arse kept up their unrelenting nagging pain, with my bottom still leaking blood. I arrived at the airport three hours before my flight to China departed. Although not in the best of shape, I was eager to leave Thailand and start afresh in the clean mountainous air of the Chinese monastery. On presenting my ticket to the smiley desk clerk, I began frantically searching for my misplaced wallet. With the contents of my rucksack strewn all over the airport floor, I discovered I didn't have my wallet, having lost it somewhere between Koh San Road and the airport. Resembling an extra out of Dawn of the Dead, I lurched my way back out of the airport, dragging my rucksack behind me to retrace my steps, realising the chances of coming across it were slim at best. The loose bundle of notes in my pocket was just enough to get the bus back to Koh San Road and, with the clock still against me, I huffed and puffed my way to the small taxi window.

To my astonishment, they had my wallet and even more astonishing, was that it was intact with cash, cards and

Oh no you're not . . .

emergency numbers. I tipped the same driver handsomely for his honesty and asked him again to take me back to the airport, promising him double if he got me there in record time. He lived up to his end of the deal with some truly impressive, highly illegal driving, getting me to the airport with minutes to spare. Pissing sweat and weeping blood from my arse, I returned to the flight desk, only to be told that it had just closed. In spite of my pleas and tales of woe, the still smiley clerk informed me there was nothing she could do apart from offering me extortionately priced ticket for the following day. As I broke down and contemplated this, it dawned on me to heed the many signs Lady Luck had sent me. So, physically weak, mentally broken and psychologically scarred, I reluctantly made the decision to purchase a ticket home, back to Blighty.

I returned home dangerously anaemic and, according to the doctor whom I saw soon after my return, was lucky to be alive. To say the whole experience had been character building would be an understatement. I had learnt more about myself in those final few weeks than I had the previous few years. My pain threshold was now at epic heights, my spiritual development had profoundly deepened, and the path ahead of me had never looked more uncertain.

Lady Luck and Me

World's end

> *'There is darkness there that never sleeps.'*
> J.R.R. Tolkien

Armed with a working holiday visa and friends to initially lodge with, New Zealand was my next port of call. Maybe the laid-back, end of the world mentality would help me realise my potential and path. Tom and Bex, my friends from Devon, had relocated there and had managed to rent a top-floor apartment in one of Takapuna's most exclusive streets. They shared the building with your stereotypical surfer types who regularly threw barbeques on the large lawn at the front, much to the annoyance of the street's other residents who felt the house, the parties and low-income youths were not in keeping with the postcode. Such was their resentment, Tom, Bex and the rest of the building had come to know the local police officers well due to the regularity of the street's phone calls to them. What added fuel to the neighbour's fire was the open-house policy they had adopted and, often, people from all walks of life and in all sorts of states came and went, usually with thumping sound systems in battered old cars. For the first week, I sofa surfed, drank beer on the front lawn and played painful football with my healed but heavily scarred fish-bitten foot, on the pristine beach directly next to the house. It was a great introduction to New Zealand and, although only there for a week, I felt more at home than I had done for some time.

It was during the second week that Keef arrived, having spent a debauched month in Thailand. Despite Keef being part of the original Devon crew and us having

Lady Luck and Me

mutual friends, I knew very little of the man himself. His reputation preceded him and his reputation was not good. He had been expelled from every school he had attended due to having a problem with authority and, since he had moved to Bristol to escape the trappings of a farming background, had become a well-known liability on the party scene. I had met him briefly on a few of my Bristol nights out and, apart from him being incoherently legless, he had a knack of rubbing people up the wrong way.

From those first impressions, we were chalk and cheese. I was massively insecure and only cared what people thought of me, whereas Keef was over confident and didn't give two shits what people thought of him. So much so, it wasn't uncommon to hear through the grapevine that Keef had over done the booze and had shat himself, stuffed his soiled pants in a cistern and then had carried on partying, fully aware it was no secret, until the doorman found the toilet overflowing and automatically came looking for Keef. But Keef was a good-looking man and no fool, and with his 'don't give a shit' attitude, managed to bag his fair share of women, usually over a wheelie bin or in a phone box, much to the boyfriend's anger and the woman's post-morning shame. With Keef coming to New Zealand, I was a little apprehensive.

I accompanied Tom to the airport to pick Keef up and, on the journey there, Tom told me of Bex's parents taking Keef to court for driving a motorbike through their family house and then getting on the roof and shitting down the chimney, much to the disbelief of the people who were sitting around the fireplace. My apprehension grew. When Keef finally came through the arrivals gate, I was stunned at the size of him. From being a relatively svelte person in Bristol, he was now a waddling, middle-

World's end

aged, pasty, fat man. The tentative, awkward hug, slurred speech and whisky fumes which radiated from him clearly indicated that he had started holidaying on the flight over. Not only that, it seemed that he was struggling to see, not through inebriation but some sort of medical condition that had forced his eyes to close and weep a gooey white/green substance. All in all, I was really quite glad that I didn't have to sit next to him on the journey back.

The following week, I monitored Keef cautiously, wary of his reputation and of catching whatever it was that was making Keef progressively blind. By the end of the week, the decision to seek professional medical advice had been forced upon him as his eyes were now in a permanent state of closure, leaking more fluid and giving the impression that he had been hoofed in each eye by a Grand National winner. On the Saturday morning, Tom drove him to the nearest health clinic and returned an hour later beaming from ear to ear. By the time Keef had struggled to climb out of the car, Tom had gleefully told as many people, stranger's included, that Keef had contracted a bad dose of chlamydia of the eyes and had been lectured by a somewhat confused and revolted young female doctor about the risks of unprotected sex and went so far as to give Keef a practical demonstration with a rubber cock of how to apply a condom. She also suggested that if he continued to pursue his bizarre fetish he should think about wearing tight fitting swimming goggles. Keef remained surprisingly sheepish during the two-week antibiotic course and only started to come back to life when his vision returned.

It was at one of the many front lawn parties that Tom introduced us to Carl, a Kiwi who, as luck would have it, was starting up his own carpentry business and was looking to recruit chippies. Now, Tom and I had worked

Lady Luck and Me

as labourers and Tom had an interest in boat building and Keef had worked on a farm but in no way were we even remotely qualified or experienced to masquerade as chippies. However, 24 hours later, that's exactly what we were doing. Overnight, I had been promoted from a labourer straight to a skilled worker, earning three times as much per hour than I had doing any other previous job. Belts dangled with an assortment of objects that we apparently needed to carry out our skilled work. The cost of our equipment would come out of our first pay check which Carl would 'sort' out.

Our first job was to weatherboard and erect the interior walls of an architect's new build, multi-million dollar house. From the off, it was confirmed that I was not the messiah as my carpentry skills were absolutely atrocious and, in all honesty, a bit of a safety risk to myself and anyone in the vicinity. I was quickly given any job that didn't require me using anything with a cutting edge. I was no more than a glorified, overpaid labourer again. As I struggled to get the least bit enthused Tom and Keef took to it well, each keeping in character with the way they went about their work. Tom was methodical and over-cautious whereas Keef's expensive and rapid trial and error approach got the job done but made costs rocket to the increasing concern of the owner.

By the end of the first month, I was going backwards in my learning and had begun entertaining myself by drawing cocks wherever I could and attempting to break records for the frequency and length of my cigarette breaks. Nonetheless, I was still getting paid for my efforts and, finally, Keef and I had enough to move out of Tom and Bex's front room and rent an apartment with Ed, a Devon friend who had arrived a couple of months earlier, a few streets away. Ed, although agreeing to move in with us, had been a bit of a Scarlet Pimpernel since we had arrived and had seduced a Kiwi girl with outrageous claims that he was a professional surfer and had pretty much moved in with her over the harbour bridge in Auckland.

I had known Ed a lot longer than Keef and the prospect of sharing with Keef alone still concerned me a little. The apartment was the middle one of three in its own road and came completely unfurnished. After Carl had taken his 'share' for our newly acquired equipment out of our pay cheque, we were left with more than enough to adequately furnish our flat and eat like kings for the next month. Well, that's what we should have done. Instead, we went to the bottle shop and bought enough booze to keep an army of raging alcoholics happy for a month and the party shop to buy several of the legal party pills aptly named 'Big E'. We also bought the local paper. We hurried back to our empty bungalow like two school girls, ready to drink ourselves into oblivion and hopefully wake up for work on Monday morning. After the first couple of beers, our eagerness to try these legal pills got the better of us and so, with both of us having had our fair share of pills in the past, agreed to double drop on the naïve assumption that they certainly wouldn't be any more potent than the numerous illegal ones we had consumed back in the UK.

Whilst we waited for these so-called pills to kick in, we drank, smoked and flicked through the local paper looking for cheap furniture. It wasn't long before our search for furniture was forgotten as our search for escorts in the back pages had taken over. Through blurred vision and with the pills beginning to seriously affect our heart rate, Keef phoned through and booked two to come round as I rolled around on the bare carpet unable to contain my drug

Lady Luck and Me

induced giggling fit. By the time they arrived and the pimp had taken the last of our money, the pills had got the better of us. There was no giggling by this point, only the odd dribble, rolling eyes and an enthusiastic attempt to chew through our cheeks from the inside out.

The two bemused semi-attractive women began to warm to us, clearly sensing we were in no fit state to have sex and initiated the most non-sexual conversation imaginable, desperately hoping to get through the hour without having to remove a single piece of clothing. By the time mine had led me into the bedroom, we were deep in conversation about Confucian Rule and Tao of Bruce Lee. I was halfway through my Desiderata recital when the pimp knocked on the door, loudly announcing to the street that our time was up and could the ladies please come out. I didn't let my lady leave until she had heard the entirety of my recital and had given me pointers on how I could improve it. I was battered.

Both bedroom doors opened simultaneously, with Keef emerging arguing with his lady that bananas have a higher vitamin C content than oranges do. Keef was also clearly battered. As the door closed behind them, Keef and I turned to each other and discussed until dawn how it had been one of the strangest encounters either of us had ever had. The pills had spanked our bottoms and for the following day and night, had left us with the worst come down known to man. When Sunday night came around, we were penniless and still living in an unfurnished flat. That was the first of many distinctly unique experiences that I had, living with Keef in that bungalow and, in the

World's end

coming months, grew very fond of him and his terrier-like loyalty.

Months went past with Keef and I living together whilst Ed remained truly elusive, occasionally popping up with partner in tow for celebratory drinks of one kind or another. As a result, Keef and I formed a middle-aged couple, with me wearing the trousers and doing very little around the flat as Keef, sometimes wearing an apron, would do the cleaning, cooking, shopping, washing and bill paying, all without a word of complaint. For the alpha male, which Keef is, it was extraordinary to witness him display such domestic instincts. While he toiled away over the cooker or on his hands and knees in the bathroom, I was guiltily sitting on the sofa, drinking and chain smoking, perfecting Tiger Woods on the Playstation. Keef and Tom might dispute this (which they have no right to) but I left New Zealand as Takapuna's Tiger Woods champion and I'll dine out on that for years to come.

Once Keef had done the daily household chores, our time was divided between the Playstation and cigarette breaks on the balcony outside the living room. As all three houses had the same set up, it wasn't uncommon to see at least one neighbour doing the same. The occupants of all three houses shared the same age bracket, and soon, we were popping into to each other's houses as if we all shared the one house. On our left lived two young couples, Kate, a thin blonde who was dating Callum, an obese Kiwi shop-fitter with an unhealthy obsession for porn and marijuana. The other couple was Justin, a relatively nondescript, young professional who was backed by Daddy's money and who was in a relationship with Sunshine, a Kiwi/Pilipino who had a mouth like a dirty pirate. She was doll-like in size but perfectly proportioned and beautiful. Keef, having

Lady Luck and Me

developed a liking for Oriental women from his time in Thailand, thought Christmas had come. I felt sorry for Justin when Keef was introduced to Sunshine; with Keef's tenacity it was only going to be a matter of time before poor Justin was replaced.

Sure enough, Keef drew Sunshine's attention by having sex with her younger sister at a fancy dress party we hosted and, a month after Keef and Sunshine had met, Justin was at the top of the road loading the remainder of his possessions into the back of a taxi, never to be seen again. The newly formed couple flitted between the houses, regularly screaming at each other before disappearing into one of their bedrooms to have loud, angry sex. At such times, Tiger Woods was paused and one, maybe two, cigarettes were smoked before the animalist grunts subsided and it was safe to once again reposition back in front of the TV. After particularly brutal nights drinking, I was often woken by the Sunshine's ear-piercing expletives, reprimanding Keef for not being able to master his own bladder. To say their relationship was volatile would be as big an understatement as saying Russell Brand is a slightly irritating, talentless twat. Justin shouldn't feel too cheated though as, against everyone's wildest expectations, Keef and Sunshine travelled and moved to London together; their relationship lasting a truly gob-smacking six years.

Whilst all this was going on with the house on the left, our neighbours to the right had acquired a stunning 23-year-old Danish, dental hygienist named Majbritt as a flatmate. She had been working in clinics around the area and, now that she had a longer term contract, had moved nearer her work. She had been the flag bearer of the Copenhagen Festival so, when she dropped in on one of her nights out, made up and in her full regalia, my knees

World's end

went weak. As all the drama seemed to unfold around me, I didn't see the need to venture out and seek it elsewhere, so stayed firmly rooted on the sofa, playing more Tiger Woods, drinking and smoking an unhealthy amount of weed, courtesy of Callum and his contacts.

Majbritt and I had our first proper conversation late one night when she was drunk and I was struggling to stand, let alone speak. The following day, she came round to apologise for her behaviour, which I gracefully accepted without having any recollection of a single word that had been spoken. She thanked me for listening so intently and coyly asked whether we could have more conversations in the future. Again, I accepted, not believing my luck but also with a sizeable dilemma on my hands. She had met me and had had this 'conversation' with me when I was absolutely battered. My tiny brain then convinced me that every time I spoke to her, I had to be battered, giving me the irrational fear that if I spoke to her sober she wouldn't like me.

It was during one of the early dates that she told me of a troublesome relationship she had had in the past with a boyfriend who had started taking drugs behind her back until their relationship fell apart, leaving her devastated and mistrustful of all drugs and their users. I was in too deep by the time she told me. I had two choices: one, confess, get a slap and confirm her suspicions that all drug users are liars and never talk to her again; or two, don't tell her, stay stoned, keep dating and pray she would never find out. Against my noble, righteous self's wishes, I went for the easy option and continued bumbling through conversations either monosyllabically or over-compensating by incessantly speaking bollocks. Nevertheless, our relationship flourished

Lady Luck and Me

and, soon, we were saving for transport to drive around the country in.

Meanwhile, tempers at work were flaring, in particular between Keef and Carl. Carl had begun to miss days to 'source' more work or, when he did turn up, did very little to help a fast learning Keef get projects done on time. In Carls' absence, Keef had taken it upon himself to talk to contractors and get a far better insight into how much Carl was being paid for Keef and Tom's work which certainly didn't equate to what we were all taking home at the end of each week. Carl justified his seemingly low wages by reminding Keef that he paid the petrol to get us from job to job. After some hasty mental arithmetic was done by Keef, it seemed Carl was collectively charging us $1200 a week for the privilege. After vile words were exchanged, all form of friendship or professionalism broke down, leading to Keef and Carl not being allowed in the same room together. We agreed to finish the job we were doing and look for similar employment elsewhere.

The job that we were currently involved in was building the wooden framework for 10 cinemas in Sylvia Park, South Auckland. At the time, it was the biggest Westfield in the Southern hemisphere and millions had been invested in it. Even with all that money and mega brain power, no-one had thought about getting the giant screens into the auditoriums until a cleaner on his cigarette break questioned the foreman on how they were going to do it. The resulting chaos of rapid demolition and rebuilding kept us in the job for a further unexpected month, perfectly ending just before Majbritt's and my adventure began. Once the cinemas were recompleted, all ties with Carl were severed, leaving Tom and Keef to hack around Auckland working unsupervised and me to gratefully escape the

World's end

building trade straight into a two-month travelling holiday with a girlfriend that still didn't know I had to be stoned to talk to her.

With heavy, hungover heads, we waved goodbye to the incestuous fold which we had been living in and embarked on our two-month road trip in a newly purchased, beaten up, sixth hand, red Mitsubishi van. Within the first hour of being on the road, my mind had already turned to how I was going to hide away so I could roll a funny cigarette and be back to the Ben she knew. In the weeks ahead, increasingly complicated plans were devised in order for me to escape and feed my paranoia. I felt I would surely be caught by her sooner or later and left with a horribly awkward conversation and very complicated aftermath but, thankfully, by means of a healthy, part-criminal mind I evaded being caught for far longer than I had expected. It wasn't until we got to Wellington at the most southerly point of the North Island that I was eventually rumbled.

One morning, while we were staying in a caravan park/campsite, Majbritt left the van and myself, towel in hand, for her morning shower. On a journey like ours, time alone was rare and so opportunities to smoke and become 'Ben' again were highly sought after. Putting the van between myself and the shower block, I sat down out of view and hastily rolled the first doobie of the day. With the morning sun on my face and an enormous inhale, I closed my eyes and felt the drug tickle my morning brain only to be interrupted by Majbritt, firstly telling me that the cleaner was cleaning the showers, and then question what the fuck I was doing. I spluttered I was having a cigarette, only to be betrayed by my legs which gave way as I attempted to stand, forcing an immediate grovelling apology. As the organic chemicals got stuck into my head I

Lady Luck and Me

watched her lips move as she berated me, the drug and my irresponsible intention of driving. We sat in silence for the next three hours until she was satisfied that the drug had worn off and I was sober enough to drive. I thought it best not to tell that her 90 percent of the time she had known me and 95 percent of the time that I had been driving, I had been under its carefree influence. Time would tell whether she still liked the 'real Ben'.

I drove as Majbritt had yet to learn and, whilst she stared out of the window or slept, I was trying to hatch a new plan to get the last remnants of the smuggled marijuana into my body. As Lady Luck would have it, I inadvertently threw the weed out along with the road maps resulting in untold anxiety being both driver and regular dope user.

New Zealand is, without question, one of the most beautiful places I have ever been to, never failing to impress with its constantly changing, awe-inspiring scenery. We travelled to all the main cities and notable landmarks around both the North and South Island, sticking, where we could, to the coastal roads. With the exception of a couple of enormous rows, we had a thoroughly good time. A week later than planned, we made it to Christchurch to get a couple of badly needed nights' sleep in a conventional bed before spending a few days very much alone, miles from anywhere in 'Lord of the Rings' country.

The first days driving into the barren hinterlands had gone well. We had, as planned, found ourselves very much lost and, since the last two hours had been spent following the van's dying headlights, we had no idea of where we had come from or how to get back to it. But we had a spare tyre and all necessary equipment to tackle pretty much any eventuality and so pulled off the track

World's end

we were on and parked on what looked like a lay-by. We hadn't seen any other traffic for the past four hours so we were confident we wouldn't be moved on during the night and settled in. Just like on Dartmoor, it seemed that the weather was capable of changing at a dramatic speed. An hour after first hearing a light breeze outside, there was now a gale force wind with marble-sized hailstones rocking the van from side to side, resulting in both of us experiencing serious nausea. The plummeting temperature had also forced us to wear most of our clothes under the duvet in order to keep us functioning as normally as possible. A couple of hours into mother-nature's onslaught, Majbritt complained of abdomen pains too serious to be sea-sickness symptoms. She had told me on one of our earlier dates that she had been born with one defunct kidney and had had it removed when she was child, leaving her with only one working one. The pain she was experiencing, I reassured her, was nothing more serious than what I was suffering and, dismissively, told her to lie back, wait for the storm to pass and try and get some sleep, which I then duly did.

I woke not long after, to the still-howling gale, my breath visible in front of my face and the silhouette of Majbritt gently rocking and sobbing in the corner. I feared now that, maybe, my earlier advice was not so sound. Her stomach pains had grown considerably worse and she was now struggling to find any position which would ease the pain. Thinking that something, very probably, was wrong, I braved the elements and carefully bundled her into the passenger seat. With the wind and rain lashing at the van, the weak headlights made very little impact in the darkness so it wasn't until I came face to face with a wall of rock that I realised that we had been parked at the entrance of a disused quarry. Only as I was making my three-point turn

Lady Luck and Me

did I see the huge drop a foot next to us, causing me to thank Lady Luck that neither of us had needed the toilet during our brief stay.

Gladly, Majbritt next to me was blissfully unaware of our near-death experience as some sort of fever had her in a foetal position, shivering uncontrollably. I didn't have time to dwell on what might have been and slowly crawled back out of the quarry and back onto a sealed road, still having no recollection of which direction we had come. I turned and drove and drove until, finally, the weather subsided and cleared just as dawn broke. It seemed that we had taken a small detour but, luckily, we were heading in the direction of Christchurch and, according to a road sign, should be there around lunchtime, good fortune permitting.

After a close fuel scare and a couple of unmissable photo opportunities taken while Majbritt was slipping in and out of consciousness, we were in Christchurch. Well, I was in Christchurch, Majbritt was in her own dark world, babbling in tongues. I was exhausted after the drive but kept awake by the very real concern that Majbritt looked as though she was dying. Our little van hurtled around Christchurch, my eyes peeled for a hospital. Finally, and just as Majbritt's breathing had become dangerously shallow, I saw the welcoming signposts of a hospital nearby. Following the car park directions, I emergency stopped outside the ambulance entrance and ran in for medical assistance, leaving Majbritt slumped against the passenger window. With not a soul in sight, I grabbed a stray wheelchair and ran back out to the van to help Majbritt into it. Back I went through the doors and wheeled her like a man possessed down a long empty corridor, until I eventually came across a receptionist sitting at her desk. It took me a couple of

World's end

minutes to catch my breath sufficiently enough to be able to explain the situation, only to be told by the calm, still-seated receptionist that this was a maternity hospital and they could do nothing to help. She told me that the hospital we needed was a kilometre further down the street and that I could not park my van where I had if I came again, otherwise it might be clamped. I took her warning badly and, as she reached for the phone to call security, I was off back down the corridor, through the doors, tipping Majbritt back into the passenger seat and sending the wheelchair rolling across the car park. The last speed bump out of the car park was particularly ferocious, catapulting both our heads into the van's low roof. Majbritt, thankfully, was still blissfully unaware of the goings-on and had now turned a rather worrying white/grey colour.

The reception at the second hospital was a lot more professional and, once I had explained the seriousness of the situation to an anxious looking nurse, Majbritt was whisked off through the doors with a small, white-coated army following her. The awful coffee which the sympathetic nurse gave me did little to suppress my worries and only increased my heart rate when she politely enquired if I had paid for car parking otherwise, she said, I was likely to be clamped.

Majbritt did indeed have a serious kidney infection and, according to the specialist, was lucky to be alive. She spent the next 10 days or so under the watchful eye of the professionals and, in order for me to be close to the hospital for visiting hours, I stayed at the nearest hotel which just happened to have a double bed, an en-suite bathroom, Sky TV and a mini bar. The hotel owner was even kind enough to throw in a free spa once I had told him of our terrible episode. I wouldn't say I discouraged the doctors to

Lady Luck and Me

let Majbritt go early but I might have leaned on Majbritt to stay there an extra night as I struggled to come to terms with spending a night in the van after this luxury.

My expensive stay and Majbritt's health brought a premature end to our road trip, so we hot-wheeled as quickly as we could back to Takapuna, staying in far from desirable accommodation on the way. To say I didn't have pangs of guilt for living like a king whilst she lay in a hospital bed would be a lie and, if I had saved some of the money, then we wouldn't have had to resort to putting on flea bite cream in the mornings.

We kept the van for a short while after returning and then sold it to another ambitious wide-eyed couple. With our visas running out and my shoulder popping out with much more frequency, the decision to return to the UK for surgery was made. Majbritt was to fly home to Denmark first and then come and join me at Mum's for my rehabilitation. Having said teary goodbyes, I sat waiting for the plane to depart, sad to be leaving New Zealand but happy I had made some life-long memories and life-long friends. Now that I was heading back home, I needed to get serious, settle down and get some sort of career going. My travelling days, for the moment at least, were suspended.

Who needs love when....?

'This love is hardcore. Let's make it soft porn'
Arzum Uzun

Settling back in Blighty was difficult. I was living with my mother and sister in a small flat in Guildford and housebound after my shoulder surgery, which I had done privately a couple of weeks after returning. Apart from the heavy-duty painkillers, wine was the other relief I had from the boredom and the growing oppressive feel of the flat. Returning from an independent way of living to being holed up and dependent on family again took a chunk out of me.

As the days went by, I missed Majbritt more and more. We were communicating almost daily and there were growing signals that maybe our relationship could be rekindled so, for my thirtieth birthday, I jilted friends and family and decided to celebrate it in Denmark with Majbritt and her non-English-speaking parents. In order to win her back, I needed to impress her and her parents and thought it necessary to invest in a new wardrobe, so wandered into Guildford on a Gok Wan mission.

Being a typical bloke with regards to clothes shopping, I had lost interest within the hour and had bought a pair of non-descript shoes and a pair of jeans, neither of which had been tried on. Happy that I had something to show for my exertion, it was time to reward myself with a swift half in one of the town's many pubs. I settled myself in a tiny sun-soaked smoking area at the rear of the pub and reclined in my chair, feeling the sun on my

Lady Luck and Me

face and running through lustful thirtieth birthday present scenarios. My erotic thoughts were interrupted by a female American voice asking whether she could borrow the only other chair in the area, which my shopping bags were on.

She must have been in her mid-forties, heavily made-up, with long brown hair and a figure hugging dress. She was attractive and, by the way she carried herself, she knew it. After taking an age to adjust her dress, cross her legs, flick her hair and apply more lipstick, she attached a cigarette to the end of a holder, leant across the table to me and asked me to light it for her. It was a like Grace Kelly black-and-white movie scene. Feeling a little awkward, I asked her to look after my shopping whilst I escaped inside for a breather, a shot of Sambuca and a rapid pint of Stella. I returned to my shopping and the waiting American somewhat more smiley and confident than when I had left.

Two hours later, and with the sun still beating down, I was dehydrated, burnt, drunk and trying my best to maintain my Queen's English accent, still in the belief that the English accent is like cat-nip to Americans. I was enduring the pain because, early in the conversation, my new American friend had casually told me she was a porn actress over from America doing a shoot in a nearby studio. That was my cat-nip and I was determined to make the very most of the opportunity. I didn't think these sorts of situations happened in real-life, only, ironically, in porn movies. My pain was rewarded when, just as I thought of throwing in the towel, she invited me back to her hotel room at the top of the High Street.

Like a puppy following its mother I was led wobbling up the street. Nearing the hotel's entrance, she told me she wasn't allowed guests so I was given her room number and

Who needs love when....?

told to wait five minutes before giving the receptionist a bogus profession and reason why I was going up. She disappeared inside and I was left imagining who I wanted to be. Heart pumping and loins throbbing, I confidently strode up to reception and informed the blond behind the desk that I was urgently required in one of the hotel rooms. I was expecting my confidence and urgency to be enough to be granted permission without any further questioning. Alas, I was mistaken: all visitors had to be signed in and vouched for by the paying guest. I was given the visitors book as she rang the room. Lowering the handset she asked my name and purpose of visit. I hadn't got this far with the role play in my head and therefore panicked. She looked at me quizzically before speaking down the phone. 'Hello, Ms . . . Dr Max Power, your personal . . . mirkin fitter is here at reception.' The receptionist's eyes didn't leave me or my shopping bags as she awaited her instructions. It was too late to change my absurd name or ridiculous profession and so, still fuelled by the alcohol and the thought of what awaited me upstairs, I stood proudly staring back at her, determined not to be thwarted by this final hurdle. The handset went down and the receptionist, still watching me suspiciously, gave me the room directions.

After politely knocking and being called in, I was not only surprised by the spacious, tastefully decorated room but by the woman who had appeared so elegant only hours earlier, who was now fully naked apart from stockings and on all fours looking at me over her shoulder. A little taken aback with her forwardness, I froze. I hadn't imagined it would be quite as . . . filthy. I thought there might have been some small talk or at least a little fluffing

Lady Luck and Me

but then, I thought, all that had taken place in the pub. It was now at the business end of the encounter.

As I stood taking it all in, much as a rabbit does in the headlights, she insisted that I took photos of her. She said it really turned her on and, if I wanted the best sex of my life, I should direct her in her positioning and tell her what I wanted her to do. Being the keen amateur photographer that I was, I was only too happy to oblige, the only problem being that the only camera I had was on my phone. She didn't mind and I certainly didn't and so began nervously snapping away. The more photos I took the more vocal she became and the more aggressive and daring I became in my directing, evolving into a David Bailey or, more realistically, an Austin Powers. Eventually my phone's battery died, leaving both of us in a horny state of frenzy.

Just as she had unhooked her knees from behind her ears and I had torn off my last sock, there came a knock at the door followed by the manager's introduction. Through the door, he asked whether everything was okay as other guests had heard disturbing noises. She, on the bed, back on all fours, assured him that there was nothing to worry about, apologised and promised to keep the noise to a minimum. He also informed us that the hotel's insurance demanded all guests and guests of guests must either have photo ID or a passport number so would Dr Max Power come immediately to reception to complete the necessary paperwork. He would remain outside the door in order to accompany me back to reception, for security reasons.

I left the hotel, shopping bags in hand and my heavy pendulous balls around my knees. The hotel manager had seen it all before, and was giving short shrift to the

Who needs love when....?

woeful excuses I was giving for not carrying the correct or, in fact, any ID. The following day, I phoned the hotel under another name, desperate to have the best sex of my life, only to be told she had left that morning. My heart sank and my balls sank even lower. I was not to see her again, despite the countless hours I've since spent trawling through the likely websites.

I departed for Denmark a few days later, surprisingly guilt free and high in confidence. I was met at the airport by a svelte, stunning and obviously very happy Majbritt. For the four days I spent with her, she and her parents went above and beyond the call of duty looking after me. It was established within a few hours of meeting the parents that they were keen to learn about me, my background and ambitions, both professionally and with Majbritt. They had even gone as far as buying an English phrasebook and dictionary which I had to thumb through, showing them individual words until understanding was achieved. Some nights, I went to bed with a dull RSI ache in my thumbs. Majbritt translated for as long as her patience let her before she left the table to pursue any other menial task.

My birthday night was spent in a pre-booked VIP area in a club, watching Majbritt dance in a skinny dress whilst the entire male population devoured her with their eyes, occasionally swinging around to measure me up for suitability. Her eyes never wandered from me once and, in spite of the many invitations she had to dance with far more attractive, better built virile men than myself, she made it abundantly yet politely clear that she was dancing for me and me alone. I fell back in love/lust that night and

Lady Luck and Me

woke the next day feeling like a new beautiful chapter was about to begin.

I bade my farewells to the satisfied and considerably friendlier parents, vowing to return and offering them an open invitation to come and visit, assuring them that my Danish would have improved, still using the dictionary to communicate it. With Majbritt, the goodbyes were more emotional and, although not having any sex in the entire time that I was there, regarded our second throw of the relationship dice to be in its embryonic stages and knew that the sex would be worth waiting for. We parted company tearfully and arranged for her to come and stay with me indefinitely the following weekend.

I returned home full of the joys of spring, buying a Danish language course on the way. It was only when I had put my bags down at home that I realised I was without mobile phone. The pictures . . . the pictures . . . oh my fucking God, the pictures. I can't begin to express what my heart and head did then, my arse however, quivered and winked rapidly. Apart from leaving the phone behind, the second stupid thing I did was not backing up any numbers. Short of going on Facebook and telling her not to look at my phone, which would be suicide, I had no option but to hope that she 1) didn't look at my phone, and 2) didn't look at my phone, had my address and would just send it. As I went through all the worst possible scenarios in my head, my eye caught the attention of the flashing red message light on the landline phone. Clearly still in a state of numbness, my auto-pilot hand reached out and pressed

Who needs love when....?

play, only to hear the dulcet Danish tones of Majbritt address me.

'Hi Baby, you left your phone on my bed. I had to go through it to get your Mum's number. Hope you got home alright . . .'

That was the first half of the message. The second half was in Danish and, again with the help of the Danish/English dictionary and more RSI injuries, roughly translated as: 'Didn't want to offend your mum, but you motherfucking c**t. I saw the fucking perverted/sick photos of the haggard/gnarled woman. Don't ever contact me in any way again you utter/monumental arsehole. Go fuck yourself.'

It took me a week to translate her hate and, from whichever angle I looked at it or what dictionary I used, there was no indication of any love or reconciliation. I lost three things in that one phone message: my future wife and mother of my children, all my numbers of everyone I've ever met and, of course, pictorial evidence and memories of the best sex I so nearly had. It seemed cupid's arrow had just temporarily wounded me.

With the help of numerous bottles of vino, Mum and I came up with property development as a career choice. The housing market was still growing and the return on 'flipped' properties was still seen as a way to make a lucrative living. With my suspect New Zealand building experience and the countless hours watching 'Homes under the Hammer', I felt fairly confident that I could make a go of it. With this new chapter in my life, I decided to get a

Lady Luck and Me

dog to keep me company and so found a beautiful, young, rescued border collie which I named Zeus.

Deciding that I should target an area that I knew, Zeus and I headed down to Devon and began looking at properties that were up for auction. After visiting a few, my heart became set on the most run down, grim, two-up-two-down, terraced house in the middle of the worst area of Plymouth. I'm sure that if Sarah Beany had the best builders in the world she wouldn't have touched it with a telescopic bargepole. I managed to acquire the property before it went to auction and at a lower price than the guide suggested. When the day arrived for me to take charge of my new property, I had to herd the occupant out with two black bin bags full of three generations' worth of family possessions into a waiting taxi.

It was only when I closed the door behind me that I realised the extent of the mammoth task that I faced. For a start, the house had never been cleaned and the previous occupant was evidently a fully-fledged hoarder: rooms were crammed from floor to ceiling with three generations' worth of . . . stuff. Clothes, magazines, empty food tins, broken motorbikes, photos, rotting food, all piled up against damp, crumbling walls and falling ceilings. Four days after having the keys in my hand, the small house still wasn't cleared and I began to feel that I had bitten off far more than I could chew. I enlisted the help of a semi-builder friend who was to live in and paid him 300 quid cash a week. We had a budget and a timeframe which, with our rudimentary building skills, was wholly unrealistic and soon over-ran.

The other growing problem that I had was Zeus or, rather, his malfunctioning bladder. Months late, budget

Who needs love when....?

blown and with Zeus's urine stains on the freshly laid carpets, we finally finished just in time for the housing market to collapse. My days as a property developer had lasted just one property which no-one wanted to buy. Zeus unfortunately lasted just as long. Wherever we went, his bladder leaked and it soon became painfully obvious that I wasn't going to be able to mop up after him for the next 15 years or so. We found a loving lady who had other rescue dogs who gladly took him in, sending us photos of Zeus, happy as Larry, continuing his life in a sort of doggy nappy.

During my brief stint in Plymouth, my physical health took a turn for the worse. I attributed my growing chest pains to the perils of fine dust and filth of refurbishment. My loving mother took it a little more seriously and before I knew it, I was an emergency case in Derriford hospital with a suspected heart attack. Both nurses and doctors were bamboozled by the ECG which suggested I was having a massive heart attack. Three hours and three ECG's later, it was clear I wasn't dying and pericarditis was diagnosed (a swelling of the sac around the heart). Common apparently. My ECG results were thereafter used for medical students I was told.

After that little excitement I convinced myself I needed a break. Not that I deserved it, or could afford the expense or the time off, I decided to go on a weeks' skiing holiday to Saalbach, Austria with a really good group of friends. I was fortunate enough to have gone on annual family skiing holidays since Mum had been married to dickhead, although all I remember about them was the three-day drive to get there and being so cold in my day-glo all-in-one ski suit that I used to look forward to my bladder filling so I could momentarily warm my bottom half. The pay-off for being permanently frozen and stinking of piss

Lady Luck and Me

was that I learnt to ski relatively well and, as it had been a few years since I had been, the opportunity to go skiing with friends rather than dickhead was not to be missed. With an entirely new ski wardrobe, again which I couldn't afford, we left for Austria.

After having initial problems with the accommodation being down a snow-covered, abandoned track, miles from anywhere, we collectively made the decision to get a refund and invest in hotel rooms in town. There were three main reasons for this: 1) night life, 2) easy access to the slopes and, the most important, 3) sanity. I think we all feared that if 8 people went in, after a week together, with alcohol, there would be just one person left alive to tell the story. The group consisted of two couples, Tom and Claudia, Dave and his then-wife Andy, and the rest of us singletons, Charlie (Dave's sister), Pete (too many teeth), Will (ex-professional rugby player, model and now investment banker . . . grrrr) and me, the knob.

As expected, the two couples got a double room each and, as the hotel was otherwise full, the rest of us got to share a family room. Naturally, Will ended up sharing the bed with Charlie (platonically) and Pete and I got two tiny old rickety single beds that were designed for small children. The combination of both Pete and my smelly socks made our room a no-go area; even the cleaners avoided it after the first day. But, as we didn't intend to spend much time sleeping, our pitiful beds didn't really bother us. From the first day it was clear what people's priorities were. Tom and Claudia, arguably the most advanced skiers, woke at the crack of sparrow's fart, shooing the rest of us out of bed like SS staff sergeants, which went down like a bag of cold sick. The strong verbal abuse which they received from each and every one of us in our slumber was a clear

Who needs love when....?

indicator to them that we were looking for a more leisurely skiing holiday and so they refrained from trying to rouse us thereafter.

Charlie, the least experienced, had absolutely no intention of making it a skiing holiday and was more inclined to make it an après ski holiday, spending her days pootling around the baby slopes or sampling the different bars' mulled wine. The rest of us took a relaxed approach to the slopes, occasionally braving the odd black run but making sure any exertion was rewarded by a drink or two. Pete was a relative beginner so it was usual that we would be waiting for him at the end of each run but this wasn't a nuisance, quite the opposite actually. It was clear from the first day that everyone had invested in ski gear, apart from Pete. Pete had managed to acquire an all-in-one sky-blue eighties suit which, along with his Davy Crockett furry hat flapping in the wind and his numerous teeth reflecting off the snow, made him an awesome sight to behold. If you can imagine a gay, eighties James Bond, learning to ski then you're half way there. Even in my darkest days that mental image always makes me chuckle. Thank you, Pete.

As dusk fell, we usually rendezvoused at a predetermined bar along with many heavily moustached aging Austrian men and, as Charlie is an attractive blond-haired, blue-eyed, amply busted ball of energy, we were never short of entertainment as random men tried their luck. After the first night, the balance of the holiday began to tilt. It became less and less of a skiing holiday and more and more of a drinking holiday. By the end, between the hangovers from the night before and the sun setting, we had about an hour's worth of daylight skiing. However, our time spent drinking reaped us rewards in the end. Not only did the local night club allow us to clear their dance

Lady Luck and Me

floors with all of us sitting down in a line, pretending to row ourselves across the dance floor to the bar but also Tom and Will, with their charms, managed to befriend the female casino owner who, coincidentally, also ran a strip club beneath the casino.

On the last night, it was decided to have a nice meal and then head to the casino to try our luck. I don't really understand casinos, so I watched Tom and Will peddle their wares and come away quids in and with a couple of croupiers' numbers in their back pockets. With their winnings, they decided to head downstairs as VIP members. As they went downstairs, I ducked out to make a phone-call and get some money. On my return, I entered the strip club to find the strippers sitting around the stage, smoking cigarettes, watching Tom and Will wearing only grass skirts gyrating around the two dance poles. They were in their element and moved like they were born to do it, like two unmade up drag queens. They were so natural that the strippers were visibly uneasy with the reception they were getting from their usual punters.

It all came to a head when they tried to get others onto the stage to incorporate them into an impromptu routine. By then, the strippers had had enough and the bouncers were called. Returning the grass skirts to the rightful owners and being protected by the salivating owner, they were escorted to seats and given free drinks to a heart-warming round of applause. It was comedy and arrogance all in one, at its very best. We all sat there watching the strippers trying to mimic Tom's and Will's moves but without success and without much appreciation from the waning crowd. The strippers who weren't performing were doing the rounds, trying their best to entice the onlookers to have a private dance and, after numerous refusals on the

Who needs love when....?

grounds of morality, Will came and sat next to me, clearly disappointed at my reluctance.

A couple of drinks later and with Will's incessant encouragement, I decided to go against my moral compass and gave in, accepting a dance from a beautiful Brazilian. She took me by the hand and led me away behind the curtain to the private booths. A couple of minutes into her routine, I think she must have picked up that I felt uncomfortable being there so changed her tack in the most unlikely way. She laid face down across my lap and insisted I spank her bare arse. Somewhat surprised at her request I asked her to repeat it and, sure enough, she wanted me to spank her bare arse. So, tentatively and gently, I slapped her arse. She looked me in the eye and loudly yelled, 'Harder, harder,' which I duly did, feeling even more uncomfortable and not at all aroused. 'Harder, harder,' she kept shouting at which point Will poked his head around the curtain, smiled and wandered in taking the seat directly opposite, not two yards away, nodding his head and smiling.

I continued slapping the stripper's arse looking at Will in a bemused way until all of a sudden the curtain was whipped back by the biggest bouncer I've ever seen. He told Will to go to the bar and then frog marched me out of the strip club, up the stairs and onto the street, closing the door behind me, leaving me to wonder what the hell just happened. Thanks to Will's newly formed friendship with the club's proprietor, I was allowed back in, but under strict instruction not to go anywhere near any of the strippers.

I returned to Plymouth to gather the remainder of my possessions and left the property in the hands of an unreliable letting agent. I was moving back to live with

Lady Luck and Me

Mum and sister again, until, at least, another idea of what to do with myself reared its creative head.

Where the streets are paved with gold

'Mind the gap.'
Neil Gaiman

With the arse falling out of the property market and with a reluctance to train in anything again, I was left with the skills I possessed to make a living. Again, after an extended red wine session with my mother, the idea of Zen London was born. With my acquired and varying bodywork techniques, sports science knowledge and Muay Thai training, I was to be a mobile Muay Thai fitness instructor and masseur. After forking out for branded equipment and a website, I sat back and waited, expecting to be inundated with enquiries. Three weeks passed with me looking hourly at my Google inbox. I was baffled that I had had only one enquiry, three times . . . by the same 64-year-old man asking whether I did oil foot rubs and, if so, that he'd pay extra for me to wear a cowboy hat. Times were hard but every man has his pride.

I knew nothing of search engine optimisation or online marketing at the time and assumed that, because I had a website, I would have clients. If you build it, they will come. Let me tell you, that's bollocks. After you build it, you've got to polish it and polish it and then polish it some more. A month on from its birth, Zen London had had 14 hits, three of those being the coffin-dodger freak, with an average viewing time of just 22 seconds; something had to change. In industries such as mine, the best marketing is word of mouth and that meant networking and networking

Lady Luck and Me

meant being around potential clients which meant a move to London. I had vowed to myself at a younger age that I would live at least a year in London and, once again, it seemed that the stars had aligned and shown me now was the time.

Initially, I was to live on Fulham Palace Road with two other girls (one being my girlfriend Jules) until the room at my friend Tom's house, around the corner, was vacated by his girlfriend who was taking my room in Jules's flat.

Jules is worthy of special mention. Australian with wavy, blond hair, big blue eyes and a brilliant brain, she was living in London working as an editor for a big fashion house. I had first met her on her birthday during my first trip Down Under and, at the time, I spent longer looking at my shoes than her after another wave of acne had crippled my confidence. Lady Luck was to be kind enough to see to it that our paths would cross again though through mutual friends. I have known Jules for 11 years and we have dated twice now. Regardless of how compatible we are it seems that that X factor is amiss, and I fear no matter how many times we revisit the idea, the outcome will sadly never change. Loving someone but not being in love with them has got to be the cruellest of all loves.

Anyway, the flat situation was a simple boyfriend/girlfriend room swap. The rent I was receiving from the house in Plymouth covered the rent I was to pay for the flat which left me with just the bills to pay and that would roughly equate to three clients at 50 quid a session to find per month. Fifteen clients a month, one every other day, would see me living comfortably. I didn't get 15 clients, I didn't get three. Despite my friends going above and

Where the streets are paved with gold

beyond their call of duty, I was very much on the bread line and constantly feeling the black paw clawing at my mind. Wee-Man, who was living in Kentish town at the time with his new, pregnant girlfriend, Pip, saved my life on more than one occasion. They fed me, housed me, entertained me, enlightened me and I'll forever be in their debt.

It was with Wee-Man that I found a Moroccan café in Aldgate East, which is sadly no longer there, and John a struggling sculptor who worked part-time there. He was clearly educated although severely malnourished. His back had become so knotted it forced him to hunch and, having had success with other hunchbacks, I offered my services. The problem was John was homeless and penniless. I agreed to work on John for free hoping Lady Luck would reward me for my generosity. Travelling from Hammersmith along the District Line to Aldgate East took an hour and cost me a fiver there and back.

In the middle of this high-ceilinged, pillared café I rolled out my mat and, to many bemused faces of all nationalities, colour and creed, began working on John. When the hour and a half session was up, and I was sweating like a caged pig, John would give me a jumper which he had found or, on one occasion, half a 330ml bottle of Coca Cola. Still thinking Lady Luck would look after me, I gratefully accepted, thinking he was in a worse position than me. Twice a week and for three months, I did the same journey and was rewarded with equally useless items in payment. It was one of the café's foreign customers' asking John about help with their college work that alerted me to John's employment and, after a couple of subtle questions, I established that John had been in gainful, full-time employment for the previous two months, earning around 500 quid a week helping foreign students with

Lady Luck and Me

translation. Ironic that I was masquerading as a successful mobile health practitioner but earning fuck all and John was masquerading as a homeless man, bringing home 2000 pounds cash in hand a month.

I didn't get in touch with John again and thought that I had banked enough Karmic points to guarantee me rich, regular customers for the rest of my life. My next customers, courtesy of Wee-Man, seemed to be exactly that and, thankfully, just in the nick of time. They were a gay couple living in an enormous house in Balham; the bread winner was a middle-aged successful English advertising guru whilst his young Brazilian boyfriend stayed at home, pottering around, waiting for his beloved to get home each night. As Wee-Man was our mutual friend, the introductions were informal and relaxed, allowing me to tell them the strife I was in and how their discounted massages would buy much-needed food and keep the wolf from the door for the next couple of weeks. I was even honest enough to tell them that I had phoned my mother on more than one occasion, asking her to put 10 pounds into my bank account so that I could get a 6-inch Subway sandwich and treat non-paying John on the other side of London. Being sure that my desperation had been heard and registered, I set about giving them extended back to back treatments which ran late into Friday night.

I emerged, drained, to a busy party made up exclusively of very camp, gay men in full party spirit. After disappointing one particularly keen reveller by telling him I didn't do extras, I sought out the hosts, looking for payment. The Brazilian told me to find his partner as he dealt with finances and, on finding his partner, he told me to tell the Brazilian to go to the cash machine which he flatly refused, offering me two grams of cocaine as

Where the streets are paved with gold

means of payment. When I tried to explain that I didn't have enough to get home, let alone feed myself, his eyes rolled and his mouth gurned, perfectly illustrating that he was way beyond capable of getting to the cash-machine. I left empty handed after being told that I should return the following day to pick up what was owed to me. By means of a loan from Tom, I was able to feed myself that night and return the following day to, once again, hassle the hungover Brazilian to walk the required 50 yards to the cash machine. Reluctantly, he did and after handing me my money, put his hood up and walked away. There was no more contact between us.

I felt jilted by Lady Luck and Karma and, after a couple of random, one-off treatments, decided to turn my back on the healing part of my business. Fuelled by anger, resentment and hunger, I concentrated on Muay Thai which, thanks to sympathetic friends, kept me going for a while longer before the stress, hopelessness and daily grind of breadline-living in London got the better of me and plunged me into another deep depressive episode. Eventually, and for self-preservation, I returned back to Guildford to live with my mum and sister and the cat. Although I had achieved my target year in London, I left under no illusion that it had been a success and, as well as being beaten by the city and its inhabitants, I felt so-called Karma and my spiritual resolve had been well and truly questioned and, it's a shame to say, had been left wanting - maybe I had already used it all up on my earlier misdemeanours. Still, to this day, I regard Lady Luck as, at best, a fickle mistress.

Lady Luck and Me

Home sweet home?

'What greater gift than the love of a cat.'
Charles Dickens

I was back home with my mother and sister, back to thinking what the hell I was going to do with my life. I was still busy angrily shaking my fist at Lady luck for not repaying me when I asked, only to be reminded by her that she pays in her own time, when she's ready.

It had been a typical wet November night and, as was customary on such nights, the wine was causing regular trips to the toilet. It just so happened that on one of these occasions, the cat appeared at the glass back door. He had been forced out earlier but had remained bone dry, sheltering under the small roof overhanging the back door. I obligingly let him in and went to relieve myself. Concentrating hard on hitting the toilet, I failed to notice the cat wander in. As his tail flicked my leg, I leapt in shock, spraying wee all over the toilet, the walls, and mirror and all over the equally surprised cat, soaking him. He shot off and I was left staring at the drenched surfaces and cursing the cat.

Having finished the clean-up operation, I returned to the lounge to see my sister cradling the cat under her chin, lovingly stroking him all the time pitying him for having been out in the horrid autumn weather. I stood there, caught between guilt and the ever rising sense of justice. Just as I was about to confess, the flowerpot over her right shoulder came into view as if it was some divine intervention to hold my silence. Sitting down, I refilled

Lady Luck and Me

my glass and relaxed, gazing into the glowing fire, smiling to myself. The cat settled in her lap and remained there purring for the remainder of the evening. That night, I had arguably the best night's sleep of my life, for the first time believing there might well be a God. With Karma's help, I had finally exacted my revenge on Charmian for all those trustingly ruined flowerpots all those years ago.

Apart from that major highlight, the time spent at Guildford was relatively monotonous. Living with my mother and sister in a bungalow didn't really allow me to get up to too much mischief and Lady Luck pretty much left me alone. However, on Thursday 14 October 2009 she was to play her hand again.

The morning had started in the most unremarkable way with the daily commute down the A3 to Putney and to the office where I was working as a temporary recruitment consultant, thanks to my good friend Tom, who had got me in through the back door. I wasn't very good, mind you nor was the job. Nine to five thirty, just above minimum wage and stuck in an office with four other people, all of whom disliked each other. Alex, the resident gay, would occasionally send emails to Tom and me describing his latest sexploits, more often than not, in such graphic detail it would have made Howard Stern blush. Matt, the son of the big boss, was so very dull he could make a glass eye fall asleep. Rebecca the Kiwi, had a positively unhealthy obsession with Tom and finally Ruth, the American boss, was a dead ringer for Lois in 'Family Guy'.

It was the same day in day out, week in week out. With nothing ever changing, it was no wonder that cracks appeared regularly, boiling over into petty arguments and nasty off-the-cuff comments. It was during one of these

Home sweet home?

purple patches that one particular day became far from normal. Ruth had headed out to an early lunch, leaving the rest of us to openly rant about pretty much everything and everyone, professionally and personally. It was a kind of exorcism or group therapy session. Feeling slightly better having vented, I headed out to grab an overpriced, stale sandwich from the garage and a gulp of fresh Thames air.

Whilst nourishing myself and in between breaths of satisfactory sighing, my mobile vibrated, 'Ben, its Ruth, I've just been told you're going to burn down the building?' Those bastards. It was true and I had said it, but, compared to other comments, it was tame and certainly not intended as a serious threat. Without giving me time to respond, she continued, 'Do not come back to the office. If you do, I will be forced to phone the police. Tom will clear your desk.' With that, she hung up.

I didn't return to the office but, if I had, I would have certainly carried out my threat. Although it was a shit job, it was still a job. I was livid, those back-stabbing bastards. Seething, I returned to my car, trying to work out the most appropriate way to execute my revenge. All the way down the A3, I was imaging weird and wonderful ways by which I could ruin them and the company; images from the film 'SAW' came to mind and, with them, a wry smile. It was the beep of the fuel gauge that interrupted my thoughts and, thankfully, the BP garage was not too far away. My car had a tendency to give false fuel readings so it always made me nervous when I heard it beep. Pulling into the garage forecourt and alongside the pump, my heart finally began to slow, relieved that my nightmare day wouldn't involve pushing my van down the hard shoulder. You haven't completely deserted me then Lady Luck, I

Lady Luck and Me

thought to myself. Having put the usual £10 worth into the tank, I wandered inside to pay.

Just when I thought my day had been entertaining enough already, the most unexpected thing then happened. The woman in front of me was rifling through her wallet when she dropped her car keys. I knew the proper thing to do was to pick them up for her, which I duly did. She smiled, thanked me and momentarily paused before asking where I was heading. I kid you not. She was in her mid to late thirties, blond, average height and buxom and, from the two massive rocks on her wedding finger, wealthy and very much married. She was in the category of 'wouldn't invite her into bed but equally wouldn't kick her out of it'. I shifted awkwardly, looking around expecting some hairy Beadle-like bloke or Mr Dale 'Orange' Winton to jump out with a camera, pointing at me and laughing hysterically. A couple of seconds passed and all remained normal. Well, as normal as such a situation could possibly be. I cautiously answered 'Guildford' and immediately regretted it, thinking that I had taken the bait, hook line and sinker but still nothing out of the ordinary happened; everything continued to be well . . . normal.

'That's the way I'm going, you should follow me.' And with that she was called to the counter to pay. Considering we were on a dual carriage-way and Guildford was the next turn off, it was hardly surprising that she was also heading that way. I smirked, shook my head, still convinced it was a wind-up and turned around to the person behind me assured that they must have heard every word of the strangest conversation ever. The young chav was completely oblivious, thanks to his iPod and the deafening music he was listening to. On one hand, I was delighted that I hadn't been exposed but, on the other, I

Home sweet home?

was aggrieved that no-one else witnessed it. Leaving the cashier, she turned, winked and simply said, 'Follow me'. I hastily retrieved the £10 note from my wallet slammed it down on the counter giving the teller my pump number and shot off after her. She waited for me in her top of the range, dark blue BMW and then proceeded to rejoin the A3, me in tow.

The firing from the job and my thoughts of revenge had subsided and had been replaced by sheer bewilderment and slight suspicion. I hadn't even heard of stories like this and that worried me. With one eye on her and the other checking my wing mirror for an irate husband or, worse still, a van with a satellite dish on top, we continued on down the A3. When the Guildford exit came and went, I began to sweat a little. Maybe I was being lured into a weird sex game with her and her husband, or led to a disused hanger where I would be set upon by some ruffians. Even worse, she was leading me to a love nest to get me naked before being humiliated by an educational television company on the dangers of following strangers. Or, just maybe, she was just taking the piss.

My eyes were becoming more and more fixed on the wing mirrors as paranoia kicked in. Following her through Peasmarsh, my heart resumed its unhealthy 140 beats a minute, rising steadily all the time. Finally, she turned off into Artington Park and Ride, halfway between Guildford and Godalming. She drove to the far end and parked in the corner, flanked on one side by a railway track and, on the other, by tall green hedges, the next closest car was a good 50 yards away, which meant two out of four of my theories were still possible. I reversed in alongside her, heart still desperately thumping to get out of my chest. I watched her shuffle around in her car before eventually getting out and

Lady Luck and Me

making her way to my passenger door. The light was fading and it was now raining. As she closed the door behind her I thought it was appropriate to introduce myself.

'Hi, my name's...'

'No names,' she said sharply. 'Believe me when I tell you I don't do this kind of thing normally; it's on a whim.'

'Sure . . . so, what did you have in mind?' I asked.

'Well, a bit of fun.'

'Ok, where did you have in mind?' I enquired.

She swivelled her head round, 'Back there.' At which point she opened the door, got out and moved around to the boot. Like an over-excited small dog, I followed, opening up the boot and rearranging the removal rugs to cover the ridged bare metal floor. Once the temporary bed had been constructed, we clambered in and closed the boot behind us. Details aren't necessary to describe how we passed the next hour. Suffice to say, I was proud of my performance.

Darkness had fallen by the time we were both satisfied, and, after redressing and very little conversation, it was time to make like Anne Boleyn and head off. It would have been a perfectly naughty crime if it was as simple as that and we had parted ways. However, Lady Luck had one final cock-kicking surprise in store for me that day. Unbeknownst to me Vauxhall vans do not have a boot release on the inside. Initially, I thought that it just wasn't in an obvious place. It then became painfully apparent that there simply wasn't a boot release. Not only was there no way to get out of the boot, access to the front two seats was

Home sweet home?

barred by an impenetrable grill. Plainly speaking, we were properly fucked.

Panic slowly but surely started to kick in. I made feeble attempts to try to unscrew the front grill using anything that came to hand. Coins, pencils, even my teeth were tried but, surprise surprise, to no avail. With rain pouring down and the car park utterly deserted, no passer-by was coming to our aid. Then, the phone calls started. It was now past six and from the frequency of the calls, her husband was getting suspicious. Phoning friends wasn't an option, she couldn't phone hers as her infidelity would be exposed and I couldn't phone mine since the closest friend I had was in London. Having reached desperation point and the very real possibility of spending an October night locked in the back of my van with a complete stranger, I had a light bulb moment: the AA, the knights of the road, thank God that I had renewed my membership the previous week. With one quick phone call, we were to be saved in 30 minutes.

Those 30 minutes seemed like days as we tried to engage in meaningless small talk, often failing as it was abundantly clear we had absolutely nothing in common. It was also clear, as time passed and the phone calls persisted, that she was becoming more and more agitated and increasingly worried about the inevitable conversation she would have to have with her husband on her return. All the while, I was fighting the onset of sleep. Finally, and not before time, the beautiful hum of a car engine was heard through the van's panels. The driver's door opened and a

Lady Luck and Me

bearded, florescent jacketed, middle-aged man peered through the grate at us.

'You ok?' he asked.

'Good thanks, mate, you just need to pop the boot. Sorry,' I said, sheepishly, with beads of sweat running down my face.

At that, he looked us both in the eyes, raised his eyebrows and withdrew from the car. I felt like a three-year-old who had just shat himself. I cannot describe how beautiful the sound of the boot opening was. Since then, every time I see a boot being opened I can't help but smile. If I was Shakespeare, I would have written a sonnet about it. Cold air flooded in, at which point, the smell of sex and exertion seeping out must have been overwhelming for our poor angel in yellow.

As soon as the boot was at its maximum, the woman bolted, like a greyhound out the traps, and was gone, no word, no goodbye, no parting gesture, just the sound of her BMW's engine roaring towards the exit. The AA man looked at me, shook his head, said nothing, climbed back into his van and left, leaving me standing there in the pouring rain, wondering what the hell had just happened and cursing myself for not buying cigarettes earlier.

The journey home was significantly more sedate than the journey there. It had been a crazy day, exhausting both emotionally and physically. Jury's out whether I can tell my grandchildren that tale, I'll let them read this at a suitable age.

Watery stools

> *'Shit happens. Doesn't mean you have to step in it. But if you do I would buy a new pair of shoes.'*
> **Kilburn Hall**

One autumnal afternoon, my sister and mother returned from their shopping excursion considerably more excited than usual. Over tea, they informed me that they had seen posters in a well-known, high street bookshop window advertising job vacancies, and then began a convincing argument of how it would be the perfect job for me. In truth, they didn't need their impressively compelling closing statement since I had always harboured a romantic notion of working in a bookshop, surrounded by eons of knowledge and imagination and having the ability to directly access anything in print that took my fancy. Within the hour, I had completed the online application form and duly waited, expecting to hear nothing for a week and then to phone them only to be told they had appointed someone else but would keep my details on record. I had had my fair share of rejections, so knew the process well. The position advertised was for temporary, full-time Christmas staff, from November until late January and, for me, as a temporary measure, it was absolutely ideal. To my surprise, I received a phone call the following day, asking me to attend an interview. Although I lived no more than five miles away, I had yet to visit Godalming and knew very little about the town or its residents.

I announced my arrival for the interview to a fellow tending the tills that was the spitting image of a young

Lady Luck and Me

Hugh Fearnley-Whittingstall. As he phoned the back office, I stood back to try and get a feeling of what it might feel like to work there. At that moment, an elderly lady wearing a head scarf and pushing one of those annoying shopping bags on wheels, rammed my shins trying to avoid a three-berth, six-wheeled pram that had an ugly pug-faced dog and two Waitrose shopping bags as its three occupants. The panama-hatted, Hunter-wellyed, middle-aged, middle-class driver clutched a large Costa coffee in one hand and laughed loudly into her smartphone on the other as she ploughed through the shop, dislodging dozens of books every time her steering elbows drove the machine unwittingly into a bookcase. Before she had left the shop, I saw one child having to leap for cover and one elderly dog which just wasn't quite quick enough get caught once and then twice by the front bumper as the driver took a re-run in an effort to clear whatever the obstruction might be slowing her journey.

As first impressions go, that single episode reflected the town perfectly. Shortly after I'd finished inspecting my already bruising shins, the Manager appeared from the office and led me upstairs for the interview. Considering I was interviewing for a temporary post, the seriousness of the whole interview took me unawares. I thought I had done enough after answering with a wink that my desert island book would be *Boatbuilding for Dummies*, but the Manager was unrelenting, forcing me to lie to her that I loved reading Tom Stoppard plays and *The Tibetan Book of Living and Dying* is my favourite bedtime read. I left the 40 minute interview kicking myself. Out of all the millions

Watery stools

of books there are, I have no idea why I decided they were my favourites.

That afternoon, she phoned and asked me to start the following Monday, much to my mother's and sister's delight. And so began the job which I currently still find myself in, four years on. Since my appointment, I have been managed by no less than seven different managers, all with their own style, vision and questionable social skills. Even the Hugh Fearnley-Whittinstall doppelganger had a crack at interim management at the tender age of 21. The moment he bashed the bell on the front desk, calling out for his 'minions', was the moment Stu, my friend and colleague (who had just finished a contract in the middle-east as a conflict resolution negotiator), and I regarded our new manager as an award-winning penis, and started doing what we could to make his new role as uncomfortable and as temporary as possible.

When our jibes or our utter lack of respect towards him got the better of him, his baby face would swell to a crimson colour before he stormed off, returning 15 minutes later in a far calmer mood and stinking of tobacco smoke. I always remember thinking I had never seen such a rapid change in mood because of a cigarette. It was only when we had successfully ousted him to a London store that his behavioural patterns were brought up over a beer with the manager. When I questioned her about which cigarettes he smoked, she laughed heartily and told me the angry cigarette breaks were not just calmed by a rollie out the back but by what he did before the rollie. It seemed that on the way to his ciggie, he would make a detour to the disabled toilet and emerge five minutes later, visibly more relaxed, even smiling, and perspiring whilst adjusting his belt buckle and awkwardly altering his walk.

Lady Luck and Me

She had bumped into him before and after his disabled toilet detour several times before working out his tactics of anger-management. Shocked but not surprised, I tried to recall how many times he had . . . self-medicated at work. I was sure that on one particularly bad day for him and especially his no-doubt tiny little cock, we had forced him to take seven or eight 'cigarette breaks'.

But as the managers came and went, the Godalming public continued to walk through the doors and continued to entertain. Working in a bookshop that has a post office attached means you get the regular oldies collecting their weekly pensions and the regular mummy shoppers, the 'Daddy's a wealthy banker' types pushing their state-of-the-art prams into people as they flick through books of past medical school test papers for little Humphrey, who's presently crawling around on the floor, chewing away on a Peppa Pig cardboard book.

From the outside, Godalming seems like a quaint, middle-class, quintessentially English town but, after spending time serving with its residents, I quickly realised all is not what it seems. The first thing to know about Godalming, is that it's one of London's wealthier satellite towns, being 45 minutes away from Waterloo and pretty much completely recession proof. The general demographic of the town is, as mentioned earlier, middle-class housewives, rich, aging pensioners who wear mustard-coloured cords, cravats and are usually titled, whether it be Lady, Baron or Doctor, and students who have had a similar education to mine but had arrived on the back

Watery stools

of their eighteenth birthday present that Manuel, their footman, was now grooming and feeding sugar cubes to.

Godalming also seems to house more than its fair share of, let's just say, unique individuals. There's Dancing Steve, who's in his early forties and, as the name suggests, dances and sings to his idol, Justin Bieber, at the top of his voice. The entire High Street knows that Dancing Steve is in town way before anybody actually sets eyes on him. His incoherent, high pitched, loud squeaks and unpredictable limb movements serve as an indicator and warning to small children that he shouldn't be disturbed when listening to his discman. His singing and dancing continue even when he's hugging the soft toys in the children's area, sending crying children back to their mothers and the safety of their absurd, Hummer-like prams. Rumour has it that if you overexcite Dancing Steve, he's likely to bite you and has been banned from several of the local pubs due to a lack of control over his mandibles. Although relatively harmless, the real enjoyment of Dancing Steve is watching other people's reaction to him. You can't help but raise a smile when his Bieber shrieks float in through the door and you automatically scan the children's area for the poor unsuspecting child who will shortly be reduced to tears. If I had it my way, I would employ Dancing Steve as a doorman and send him over to the kids' section every time a spoilt, precocious child misbehaved.

Although local, Dancing Steve is not, unfortunately, a regular and I sometimes have to wait weeks to be entertained by him again. But there is no shortage of other, slightly strange individuals who we see on a daily basis. There is a mother and daughter who come in every morning to use the post office and keep us updated on the wellbeing of their pet rats and rant about the new shoes the mother's

Lady Luck and Me

cross-dressing father has just bought. They follow any one of the booksellers, working like a double act, incessantly talking and interrupting each other to comment on every book they see. All conversations lead back to their rats though. Never have I known anyone to be so enthused and affectionate about what is commonly perceived as dirty vermin. Nor have I ever heard of somebody going through their so-called loved pets at the rate at which they do. Every couple of days, there is another fatality and another moan about the extortionate vet's fees. Although I have absolutely no affinity with rats and can't understand how anyone can, it is still difficult not to be sympathetic towards the mother as tears fill her eyes when she describes Horatio's or Merlin's last dying moments. When three successive rats all died with swollen stomachs, I began to question the mother on the rat's diet, only to be told that they had been given an avocado stone to gnaw on. She disagreed with me and the vet that that could have been the reason they were dying and will continue to feed future pets the same diet because, as she says, it makes them smile.

The more I lent a sympathetic ear to their pets plight, the more was expected of me when they died. I have now had to write in three separate cards; how much I will miss Hector, Horatio and Merlin and what a profound impact they had had on everyone's lives. I have even been given advice by Hector, who visited the mother in one of her dreams, and told her to tell me that I should pursue a career in pottery. When she came in crying, telling us she was struggling to deal with the loss of Merlin, I actively started to distance myself from her. She did not at all understand why the Samaritans volunteer had hung up on her after he had explained there was no more he could do to help her recover from the loss of Merlin and so she

Watery stools

was in the process of writing a letter to David Cameron explaining her disappointment with the service.

Another regular that we do our best to avoid is a wheelchair-bound, elderly gentleman who refused to wear a hearing aid or a bib. He sits dribbling, smelling slightly of death and enquires, in a booming voice, whether we have an erotic fiction section. If we don't answer quickly or loudly enough, he forgets what he has asked and asks us what he has asked for, to which we have to shout back, that he is looking for the erotic fiction section, and no we don't have one. He then booms out that it isn't for him, but for his nephew in Italy and can he order one which we think would be most appropriate. Taking details equates to getting drenched in his saliva and in a pointless ear-piercing exchange of fictional information. It has been decided the best way to deal with him is stand way back from him and go through the motions without actually ordering anything, safe in the knowledge that the same conversation will arise the following day. I think I would be more compassionate towards him if he didn't regularly tell us how bad we were at our jobs and didn't purposefully ram us with his chair if we aren't being attentive enough.

It is funny working in a bookshop, though, and has turned out to be a vastly different experience to what I was expecting. The general population seems to think that bookshop employees are all oracles and know all the answers to any question, book or non-book related. Twice I have been asked by customers what the stars hold for them in the coming week and three times I have been asked by an expectant mother what they should call their first born. People seem to think that if you work in a bookshop, you've read every book in there and can give accurate advice on literally any subject, regardless of how

Lady Luck and Me

obscure. A common question asked by the older generation is, 'I read a book some 50 years ago. It had a blue cover, no, a black cover with faded writing on the cover. I can't remember the title, the author or what it was about, but I do remember enjoying it. Do you have it?' With needle in haystack odds of finding the book, I carry out dutiful customer service by asking irrelevant questions, stroking my chin pensively and consulting the BBC's live test cricket webpage, umming and ahhing as I wait for the next update. Other surprisingly common questions include: Do you sell motorcycle helmets?, Which one of these hasn't my son/daughter read?, and the same repetitive question from the same mentally unstable customer, 'Do black people need to top up their tans?' My black colleague has the patience of a saint as she explains it to him for the tenth time that month. There's also 'Dictionary Man' who comes in every day at five without fail. A slight man in his late sixties, who wears his trousers around his nipples and peers out over his half glasses, through his thinning grey hair and wispy beard, sniggering at random words in the dictionary or, more recently, the Bible. He has yet to speak or buy a book and has the kind of face you would expect to see on Crimewatch. Let me put it another way, if I had children, I certainly wouldn't be asking him to babysit.

Despite his somewhat strange behaviour and photo-fit face, he is at least hygienic, which is more than can be said for many of his peers. Whether it's because of aging bowels, a desensitised nose, a complete disregard for those around them or, most likely, a combination of all three, elderly people seem to be oblivious that they're breaking wind. I've been on my knees shelving books when somebody in the latter stages of life slowly shuffles past, releasing loud and often noxious fumes directly at my

Watery stools

head. There's no apology, no awkward embarrassed looks, not even any acknowledgement of what they have done and they creep on, blissfully unaware of their noisy, rotting bottoms and the unsavoury stench it leaves behind.

It was sooner rather than later, months rather than years, that my illness was triggered again, I think by means of monotony. I had been working in the bookshop as a temporary assignment so neither wanted nor thought I'd be there long enough to try and work my way up the exploitive ladder. I had stupidly and lazily forced myself into limbo. I wasn't looking for another job, nor was I challenging myself but going through the same conversations with the same arseholes that have the most money and least respect. Conversation and memory faded rapidly, often leaving me staring at the same book spine that I'd been trying to shelve for the past 10 minutes. Occasionally, eye-contact was impossible. I hadn't the strength or the courage to fix a gaze and, if any question required more than a one-word answer, I was in real trouble.

The breaking point came when a customer asked me where she would find Jeremy Clarkson books. I have nothing against Clarkson but, for some reason, that query sent me off the shop floor bawling my eyes out, having to be escorted to the car by my mother half an hour later, much to the bewilderment of the spectating public. The tears were uncontrollable for hours. The heavy, invisible black coat that had descended upon me gave me the posture of an 80-year-old man. There was no definitive reason for the overwhelming sadness which had suddenly taken hold of me, but it lasted for days as I watched countless hours of

Lady Luck and Me

TV with the curtains drawn unable to set foot outside my four-walled world. It became very bad.

Black, inside and out

Only black

For days

Sobbing

Dark, final thoughts

Doctor, more medication

Psychotherapist, stronger medication

Train timetables

Knife, arm, bandages

Watery stools

Hopelessness

More black

Birdsong

Clouds

A smile

With my mind stabilised on daily medication, I was able to return to work. Still not knowing what I wanted to do in life and determined not to be under the control of another confidence-sapping agency, I continued on in the bookshop, albeit with diminishing enthusiasm. The company itself had yet another Managing Director. This one, however, treated his bright, dedicated workforce with condescension and so many broken promises no-one I've spoken to within the company gives a shit anymore. He became known for saying ridiculous things such as 'I can't wait to be back on the shop floor as a bookseller again' and, in an email, explained that bonuses were being stopped.

Lady Luck and Me

This, I'm sure you can imagine, did little to motivate the skeleton teams up and down the country who were putting countless hours of their own time in in order to achieve their 'happy coincidence' meagre pay-out at the end of each month.

After one particular Christmas, I was asked to come in on my day off as the Regional Manager required a word with me. A little nervous but fed up with the way we were being treated, I came in, worked and waited. As the doors were closing at the end of the day, the Regional Manager appeared. He didn't come in to the shop but stood on the pavement outside, thanked me for all my hard work during the festive period and, as a token of his thanks, handed me a small envelope and left. The meeting had lasted no more than 20 seconds. Inside the envelope was a company gift voucher to the value of five pounds. Even with my discount card, I would still have to use my own money to buy a book. Probably, and I challenge you to beat it, the worst Christmas bonus ever.

As frustration built with management and dwindling staff numbers, I found sanctuary at the end of the day in a pub midway between work and the train station. At first, it was on the odd day, staying for a couple to ease the woes of the working day before heading home but soon that snowballed and I found myself spending nearly as long in the pub as I had working. Not only did the alcohol consumption increase but so did my regularity, often spending days at a time being feral on my newly acquired friends' couches before rolling into work late, un-showered and, clearly, still pissed.

The more often I visited, the more familiar the faces became. Soon I was part of a small, pub family and,

Watery stools

on the odd day that I didn't go down, I would miss them. I had never heard of cock conkers before, but was reliably informed that the barman was the Surrey champion and always looking for people to spar with. Not surprisingly, he didn't get too many challengers. His usual sparring partner, Adam, had disappeared overseas to work on yachts and periodically came back to give Bertie a damn good run for his money. Adam was also the second part of the human centipede, which they attempted after emerging naked from a hot tub. By all accounts, the horrified onlookers could only grasp as they saw a naked Adam get on all fours, pull his bottom apart for a naked Bertie, also on all fours behind him, to try and push his head up it. After several attempts, either the pain or the reality of the situation got to Adam and he pulled out, so to speak, before Bertie wore him as a human hat. Bertie's escapades deserve an entire book themselves. The man is a force of nature. Never have I laughed so hard so often. The laughter itself has staved off many a potential darkening of mood. You can keep the therapists and the medication; I'll take Bertie's humour every day of the week — laughter is the best medicine, as they say.

Bertie's not alone in helping me get through the darker days. My hours propped up against the bar led to many good meetings, not that they always started off so well. The first time I met Ian, I wasn't having such a good day so had set out to drink my mind into numbness. I was close to that state when Ian and I had our first conversation. It wasn't so much a conversation but an aggressive rant once he had told me that he worked for the same American retirement home company that had treated my grandmother so appallingly. Reminiscing, I'm still surprised he didn't use any of his six-foot-five frame

Lady Luck and Me

to stop my 20-minute accusation that he, personally and purposefully, had neglected my grandmother and that I demanded an official apology on company-headed paper the following day. I was drunk but that's no excuse for behaving like an utter knob. The next time I saw Ian I was the one issuing an apology. To this day, he's the first and last who reminds me of my under-achieving and, with sensitivity, goes about finding practical and realistic ways in which I could be happier.

My first encounter with Nick the Greek was a strange one too. With half a pint of mead in each hand I listened to how he had spent the previous evening off his tits, trying to seduce a headless mannequin at the Guildfest music festival. He was eventually ejected from the venue for repeatedly prodding a bouncer's face, convinced that he was actually Mr Blobby in a tailored suit. Nick's one of the last of the old-school hippies. If he's not on the river renovating a canal boat, he's witling ornate picture frames whilst burning Nag Champa and listening to Buddha radio. It's with Nick that I have some of my best conversations. During an evening, we regularly pop out to the outdoor office (an elevated, manicured lawn overlooking Godalming) for a spicy cigarette. By the time we've finished, mysteries such as Stonehenge, God and how Kerry Katona ever managed to get into *OK Magazine* all have answers (all but Kerry), which are pondered upon and then quickly forgotten as another mead slips down.

Vegan Chrissy has been a stalwart for me for the last five years. Her adventures dressed as a badger protesting for animal rights both entertain and impress. Her unwavering strength in her beliefs is difficult not to be admired and, without causing arguments or offence, speaks passionately about her way of life. It should be noted that I write and

Watery stools

think about her so fondly because I have and always have had a soft spot for her. Her compassion, sense of fun and ever-buoyant personality make her company addictive. Simply put, she very much makes me smile.

Whether it's Bertie with his humour, Ian with his inspiration and motivation, Nick the Greek with his brilliant conversation or Chrissy with her strength of character and compassion, they have all been pillars for me during the last five years. There are, of course, others that make up my pub family. Jonnie, who gives the best hugs, hoodie Dave and Gareth with their sympathetic ears, George with his philosophy, Viking Dave with his extraordinary beard and the list goes on. I thank all of them for always being there, often when they weren't aware of just how much I needed them and sincerely hope that one day I will be able to repay them, individually, for the love, kindness and support that they have generously shown me.

During these work/pub years I thought Lady Luck had abandoned me. She neither helped nor hindered in my life and, like imaginary friends during childhood, I had begun to think she had deserted me. She hadn't. She had been there all along, watching and waiting, biding her time for a dramatic comeback, and that comeback came on the last weekend of the Six Nation rugby matches. The final Saturday arrived in what many saw as the most exciting finale in decades as Wales took on England to see who lifted the trophy. I hadn't been caught up in the nation's rugby fervour but what it had presented, which was an opportunity for a 14-hour drinking marathon down at the local. By half past eleven breakfast had been served simply by popping open a packet of salt and vinegar crisps whilst washing it down with the third pint of Kronenberg of the day. I was bordering on finding BBC 24-hour news

Lady Luck and Me

funny through the sea of glasses in front of me when they thankfully turned it over for the first, mid-afternoon match of the day.

By the end of the Italy–Ireland game, I was convinced my three-legged stool had developed a limp, requiring me to firmly place both my feet on the ground to help stabilise it. With the beer coursing through every cell of my body, including my retinas, I could feel myself getting swept up in the rousing patriotic chants, occasionally joining and firing derogatory comments at the two quiet Welshmen who had almost been forced to hunch in the inglenook fireplace. As soon as the ref blew his first whistle, the chants began to dwindle and, by the last whistle, had well and truly died, leaving the quiet punters to continue their rapid, deliberate, angry drinking. Everyone except the two Welshmen, who had emerged from their cave and were standing bang in front of the TV, raucously celebrating and risking several weeks in hospital. My stool had by now become properly limp and seemingly redundant as I was now being supported mainly by my arms, chest and forehead on the bar whilst my feet were determined to lead my body in several directions all at once.

As I watched the mob get increasingly restless and tried to gain control over my feet, a brilliant idea came over me. I *needed*, not wanted, weed. That will help sober me up, I thought. Arguably the worst idea that's ever come to man but, at the time, it was a stroke of genius. Incapable of verbal communication, I was left with one possibility to get my hands on what would surely straighten me up and that was by train. Having often made the journey to the station in 25 minutes on foot, I was confident that I could shave at least 15 minutes off that if I ran like the wind. According to my one eye that read the time on my phone, I had six

Watery stools

minutes to get the hourly train. I'm useless at maths but even I can work out that that meant I had missed the train by four minutes even running like the wind. No matter, it seemed, as I lurched off the bar following my leading head to the nearest exit. Out in the fresh air, I took time to zip up my inner coat, my outer coat, readjust my scarf and also retie my laces on my two-pound Timberland boots.

Off I set, half on pavement and half on road, trying to mimic Usain Bolt's technique. After 200 yards the first beads of sweat ran down my forehead, bypassing my eyebrows, straight into my eyes, causing me sudden blindness and a massive change of direction, ending in me backing out of a particularly aggressive hedge on the side of the road. Refusing to be beaten, I was back on my weaving run with my technique resembling an old drunk man running for a bus. What I hadn't accounted for was the size and sapping qualities of the hill that takes up the majority of the route to the station. Still, I persevered, but now with an ever-dawning realisation that the wind beneath my sweat sodden, now three-pound boots had clearly blown itself out. I eventually arrived at the station 28 minutes after breaking out of the pub, making my Usain Bolt inspired run three minutes slower than if I had just walked.

I stumbled over the bridge to my platform making dying donkey sounds as my lungs did their best to recharge themselves. Thankfully, the station and its platforms were abandoned, leaving me wobbling underneath the information board, trying to make sense of what it was telling me. By some miracle — no, miracle's too strong; it is British rail after all . . . By some coincidence, my train hadn't arrived, having been delayed and was due to turn up in the next five minutes. Hands on my knees, still breathing heavily, sweat pouring off me in torrents and

Lady Luck and Me

with a lengthening strand of snot dangling from my nose, I did my best to thank Lady Luck for looking out for me.

It was halfway through my mumblings of gratitude that my stomach made an almighty shift, unsettling its contents and driving them straight to my bowels with a thunderous groan. The unmanned station facilities closed daily at six p.m. leaving me in a bit of a quandary. It seemed my bowels had no patience for my decision making and began to go ahead with their evacuation without my permission, forcing me up the small grassy bank that runs adjacent to the platform. Unable to make it barely a yard up the bank, I was tearing desperately at my flies. I squatted on the incline just in time, managing jean clearance as the first gallon of beery, rusty water flooded out of my arse and flowed its way between my feet down the bank to the platforms edge where it began gathering in a dirty pool. As the evacuation continued, I found myself grasping on the tall grass either side to prevent myself from losing balance and inadvertently sliding down my mess onto the platform. Just as I had achieved the necessary centring, the unmistakable sound of the train rolling into the station filled my ears. It was four minutes earlier than the bastard information board had told me. My bowels were still open and, judging by the volume that was still steadily descending down the bank, weren't about to close anytime soon. I grasped the grass in horror unable to move as the carriage lights gave me my very own spotlight in the surrounding evening blackness.

The train stopped and, not three yards away, two children's heads popped up and peered out of their window, shielding their eyes from the polluting carriage light. I found myself awkwardly trying to look away, much like a cat or a dog does when they think you're watching

Watery stools

them have a shit, and pretended the children hadn't seen me. From the odd glances I stole back at the carriage, it was clear they had spotted me. Not only had they spotted me, they were now pointing at me and crying, properly crying and pointing. The parents joined them at the window to see what had thoroughly disturbed their two innocent children. The terrible image of a grown, bearded man straining, clutching onto grass, trousers down, cock and balls out, pissing sweat and shitting beer with half a hedge stuck to him answered them. The father bolted off leaving the mother to drag their visibly distraught offspring away from the window and console them on the seat, out of view of the feral, defecating stranger.

Just as my bowels had exhausted themselves, I heard the beeps of the closing doors. The beeps of the opening doors were only a few seconds earlier so for the doors to be closing so soon indicated that the train didn't want to hang around. As the train crawled out of the station, I saw the father and the conductor in agitated conversation with the conductor reaching for his phone. The father stood at the door, hurling verbal abuse at me. Dodging my effluence, I staggered back on to the platform and watched the train's lights disappear into the night. With the next train being in half an hour and the police very probably on their way, I decided it might be best for me to head home. On my shameful journey back, I was trying to think of the best stain remover for the back of my trousers and hideously soiled boots.

Welcome back Lady Luck, can't say I've missed you.

Lady Luck and Me

Black dog days

'It always looks darkest just before it gets totally black.'
Charlie Brown

Christmas was once again upon me. I was still living at home with Mum and my sister, although they had flown over to Australia for two months to reconnect with Emma, Lynden and their children, leaving me to look after the cat and myself. I'd been travelling and scoffed at my mother's and sister's concern about my ability to look after both myself and the cat. I relished the opportunity to have time to myself and create my own little nest, safe in the knowledge that any interruptions would be scarce. As the winter blanket descended, so did optimism and health. The poor cat developed a truly disturbing body cough that made his entire body heave, closing his eyes in order to prevent his eyeballs popping out of his head. It became unbearable to watch. The vets, their medication and robbing fees didn't help, so I returned home most evenings to have my dinner on my lap, watching whatever was loud enough to drown out the cat's pitiful gasps for breath. I felt tragically helpless. I told myself at the time it was for self-preservation purposes that I looked away. In reality, I felt ashamed that I was unable to do anything to stop this fragile creature's body from convulsing. Endless, dull, dead, meaningless days watching a cat struggle for life was more than enough to wake the noir hound from his slumber. Once awoken, there was only going to be one winner. It prefers no distractions and craves isolation in order to have your undivided attention. Occasionally, ideas

Lady Luck and Me

break through the blackness. It was only last month that I had such an idea. Turns out they aren't always good ideas.

For the first time in weeks I had mustered enough strength to leave my four walls and drawn curtains and thought it best to reintroduce myself back into society by hiding away in a darkened corner of an unknown pub, watching the world go about its business. I found my corner and tried to avoid making any eye-contact. It made me feel like a criminal. The more I shied away, the more I felt strangers eyeing me suspiciously, building my paranoia to sickly proportions. The more it grew, the more I frantically searched for the nearest, most inconspicuous exit route. I could feel the enormity of the task I faced crushing me, wishing I could turn all of me off and disappear there and then rather than draw any attention to myself by standing, walking or even breathing. I began to panic. As I tried to sort the persistent, abusive, ramblings in my head from the practical process of escape, my heart pounded, getting heavier and heavier, louder and louder, until I could see the table begin to rhythmically shake as the beat resonated through to the soft furnishings making the beermats in front of me jump. The light seemed to get brighter, the air thinner, the temperature hotter, the self-loathing stronger, the train tracks more attractive.

I shouldn't have come. I was struggling to go. It was stupid, thinking being around people might help, stupid thinking that their normality would somehow rub off on me, stupid thinking that the distraction of being in public would interrupt the incessant dialogue affirming my failures and disappointments. I was stupid. I was broken. My brain didn't work like those people around me. I was different and not in a good way. I didn't deserve to be there. Someone else should have had the education and

Black dog days

opportunities that I had had. Everyone would have made a better, happier, more fulfilled life than I had. I was a failure.

I wanted to plunge my hands into my skull and pull out the brain, the blackness and the beast with all its claws, teeth and venom. I didn't care for the end result, I just didn't want it there, battering away mercilessly, day and night. I wanted to tear my skin off and scream at the top of my voice as I liberated as much of me as I could. It was inseparable, indiscriminate. It was me and I was it. It was in everything I saw, everything I thought, everything I tasted, the only thing I felt. It was inescapable and it had been for months. Today the environment was different but the all-encompassing, vacuous black continued its relentless march through me, minute by minute taking more and more of me.

It was just another day to try to get through. I had given up with hope, I was too tired fighting to try and resurrect it. Very occasionally, I would think that I had caught the black dog napping and find myself in such places like the one I was currently in, only to be reminded, sabotaged and punished for disrespecting its authority and power over me. Here we were once again, with it deafening my mind, almost laughing at me and my pathetic attempt to lose it. It knew my fears and my weaknesses far better than I did. It relished getting to the most sensitive and painful areas, probing, twisting until I bent to its will and let it run riot, polluting whatever reserves of strength I had left. Chip, chip, chipping away until the growing ball of blackness inside utterly consumed me, even took control of my heartbeat, driving me, pulse by pulse, to do what it

Lady Luck and Me

wanted, what it's always wanted: nothingness, permanent darkness.

If the medication, counselling and psychiatry didn't work in breaking its hold, where else was there to go? What else was there to do? It was comfortably winning. In fact, it was galloping towards the line, towards total and absolute control and, with me leading it there, towards the train tracks. To date, it's only led me that far once. I don't remember the journey getting to the platform, I don't believe I was in control of myself but I do vividly remember a young girl no older than five holding the hand of her father, staring at me quizzically. As the train and my death approached, her gaze averted not once. I couldn't do it, I couldn't do it to her, not at that age, that would be a bad introduction to the darker side of reality and I wasn't going to be responsible for the permanent psychological scarring. She, or rather her eyes, saved me that day.

No tracks today though, I just wanted to be back on the sofa, drinking long and enough to keep my tears company. The illness loved me to drink and drink heavily, feeding its hunger for my irrationality, my insecurity, my self-worth, my demise. It made me love feeding it. It made me need to feed it. I needed to feed it now. I needed to be hidden away, back in a darkened, unclean room, away from everything and everyone, nothing to distract me from drinking, sobbing and listening to it telling me of the pain I've caused, the lives I've hurt, the pointlessness of my existence. I had to feed it. I had to get out. By the time I got to the door, I was visibly shaking and erupted into the mid-afternoon greyness, sweating and weak. I don't remember getting home, I didn't remember any of my actions. I was on ghostly auto-pilot with time and memory having no role. I wasn't me, it was me. Before the wine had been

Black dog days

poured, the first tear had fallen. With no phones, no light, no interruptions and no choice, I was its captive audience, until I passed out or it had won. I took a huge gulp and sat back, ready to take another defenceless beating.

The more I drank, the blacker it became. Mercilessly, it drove on, burrowing under and taking over every recess of my mind. It jeered at me for my lack of control over my own mind, reinforcing its hold over me, mocking me. The tears relieved nothing, they weren't enough. It wanted me to feel it, not mentally anymore, but physically as well, reminding me it had complete control over every aspect of my being. If my legs had worked, they would have taken me to the train tracks but, thankfully, the fourth bottle had rendered them useless. It was usually after the fourth that I passed out, fully dressed and occasionally losing control of my bladder.

Days and nights came and went, morphing into one another. The longer it controlled me, the tighter its grip became, isolating me from myself and the world around me. By now, I was severely depressed, relying heavily on alcohol and weed to comatose me quickly in order to have a respite from the never-ending, poisonous dialogue that flooded my mind during my waking hours. Depression and addiction, I found, can very quickly lead you down the path of loneliness. I didn't want help, I didn't want others to worry, I didn't think I was worthy of others worry, I didn't think others would understand. I thought my illness was unique, incurable and would have an inevitable ending. But this chronically unhappy, lonely, damaging state of mind wasn't entirely new. In actual fact, I found sanctuary in the loneliness. Loneliness had been my constant companion for as long as I could remember. From my early years living alone at school to the friendless

Lady Luck and Me

school holidays in Germany, loneliness held my hand, it gave me emotional self-sufficiency and security and when I felt abandoned, unwanted and unloved, loneliness was always present, always reliable and always jealous of anyone trying to get too close. Relationships both past, present and future, don't drive me as they drive others. I have loneliness which has never abandoned me, never let me down, never physically beaten me and will always welcome me with open arms.

Eventually, the alcohol, weed and loneliness drove me into numbness. With such complete numbness, the only assurance I had that I was still physically alive was the feeling of the kitchen knife being repeatedly plunged into the top of my arm and dragged through the skin and muscle until blood ran freely down my arm and off my fingers. My deterioration triggered Mum to cut her trip to Australia short and she returned home to care for me and arrange medical appointments. As much as I needed help, the realisation of being unable to look after myself reinforced my sense of failure and uselessness.

Over the next few months, I saw a host of doctors, therapists, counsellors and psychiatrists, all adamant that their expertise and mind-boggling fees would set me on the road to recovery. As these so-called experts delved into my background, quoting Freud and Jung at me, my medical debts grew and grew, adding further mental anguish to an already broken mind. By the time my debts had run into thousands, I had lost all confidence in anyone being able to help. Irrespective of the certificates that adorned their ornate office walls, their trial and error methods beggared belief. One counsellor accused me of 'playing him' and, as I walked through his lavish front door for the last time, I had to remind him that I had paid hundreds of pounds for his time and expertise and was in such a place that I could barely dress myself, let alone construct a pointlessly elaborate mind game.

With my reluctance to see any more therapists, the consultant psychiatrist at The Priory increased my daily medication to 300 mg of Venlaflaxine which is what I'm still on today, plus other medications. Despite the many side-effects and physiological damage they're doing to me, I prefer them to the sinister thoughts that the illness brings. Chances are I'll be on the pills for life, as coming off them can be equally as dangerous as the illness at its very worst.

As for my current situation, well, four years on from starting what I thought would be a note to my family justifying my physical ending, very little has changed. I'm still living at home with my mum and sister; I'm still working at the God-forsaken bookshop, and I still have no purpose, direction or meaning. As Rollo May said, 'Depression is the inability to construct a future.' Thank you, Rollo, I couldn't have put it better myself. The final suggestion the last panel of psychiatrists offered was for me to change my life fundamentally. After all the hours I've spent wrestling with my mind and listening to counsellors, I'd never thought of that and can clearly see why they have a string of letters after their names. If that's the best advice there is available, my condolences go out to other sufferers. I will listen to their pearls of wisdom and do as they say: I WILL make a fundamental change. Lady Luck, lend me your hand and show me where I left that train timetable.

THE END?

CPSIA information can be obtained
at www.ICGtesting.com
Printed in the USA
LVHW041353210621
690761LV00018B/408